Management for Professionals

More information about this series at
http://www.springer.com/series/10101

Sharda S. Nandram

Organizational Innovation by Integrating Simplification

Learning from Buurtzorg Nederland

 Springer

Sharda S. Nandram
Praan Solutions
Amsterdam
The Netherlands

ISSN 2192-8096   ISSN 2192-810X (electronic)
ISBN 978-3-319-11724-9   ISBN 978-3-319-11725-6 (eBook)
DOI 10.1007/978-3-319-11725-6
Springer Cham Heidelberg New York Dordrecht London

Library of Congress Control Number: 2014956866

Printed on acid-free paper

Springer is part of Springer Science+Business Media (www.springer.com)

To those who try to be the transformation they want to see

See the Self, by the Self, in the Self
From: Bhagavad Gita, Chapter 6, verse 20

Foreword

In 2006 Buurtzorg Nederland was established. Some friends with a big ambition wanted to change the Dutch homecare into community care. Many patients were troubled by the fragmented way care was delivered and many nurses were frustrated because they couldn't perform the way they wanted to. We chose for an Organizational model which focuses on meaningful relationships and no hierarchy. We wanted to use IT in a way that it served the nurses. We wanted to work with people who could be proud of what they achieve: day in day out! We wanted to show that it's much more effective and sustainable to work this way and yes: we wanted to change the world (a little bit).

Sharda Nandram succeeded very well in describing and explaining this adventure. The way she developed a new Organizational Theory was very inspirational for a lot of people working for Buurtzorg and myself. I think a more humane or humanistic approach is needed in management so that people can be the owner of their daily work, can enjoy their results, and can contribute to society with meaningfulness. Sharda explains what the principles are for the Buurtzorg way of working. From different perspectives she shows what is needed to build a non-hierarchical organization. By letting the nurses talk about their daily work and tell what it means for them, these principles become very clear. At the same time it provides us with a lot of scientific knowledge for further research and applications in management.

I hope that everyone who reads this book enjoys the stories, the reflections, and the theoretical insights. It was a big honor to work with Sharda!

Sincerely,

Almelo   Jos de Blok
July 27th, 2014

Preface

I am truly grateful for having met many new people, for their stories, opinions, and inspiration in developing this book.

While I am writing this acknowledgment the first draft is ready. I realize that writing this book gave me the fulfillment that I needed in this stage of my scholarly life. I am grateful to many people, too many to mention by name. I recall those who participated as respondents during the research; those who showed a sincere interest in the project; friends who frequently called to ask how I was doing, some who invited me or dropped by for a chat. Writing such a book makes you at times invisible for the outside world. The computer with your data, the Internet, and your own creative sources become you best friends. By showing attention, friends reminded me of the external world out there.

Life is for learning and the greatest gift one can get is meeting people who contribute to this learning. Each of them, in their own way, has contributed to my learning. I think I have met many like-minded people with the aspiration to contribute to what really matters in private and professional life. I have seen how they take responsibility for getting things done. How they rethink situations to find solutions for problems; how their striving for work efficiency goes hand in hand with humane values; how they are pragmatic, using their common sense; and how they honor simplicity.

When I wrote down my findings and reflected upon them, I realized that this book project was a special one, personally and professionally. Personally, because I could relate findings to my experiences with the community care system in the Netherlands. My Mom was suffering from Progressive Supranuclear Palsy (PSP), an illness without effective treatment in the period of 1997–2007. In those years we witnessed the deterioration of her brain's functioning and the increase of care dependency. Hailing from a culture where collectivism and caring for family are important values we tried to avoid too much dependency on professional health care. But when her care demand increased at a certain point in time, we had the choice between finding her a place in an elderly nursing home or keeping her at home and ensuring the care she required in the home environment.

As the first option was not really an option for us, we had to enter and experience how the healthcare industry was organized.

We encountered unfeasible advice from healthcare agencies and oftentimes we noticed the low motivation and the low quality of service amongst nurses and nurse assistants. In those days, there was no Buurtzorg, but I am sure its client's focus would have eased her life in several ways. Instead of a relief, during many visits by care professionals, the complexity and frustration for my Dad increased. Appointments were not met, on some days no professional caregiver showed up, some days we found our Mom half-dressed because the caregiver had to leave, some days they skipped part of her breakfast routines due to their busy schedule, every week many new nurses and caregivers entered the residence, each with their own ideas of how to take care of her and what would be good for her, and also medicine was often not given on time. We followed our hearts and decided to consider alternative ways for making her life as convenient as possible given the circumstances she was in.

Together with my 8 siblings, my Dad, and a few other family members and a small part of professional care offered by private care agencies, especially for those services we were not trained for, we created a team and tried to give her the best possible care, love, and as much comfort as possible. This was the best possible solution we could think of. The higher purpose at Buurtzorg is delivering the best possible care to the client. Our higher purpose was the same. Not every client has so many children able and willing to take care of them. Buurtzorg is then a good alternative, based on what I have seen during my research and the understanding of its approach: it is personal and professional.

Also professionally this project was enriching to me. Those who know my work are aware of my drive for contributing to build an alternative paradigm for management. Having the opportunity to study Buurtzorg has confirmed that some of my previously developed assumptions on entrepreneurship and management are not utopian but could be put into practice: economic and humane outcomes; matter and spirit; discipline and letting go, as two sides of the same coin.

I sincerely hope that this book will contribute to your learning and inspiration on alternative ways of organizing management.

Amsterdam   Sharda S. Nandram
July 7th, 2014

Contents

Towards a New Way of Organizing

1

Abstract

Driven by the conviction that a governance and organizing structure in organizations has a huge influence on human behavior, organizational efficiency and effectiveness, Jos de Blok started to think of alternative organizational structures for community care. He knows the ins and outs of the community care needs and experienced the calling for social change in this industry which he initiated with the start of Buurtzorg Nederland, a new community care organization as an alternative to current organizations (The Dutch name Buurtzorg could be translated by Community Care). Buurtzorg is one of the most talked about and revolutionary cases in community care, the successful and award winning practice of Buurtzorg forms the backbone of this book.

Its achievements have attracted attention nationwide and internationally. While many organizations have been facing the negative impact of the financial meltdown, starting from scratch late in 2006, Buurtzorg has shown a huge growth in turnover, an increase in personnel, as well as good financial results and overall a cost reduction of 40 % compared to similar organizations in community care (More details about the outcomes could be found in the following study: Social Business Case ("Maatschappelijke Business Case". Netherlands: Transition program/Buurtzorg; 2009). June, Available from: http://www.transitiepraktijk.nl/files/maatschappelijke%20business%20case%20buurtzorg.pdf).

His calling for social change is something many other entrepreneurs, managers, and professionals experience in various industries. An underlying assumption they have is that available resources could be used in more effective, efficient and meaningful ways to solve many types of problems for their customers. In their discussions they often recall Albert Einstein's saying, 'that we cannot solve problems with the same thinking we used when we created them'.

Many of them realize that change is not enough. It is transformation which is required. While change is about doing things a bit different here and there but

© Springer International Publishing Switzerland 2015

S.S. Nandram, *Organizational Innovation by Integrating Simplification*, Management for Professionals, DOI 10.1007/978-3-319-11725-6_1

within the same structures, transformation comprises of a fundamental shift in consciousness and creativity and it requires a holistic process and structure. This is about conversion of the mindset in the process of using the available resources to solve a problem while synthesizing existing resources with new activities to give birth to new structures.

The case of Buurtzorg shows how such a transformation looks like both for the individual professional, the client, and for the type of organizational architecture and how converting the mindset and integrating activities are key processes of social change and organizational transformation.

Those who are driven by social change and transformation could learn from and get inspired by the underlying principles, a new theory, that has been induced from the case of Buurtzorg.

1.1 Introduction to the Book

This book introduces the Integrating Simplification Theory (IST) and its main concepts and processes, as a contribution to the current discussions in management on a new paradigm for enhancing organizational performance, employees' meaningfulness and sustainable outcomes. This new paradigm embraces organizational innovation as a special form of process innovation as a response to the VUCA management world. VUCA stands for volatility, uncertainty, complexity and ambiguity as main management problems. Reflections about this VUCA world and how this book contributes can be found in Chap. 10 of this book. The Integrating Simplification Theory is induced from an evidence based management approach that is characterized by the following organizational outcomes: highly satisfied clients, immensely gratified employees, low illness rates, less sick leave, good production rates and business performance as well as continuous innovations. A full attunement to the client, self-managed entrepreneurial teams and a flat control mechanism without or with only minimal management layers, as well as Yogic Leadership and professional intrapreneurial freedom based on trust, Craftsmanship, the coordination of communication, knowledge sharing mainly through a virtual platform and serving the client as a higher purpose, are proposed as the main building blocks of the architecture of a new management paradigm.

This book is based on research using a Classic Grounded Theory (CGT) methodology. This methodology has been applied to identify the main concern, the core category, the core concepts, their properties and theoretical coding to build the Integrating Simplification Theory and introduces it to be broadly applicable in management. The Classic Grounded Theory is an inductive research method and falls under the qualitative research designs. In the appendices a detailed description of how the research was conducted, has been presented. This approach comprises the unfolding of the subtle aspects in the Craftsmanship of the professional employees by focusing 'within' their own expertise and exploring entrepreneurial opportunities to enhance a client focus. Furthermore it allows the emergence of main concepts regarding the organizational architecture to be used as explanatory factors for the client care focus.

In the proposed theory, management is seen as an enabler rather than a main process. Thus management is legitimate only if it serves the main purpose for a company's existence. Management that does not serve this main purpose leads to disintegration in terms of too much control, power, and lack of trust amongst stakeholders. In recent decades, the art of management has been lost due to developments to foster efficiency and productivity as the main aspirations in several organizations. Efficiency and effectiveness seem to be understood as synonyms. Peter Drucker's quote reminds us that "efficiency is doing things right, while effectiveness is doing the right things". Why management practices have been developed and how they realize effectiveness, is often not a question. Main attention in management education, training and in practices has evolved to doing things right, thus efficiency. The beliefs of managers are leading in such practices. Often individuals at the workplace are being studied in the way they behave without raising questions if scientists should also elicit discussions on whether the behaviors are right, justified and appropriate in the particular context.

1.2   The Case of Buurtzorg Nederland

The proposed approach in this book is based on the practice of community care at Buurtzorg Nederland. Buurtzorg focuses on re-constructing and renewing existing approaches to organizing the Community Care Industry in the Netherlands. The founders started their foundation with the question of how to foster organizational innovation in the healthcare industry for elderly care from a meaningful view by prevailing humane values over bureaucratic organizational structures and institutes. This view embraces an integrated alignment to clients' needs and employees' Craftsmanship.

While establishing the foundation they had to deal with the questions of how to create, organize and maintain high quality care, prevention and nursing to be offered to clients in their residential contexts. They had to consider how to attract and keep qualified healthcare workers, nurses and nurse assistants committed to adapting to the community care work method and how to organize the management tasks in a frugal way to optimize the primary process which is delivering quality care. They focus on discovering how to achieve effectiveness while realizing productivity, creating entrepreneurial space and autonomy of the employees. In this perspective the client is recognized as a whole person and thus perceiving his social, spiritual and emotional needs are as important as the medical needs. The client's family, his or her social or wellbeing ties of significant others including other professionals such as physiotherapist, social workers, hospital nurses, nursing homes and general practitioners (also called family doctors), may all be considered as relevant stakeholders in the type of solutions that are co-created in dialogues with each client.

The book describes how Buurtzorg is succeeding and the achievements it has realized so far. Through the theory and its building blocks that have been induced from the research, the management processes at Buurtzorg are described and explained in the perspective of solving the main concern. The main concern in the study was: 'what does an organization (Buurtzorg) do, to deliver services that are fulfilling the client's/customer's needs and how does it design and organize its activities for realizing a client focused service'. In practical terms, at Buurtzorg this is about a client care focus. Since the organization has not standardized this process of care delivery, in practice every team and the Headquarters deal with a question like: 'what do we need to do, to deliver care that is client focused?' The underlying assumption at Buurtzorg is that a client focus is the best approach to serve the client's needs. The term main concern hails from the Classic Grounded Theory (See Appendix A.1). Furthermore these findings are linked to current management theories, practices and debates which can be found in scholarly management literature and at mainstream management conferences. From these descriptions the reader will be introduced to the innovative characteristics of the so called "Integrated Simplification Theory" (IST).

1.3   Structure of the Book

The chapters will follow the building blocks of the theory.

Chapter 2 describes **the startup process and organizational structure**. Topics addressed are: the motivation behind founding Buurtzorg, how ICT became a necessary ingredient for the startup process, the steps taken for developing and introducing the design for organizational innovation, the organizational structure and main accomplishments of Buurtzorg in the past 7 years and a brief description of the organizational outcomes.

Chapter 3 addresses **the foundations of Integrating Simplification** as the core category of the theoretical framework. The main issue that kept the respondents busy was: what to do to serve the client in the best possible way. After formulating the main concern based on the Classic Grounded Theory formally the main concern turned out as follows: 'what does an organization do, to deliver services that are fulfilling the client's/customer's needs and how does it design and organize its activities for realizing a client focused service'.

In the research interviews, the focus in the open questions was put on what do people who work at Buurtzorg do (how do they design and implement their tasks) to serve the client in the best possible way to maintain their quality of life and how is the Buurtzorg innovation being organized to deliver a client focused service? The theoretical approach of the Classic Grounded Theory has been applied for inducing the building blocks of the model. This method fits very well in the context of Buurtzorg's bottom up approach. The theory is being derived (in scientific terms: induced) from the data and thus the theory is grounded in the daily practices at Buurtzorg. There are no pre-conceived notions of how organizations work; it is simply an attempt to conceptualize what could previously be found and what has worked at Buurtzorg.

For this study several resources were used: face to face interview sessions with founders, a variety of employees from the small Headquarters, nurses and nurse assistants in team sessions; interviews with clients and clients' visits, observations during internal meetings, the internet conversations, the media exposure, company documents, and reports of the case in other books. A detailed description of resources has been provided in the appendices of this book.

The proposed management *Integrating Simplification Theory* will be described and explained in detail by providing several examples found during the research at Buurtzorg Nederland. Integrating Simplification has been defined as a form of organizational innovation consisting of three core concepts:

(a) Systematically identifying and assessing what is needed by asking the questions: What are the needs of the client? Why do we do things as we always do? How does it help the client? This is the *needing principle.*

(b) Continuously connecting to different types of cues and reconstructing the perception of reality by asking: What is really going on? Is there a simpler way of doing things? How would this improve the client's quality of life? This is the *rethinking principle.*

(c) Designing and implementing tasks according to the current circumstances or new perceived reality until this doesn't work because the context has changed again or someone has a better alternative. Questions that are being asked here are: What do I require for this novel approach? How do I bring this simpler method into practice? How does the new practice improve the client focus? This is called the *common sensing principle.*

Integrating Simplification aims at avoiding what could lead to disintegration in the primary organizational process and avoiding any kind of wastage (in time spent, money and material) in terms of unnecessary complexity in realizing organizational goals. It has as main building blocks or dimensions, a smart assessment of management resources, structures, and processes. Translating this into pragmatic approaches it creates room for: an intrapreneurial mindset to enable innovation; a deep understanding and mindful assessment of the nature of Craftsmanship; a holistic, physical and emotional evaluation of the needs and capabilities of the client (as a whole person) and a dedication of the leader to a common higher purpose leading to creating space for contribution by those who get themselves involved in the organization.

The following core dimensions where the principles of the theory emerged to solve the main concern will be addressed in separate chapters:

- **Chapter 4 Attuning to Clients.** In this chapter the approach toward the client is explained. Many clients reach out to Buurtzorg because of word of mouth marketing. A main enabling process toward the client's focus is the assessment of his capabilities. The focus that is being applied is one of empowering the client to become independent as soon as possible. The client's context is being assessed by considering the potential role that can be played by significant others such as family members, friends, neighbors and volunteers. In cases where significant others could be involved to assist the speedy recovery of the client, yet with low complexity, they are integrated as important stakeholders. However, just taking the client and their whole situation into consideration is not enough. It should be perceived as the main purpose at all levels of the organization. Rather than considering the client as a sick person or a person who needs help, the client is perceived as a person with capabilities; as a person with significant others around him; as a person with certain belief systems. The scientific concept of entrainment has been applied to position the different types of attunement that have emerged from the data. A few examples will be provided to explain how the types of attunement to the client work.

- **Chapter 5 Subtle Craftsmanship in Communities.** This chapter describes the practice of Craftsmanship. Craftsmanship has been defined in the Oxford Dictionary as the skill in a particular craft. Here we refer to the craft of nursing and caring. From the data, the concept of Craftsmanship has emerged as an important factor for describing the client focus approach at Buurtzorg. The Craftsmanship at Buurtzorg does not only involve individual oriented skill to work as a professional. As Self-Managed Teams form an important organizing structure at Buurtzorg the Craftsmanship in the team context will be explained in addition to the individual skills that nurses, nurse assistants and healthcare professionals require. A detailed description has been provided for the Self-Managed principles, the way team members reach synergy in their work approaches and goals for the team in serving the client in the best possible way. Furthermore the subtle expertise will be explained as a relevant concept of 'subtle Craftsmanship'. Nurses, nurse assistants and community healthcare professionals have developed several professional competences but simply just using them may not be sufficient for realizing the Buurtzorg vision. Accomplishing this requires a deep understanding of the client and the circumstances around them eliminating irrelevant information and using subtle cues for decision making processes. These subtle cues are taken into account in addition to their professional expertise.

- **Chapter 6 Intrapreneurial Team Freedom.** This chapter describes Intrapreneurial Freedom as one of the core dimensions of Integrating Simplification at team level. This dimension is about providing the freedom and responsibility for running the Self-Managed Teams by allowing entrepreneurial behavior; creating conditions and maintaining the freedom so that they act with entrepreneurial spirit to innovate and create new solutions for problems and needs with decisive power within an existing organization. It requires a behavior to re-construct reality in interaction with those whom it concerns in order to foster speedy and well thought decision making. Intrapreneurship is often associated with creating a venture within an existing venture but recent developments have shown that the term has become polluted by its main focus on the entrepreneurial behavior that it requires from the intrapreneurs rather than experimenting with a venture with assistance of an existing firm. In this respect entrepreneurial behavior is about having ideas and using initiative, resourcefulness and determination. This then generates something of value for the clients, nurses, nurse assistants and the organization. In addition to behavior it requires certain conditions such as structure and planning. While in pure intrapreneurship the aim is to create a venture within a venture, but here we suggest introducing Intrapreneurial Team Freedom to focus on the process rather than the results in terms of creating something of economic value. In both the collected data and employee surveys two phrases consistently occurred: working for Buurtzorg gives freedom and the feeling that you are running your own office or company. Combining both aspects results in Intrapreneurial Team Freedom.

- **Chapter 7 Pragmatic Will with ICT.** In this chapter the antecedents (the explaining factors) of the ICT management architecture are being explained. The processes in the ICT architecture comprise the three main properties. The first one is flexible support to the primary process so that nurses can flexibly access the necessary data and information for reporting time spent at clients, as well as the possibility to report and monitor client information any time and at any place to serve the client in a holistic way. The second one is a step by step introduction of creative solutions for the ICT-users which is time saving, iteratively developed with users and which helps reduce complexity. The third property is Systematic Assessment. This is about continuously asking yourself and colleagues: How does my activity serve the mission and could the impact be made transparent? Without an intentional description of how things should work, these questions themselves induce certain behaviors in the organization. Systematic Assessment of data is required to build a common foundation amongst the professionals in serving the client to fit the organization's philosophy of trust building through Craftsmanship (Chap. 5) and enhancing Intrapreneurial Team Freedom (Chap. 6).
- **Chapter 8 Leading a Higher Purpose.** This chapter describes the leadership features at Buurtzorg and how the common purpose resonates in the organization and becomes a higher purpose to which everyone tends to contribute. Leadership has the feature of integrating roles. Three concepts that are induced from the research data are described in more detail and a literature review is presented as well. These concepts are expressions of the three principles of the Integrating Simplification Theory: needing, rethinking and common sensing. The first one represents expressions of the belief system of humanity over bureaucracy, stressing humane needs of clients and how this relates to the higher purpose of serving the client. The second concept refers to the various roles of the founders and the ability to integrate thinking processes and generate re-thinking for realizing innovative approaches. The third concept is the communication style and how using common sense and pragmatic approaches help in reaching out to all employees. The higher purpose resonates because of the lucidity in structure of the primary and secondary processes in the organization

- **Chapter 9 Scientific Contribution of the IST in the context of Organizational Innovation**. In this chapter a reflection on relevant theory will be presented to suggest how the theoretical framework adds to existing theories and insights. Here the related academic management and philosophical literature and concepts are reflected upon and the added value of this theoretical framework to management. The Knowledge Creation Theory, constructivist view of Piaget's theory, a Vedantic philosophical view and Effectuation Theory are the main theoretical frameworks in this chapter.
- **Chapter 10 Implications and Discussion**. In this section the following issues are presented: How do the findings help in navigating the VUCA management problems? What are the practical and scientific implications for the context of management?
- **Chapter 11 Reflections and Conclusion**. In this chapter the author provides several reflections on the findings and observations that were drawn during the research in respect to organizational theory development and for management education. The questions are: what are possible limitations in applying the Buurtzorg approach for the long run or in other organizations? What is the role of human values in implementing the approach? How could spiritual reflections help in achieving a sustainability application of the approach?

The **appendices** give a detailed overview of the research methodology and some additional overviews for the reader who requires more in-depth understanding of the research and its findings.

In the **epilogue** an analysis and reflection on the founder's leadership role is being described.

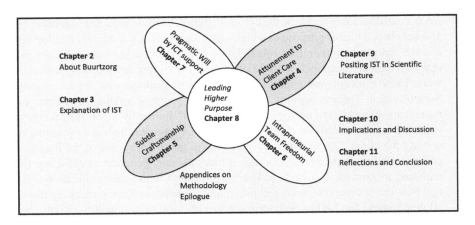

Fig. 1.1 Overview of the book

1.4   Navigating the Book

This book aims to reach out to a broad audience who is interested in organizational innovation, social change and community care. Those who are interested in community care and the processes at Buurtzorg may feel attracted towards Chaps. 4–8 as these are presenting the building blocks of the theory in the Buurtzorg practice. Those who are interested in a brief overview of Buurtzorg should read Chap. 2. The more scientific driven scholars in management would enjoy Chaps. 3 and 9. As the methodology that has been used in this book is not a common practice in management, the appendices chapter will give the detailed background of the procedure, probably of interest to researchers and management scholars. Management practitioners may especially enjoy Chaps. 2, 10, 11 and the epilogue (See Fig. 1.1).

Buurtzorg Nederland: Start-Up Process and Organizational Design

2

Abstract

Buurtzorg's practice has been labeled as an innovative management practice. Management innovation refers to the introduction of novelty in an established organization, mainly representing a particular form of organizational change (Birkinshaw et al. 2008, p. 826). Birkinshaw et al. (2008) define management innovation as 'a difference in form, quality, or state over time of the management activities in an organization, where the change is a novel or unprecedented departure from the past' (2008, p. 826). They describe management innovation as the invention and implementation of a management practice, process, structure, or technique that is new to the state of the art and is intended to advance organizational goals. The topic of organizational innovation has not received as much attention as other types of innovation such as technology driven, process innovation, strategic innovation and service innovations (Birkinshaw et al. 2008). Given the purpose of the current book it is interesting to see how Buurtzorg's organizational innovation identifies with the main concern of a client care focus and how it fits in the current management debates on organizational innovation and how it can contribute to the existing knowledge. An in-depth reflection will be presented in Chap. 11 of this book. This current chapter aims to provide some background of Buurtzorg and addresses the following questions: What did the motivation phase for starting Buurtzorg look like? What are the main phases of its organizational innovation? How is Buurtzorg organized? What are the lessons from Buurtzorg's start-up process of management innovation?

© Springer International Publishing Switzerland 2015
S.S. Nandram, *Organizational Innovation by Integrating Simplification*,
Management for Professionals, DOI 10.1007/978-3-319-11725-6_2

2.1   The Motivations for Founding Buurtzorg

2.1.1   Revitalizing Community Care

Buurtzorg Nederland was founded in 2006 as an alternative to existing home care organizations. Until 1990 the Netherlands was known for its good system of healthcare. The healthcare of those living at home was organized by nurses, community nurses, social workers and family doctors. Only those with a few years of professional experience in hospitals, additional completion of a 2-year specialist degree and high working standards were qualified as community nurses. These community nurses were responsible for home care, often for the elderly or they specialized in specific areas including healthcare for children. They worked in small teams in a community or district within a city. They were responsible for home care, prevention and healthcare in that area. They were employed by local private organizations. These organizations were structured based on several Christian religious beliefs, in the so-called cross organizations identifying themselves with a green, white or yellow cross (De Blok 2011). There was a national cross organization which administered the national standards for the services they provided to patients.

Due to reforms in the 1990s, different home care groups merged, followed by mergers between these new groups and Elderly homes, often with the aim to create economies of scale. This resulted in turning home care organizations and Elderly homes into primarily large organizations often tending toward bureaucratic organizational structures. The original contribution of the community nurse, who with colleagues, was responsible for a community or district and had the overview of the needs and what was really going on, got lost in the new structure. Their image and added value declined as their job roles changed in content and structure. The reforms were also applied in the education of nurses resulting in new types of nurses with less holistic competences and responsibilities.

At the same time, due to aging of the population, the demand for home care agencies to provide assistance with such things as bathing, giving injections, and caring for wounds has increased. However, the quality of care has become fragmented and ineffective. Patients often dealt with more than 30 different nurses in a month. The reforms also incited a change in attitude and approach of the healthcare. The image emerged as if this industry could operate on pure economic principles and business goals in terms of maximizing profit while the customer was not the same type of customer who was operating at the free market. The customer in healthcare was the patient who needed the best possible care to become independent and empowered again to live a life according to the highest norms in quality. Instead, due to the reforms, the overall view of the patients' needs were lost or ignored. The role of the community nurses changed. The autonomy they were used to decreased over the years and economic principles became more important than good care.

Jos de Blok, both as a community nurse and manager in different home care organizations, realized that economies of scale cannot be the sole initiative as it does not serve or lead to achieving the original purpose of the home care industry. It is interesting to note that the reforms did not lead to effectiveness or profit but rather it has resulted in loss and higher budget needs. Unfortunately, the healthcare agencies and insurance offices moved further away from the primary process where the main objective was serving the patient in the best possible way. While thinking that business principles and approaches would solve the issues in healthcare in terms of efficiency and effectiveness, in fact none of these were realized. Instead, the expenditures were continuously increasing, patients were complaining and nurses experienced strains and a decline in job satisfaction and job pride occurred.

Considering this, Jos de Blok founded Buurtzorg Nederland. His former colleague Ard Leferink was involved already from the start. Ard contributed with his ICT expertise and creative thinking abilities while Jos could provide his strategic ideal to revitalize the community nursing practices and nursing expertise. From conception, his life partner Gonnie Kronenberg contributed with her extensive insight and expertise in administrative organizing and her pragmatic down to earth attitude. Jos introduced the idea of establishing a foundation as the most suitable business entity for Buurtzorg. He received many objections for this idea throughout his network. Some were advising a private limited company as the most suitable form. He noticed how dominant the economic model of profit making was in many minds around him. This suggestion was also raised several times in the supervisory board which was formally established a few years later, as of January 1st, 2009. It was Gonnie from whom he received full support to keep the foundation as an entity instead of a private limited company.

Jos, being a strategic thinker, community nurse, former manager and a person with a high drive to be a change agent could integrate his vision with the contributions he received from Ard and Gonnie beyond the start-up phase. Now seven and a half years later, in practice Jos, Ard and Gonnie form the main players when important decisions need to be made. Ard contributes as driving force for innovations under the label of Buurtzorg concepts while Gonnie is the managing director for all internal affairs. When it comes to strategic decisions and corporate communication, it is Jos who plays the most important role. In practice he usually asks for advice from external sources as Buurtzorg has a flat organizational structure, trying to keep hierarchy out as much as possible.

2.1.2 Founder's Drive Towards a Higher Purpose and His Entrepreneurial Drive

Jos de Blok's actions as the founder of Buurtzorg are based on a deeper drive of serving a higher purpose. His humanistic and positive psychological perspective on human nature and relationships are perfectly adapted to his goal to deliver the highest quality of care. Jos de Blok grew up as a devout Roman Catholic. As a teenager, he noticed, even the most religious people often do not practice what they preach. He became disillusioned and took a distance from the Church. At 19, he described himself as an atheist. He often reflected upon inequality issues and problems in the community. In college, he excelled at economics and earned a living doing bookkeeping for companies. He felt depressed due to a lack of sense of meaning in his work and life and dropped out of university. He found a job in a hospital and finally experienced a feeling of fulfillment and 'being at home' that he found contributing to people's lives. He often reflected on problems which lead him to deep thinking about organizational issues such as: power, bureaucracy and inefficiency. His sense of solidarity with disadvantaged people, his drive to help and connect with people, his urge to understand how to lead people in a way that inspires them to bring forward their best potential and act as authentic human beings and not as machines, made him realize how much impact an organization's structure has on people's behavior. He was inspired a bit by the philosopher Sartre's ideas on co-existence and the potential each one of us has to make choices. He realized that it is something that holds for all cultures and all religions. He has a deep longing for understanding how things work and how things are related to each other, how to empower people, how to make them realize their potential and to gain a big picture perspective on existence.

He found ways to bring all of these ideals into practice at Buurtzorg. As a result, its employees think of it as a kind of freedom movement in the home care industry. The environment at Buurtzorg has created much hope, is refreshing, and confirms that giving attention to people and being authentic is effective. Providing space for freedom, creativity, love for your profession and simplicity can lead to a positive economic outcome along with experiencing a sense of meaning and serving a purpose.

While he does not have extensive experience in managing organizations his strength is his deep knowledge of the industry and a mature understanding of the community nurse gained from many years of personal experience as a community nurse himself. He has obtained some training and education in management and based on that learning he has developed his preferences for a management style that puts humane values above the bureaucratic administration; simplicity above complexity; practical above hypothetical. He is continuously open to new insights from management but his main concern lies in reforming the Healthcare Industry. Therefore on a daily basis he engages himself in institutional issues and examines the role of governmental bodies, insurance companies, doctors, the position of nurses and client related policies and the role of other relevant stakeholders involved in healthcare. This insures that he knows his market and its developments very well. While in the early years he devoted much time in presenting his ideas to other healthcare organizations, nowadays his focus lies on influencing the conversation at the institutional level (industry stakeholders, national and local governments and ministries); sharing his best practice at an international level and initiating discussions on establishing nursing education according to the principles of Buurtzorg as he predicts a shortage of community nurses in the future.

Jos de Blok and other community nurses suggest that the current universities of applied sciences do not pay enough attention in lessons for analyzing and solving clients' problems from a holistic approach and with practical assignments as was done a few decades ago. They are more trained as specialized nurses while Buurtzorg's concept requires a generalist. From the nursing population who were trained as integrated community nurses it is estimated (based on the interviews with community nurses and the founder) that about 55 % already works for Buurtzorg.

Therefore, Buurtzorg has a matured working population compared to other organizations. Due to the aging forecast of the population the relative need for home care will increase. And due to expected reforms of decreasing the number of elderly home organizations there is another reason that the demand on home care will grow. This suggests that next to the higher purpose, the founder has an entrepreneurial orientation (taking initiative, open to risks and innovative).

2.1.3   ICT as the Necessary Wing to Take Off

Before Buurtzorg was founded in 2006, according to Ard Leferink, ICT was mainly applied as a control mechanism rather than a supportive tool in the Dutch Healthcare Industry. The ICT instruments were used to manage the increased bureaucracy and comprised mainly of administrative systems that helped to generate statistics for the two financing bodies: healthcare financing agencies and local municipalities. It became obvious that their entrepreneurial rational was essentially commercial and opportunistic oriented. Commercial entrepreneurship became their norm.

Failing to solve problems of the clients was not the main process of concern but whether your productivity as care provider was high enough. Thus cost efficiency became the main focus. Expenses grew as the need for care started to rise and technological advances created more possibilities, thus also more demand. At the macro-economic level the expenditures are higher than the income. As healthcare is a public service in the Netherlands the high expenditures raised several public debates as well. This resulted in a common belief that a market-driven and commercial perspective would solve the inefficiencies and lower the expenditures. At governmental level, expansion by merging care providing organizations was seen as one of the most feasible and efficient solutions. But instead, they became bureaucratic systems that were difficult to manage in the same way as when they were smaller. The shift from healthcare as a public services to a more entrepreneurial approach was a trend in many EU countries.

As a consequence borrowed terms like product, target and deliverables emerged in the Dutch Healthcare system. Ideas were implemented from bureaucratic organizational systems such as the introduction of various management layers next to professionals who were part of the primary process responsible for delivering care. Subsequently, within a few decades, there was a fundamental cultural shift from a social and public health management orientation to a pure economic orientation in the Dutch Healthcare Industry. This change in culture could be recognized almost everywhere in the healthcare industry. When assessing and evaluating healthcare providers, the financing bodies created to measure their performance, mainly by business indicators, lost perspective of the specific context of the client who needs care, nursing, guidance and other support. Nurses were seen as providers of products.

The accountability system facilitated by ICT became more sophisticated, yet it moved further away from its contextual practices. The main problem it created was the existence of two independent processes in most of the healthcare organizations. There was a primary process for serving the client by nurses and nurse assistants and an accounting process for generating statistics on finance. The primary process was facilitated by written material archived in files while the accounting process was facilitated by expensive ICT programs. There was a gap between the language used by the care providers and that of the financing bodies. While more data was collected the complexity of the ICT systems increased. Hence less insight could be gained from the statistics produced by these systems. Healthcare providers often could not induce their performance status from these statistics. Consequently, we knew exactly how much care was provided but not the impact of it. Nor could we identify what the differences were between the various healthcare providers, because the ICT support did not aim to gain these types of insights. "It was meant for the automation of the bureaucratic system and not for gaining data in order to support the primary process," Ard expresses.

Therefore this turned out to be a big challenge for Buurtzorg who wanted to make and be the difference in the healthcare industry. The main ICT task therefore was developing and implementing tools to support the primary process in which the government and financing bodies could be convinced that such an approach could lead to transparency and more insightful accounting.

As there was no software available that suited the Buurtzorg profile it was decided by the founders and the creative thinker, Ard Leferink, that they start an ICT company focused and capable of working according to a few principles. Given the fact that the architecture of the organizational structure was built on Self-Managed Teams the system targeted to fully facilitate this process. As the Self-Managed Teams would be located in small offices throughout the Netherlands there was a need for web-based software applications that were easily accessible. Nurses needed access to all information required for autonomous functioning while working locally in offices, on the road and in patient's homes. The idea also created reduced wastage and inefficiency by minimizing paper flow and effective use of time for the client. Another idea was to develop and build a user interactive system. The ICT was an important division in facilitating the launch and served as enabler for the organizational innovation which targeted the following features: a bottom up approach; trust rather than control; a client-professional relationship; Self-Managed Teams; knowledge sharing with room for the power of a crowd rather than the power of a few experts who serve from a hierarchical setting. In Chap. 7 of this book the role and implementation of ICT as the Pragmatic Will of Integrating Simplification will be discussed and presented further.

2.2   Phases in the Start-Up Process

The founder was motivated to create a home care organization in such a way that he could revitalize community care by re-introducing its original working principles that existed in previous decades. He aimed to create room for the core focus which was, care to the client. He believed that such an approach would solve the problems

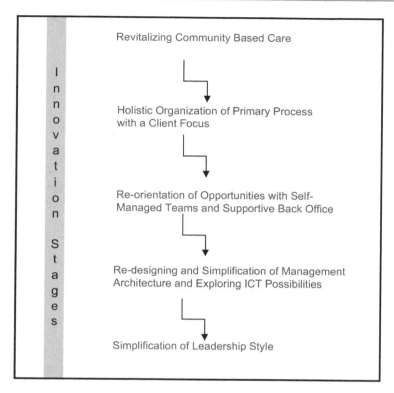

Fig. 2.1 Organizational innovation stages at Buurtzorg Nederland

faced by clients and align with the needs they experienced, as well as nurses and nurse assistants could center themselves on what brings them their professional pride, which is often to serve the client to the best of their ability and expertise. He imagined the possibility of a holistic approach to the client and a community based care. He also identified the opportunity to realize this by simplifying the financial structure. He introduced a financial structure for the home care sector by integrating all related tasks and created the community nurse position (a general position instead of various specializations).

Furthermore he redesigned the architecture by introducing the idea of a management practice of Self-Managed Teams. Ard Leferink helped him to explore ICT possibilities. Together they conceived the idea of leading management processes through a virtual web that integrates and connects the knowledge available in the organization and that inspires new ideas to improve the core business which is care. For realizing this he introduced a simple leadership style that limits management layers and management positions (See Fig. 2.1).

He suggests re-introducing the original principles of community care which fits the natural instincts of community nurses. It would give them meaning at the workplace, create professional pride, uplift the employees' spirit and it will lead

Table 2.1 Reimbursement fees for nursing, personal care and guidance

Activity	Fee in Euros
Nursing	76.02
Personal care	51.35
Guidance	55.34

to fulfill a purpose in life which is caring for the client based on humane principles. The ICT possibilities are explored and renewed as the organization grows and new needs are created. Buurtzorg has close ties with Ecare, the organization that supports all areas related to ICT designing, implementation and maintenance.

2.3   Main Approaches in the Start-Up Process

2.3.1   Integrated Fee and Simple Business Model

Let us look at the financial strategy which is very simple in nature but was not considered or implemented by others in the home care industry. How to simplify the financial structure was one of the founder's main concerns. Currently, there are four parties involved in paying for the care services, in the Dutch reimbursement system.[1] On average the nurses and the nurse assistants are providing three types of intervention and the average costs are indicated by the Dutch Healthcare System, the fees given to every healthcare institute varies for these interventions. The following fees per hour are based on information of 2014 (Table 2.1).[2]

The assumption behind these fees is that nursing is done by nurses and personal care is done by nurse assistants. This resulted in fragmentation of the care for the client. The client is not being considered in this view. It is not based on the problems that the clients are facing and how they could be helped in a holistic way to solve their problems. The assumptions made for specializing the fees was not based on the client's needs but rather for controlling the expenditures. In the tendency to gain efficiency by applying business principles only, the dominant rule became saving costs. Intensive work was carried out with lower educated people to keep the costs down. Originally in many institutes nursing was done by nurses; personal care activities and guidance were done by nurse assistants. During the reform, to follow the tendency of efficiency as was advised by accountancy firms, nurses were required to do jobs other than for which they were trained. They became managers with tasks such as arranging schedules, maintaining contact

---

[1] These are: ABWZ, Insurance, WMO, and clients.

[2] Nederlandse Zorgautoriteit, Bijlage 13 bij circulaire CARE/ABWZ/13/05c. Prestatiebeschrijvingen en tarieven extramurale zorg 2014, pp. 1–30.

with the family doctors, administrative and coordinative tasks. The idea was that their job became more complex and justified for the hourly rate paid by the reimbursement system. The consequence was that nurses were kept away from their main expertise and chosen profession which was nursing, not management or administration. The actual care giving work at the clients' homes was done by the nurse assistant.

Driven by efficiency and saving costs the healthcare organizations started to schedule their work in such a manner that going cheap became the main policy. The consequence for the client was that he received care by several nurse assistants who were scheduled in such a manner that tasks were specialized to spend as little time as possible, often resulting that for each activity another nurse assistant was responsible. At the end of the day the client felt how fragmented the care he received had become.

However, in practice, nurses and nurse assistants do not care so much about the fees that are paid for the activities they need to conduct. When they face a client with a certain problem, they are trained to come up with a solution to solve the problem. That is their natural tendency: to give the best possible care. They do not think, now I am hired for a certain task and I need to look only at that aspect of the client; another colleague from personal care will come and do the other tasks or she will solve other parts of the problem. The system however, driven by the efficiency perspective asked them to act opposite to their natural tendency which resulted in strain and stress.

At Buurtzorg the following innovative solutions were implemented regarding the financial structure.

a. All the services were grouped together, resulting in an average fee of around 57 Euros per hour and then the tasks that could be delivered for this fee were scheduled and offered while keeping the client as a main focus.
b. Attention to overhead was observed and it was considered that high expenditures were partially caused by the increase of healthcare managers in many organizations. An aim at Buurtzorg was to keep the overhead costs as low as possible.
c. It was also decided to keep the organization of the work as simple as possible while bearing in mind the needs of the client to offer him the best possible care.
d. Another aim was to reduce the fragmentation of care per client by scheduling the work in such a way that the number of nurses and nurse assistants per client is reduced.
e. The profession of the nurses was arranged in such a way that there was room again for their natural tendency to serve the client in the best possible way which will revive the meaningful work they were trained for.

The simplicity in the business model at Buurtzorg, led to both efficiency and effectiveness. Assuming, a productivity rate of 60 % and a reimbursement of 57 Euros, they save 3 Euros per hour. If the total number of hours per year is about 3 million hours, the profit is 9 million Euros. This productivity is chosen on purpose to give nurses enough room to do their work effectively while also establishing and maintaining their local networks. In many healthcare organizations the manager targets a productivity of 70 % often leading to high constraints, poor quality of the work and high levels of stress. At Buurtzorg the perspective is that managing on productivity only will not gain sustainable results for a client care focus: nurses should have enough time to know their client. It should be noted that at the same time Buurtzorg aimed low overhead costs and the Self-Managed Team structure without management layers contributes to the positive impact of the simplified business model.

Every team is aware of the productivity indicators and has internet access to the numbers per team so they can follow the developments. Each team knows how much can be spent for renting offices and other expenses. There is also account-ability on how profits are invested, for example for innovative projects, education and training.

2.3.2   Self-Managed Teams

At Buurtzorg there is a management structure in the organization which is particu-larly suited for the business of community care. For implementing the idea of Self-Managed Teams, a concept that already existed in a few organizations, Ben Wenting and Astrid Vermeer from the institute IVS, were asked to guide the teams. As experts in coaching and team building they had experimented with the concept of Self-Managed Teams in other organizations in the past. At Buurtzorg they could more efficiently test whether the way they implement the concept was valid because Buurtzorg was a new organization where they could more easily apply several aspects of the concept compared to an established organization. In the past 7 years they have experienced how the Self-Managed Team approach works more effective and under what circumstances it does not. They followed a process of trial and error which provided valuable lessons and helped them to develop the concept further. There was no predetermined model for Self-Management available to follow, only a few basic principles. In some teams personal characteristics of team members did not match well and teams experienced conflicts. Some team members were not used to sharing the decisive power and tended to coordinate instead of sharing the tasks and responsibilities. Other teams grew fast and therefore had to establish an additional team. Some teams flourished right from the start while others required more time to adjust to each other's strengths and weaknesses. Based on their findings, Ben and Astrid have written instructions on the internal website and in booklets about the principles of Self-Managed Teams. Every new team is requested to ask for their guidance. Some ask their input at the start-up while others do this at a later stage of their team building process.

2.3.3 Virtual Platforms

At Buurtzorg there are virtual platforms to enable effective schedule planning for the nurses, a forum for sharing experiences and developing innovative solutions to problems through joint effort, sharing knowledge and E-learning modules. As a result, while nurses at other healthcare organizations need to fill in printed forms which, in turn need to be administered by others, nurses at Buurtzorg, can log in to their system whenever they need to retrieve or add information such as client registration, treatment times and communication history. Due to ease of use and access, this frees up nurses to do this at their leisure. This creates flexibility and the feeling of autonomy. In order to achieve a standard of quality, Buurtzorg uses the Omaha system that has been developed in the USA. This system includes practices guide, documentation methods and a framework for information management. Omaha is a computerized management information system that incorporates and integrates clinical information about clients and the services they receive (more about this in Chap. 7).

2.3.4 The Regional Coaches

The professional coaches act as facilitators to the teams. They usually have a background as community nurse as well to ensure that their facilitating expertise suits the context of community care. Their main tasks are:

- Support new start-ups as well as established teams.
- Encourage taking responsibility and problem solving abilities within the teams.
- Coach and support teams and individual members in increasing their productivity and realizing other team output.
- Coach a team in coping with illness absences.
- Discuss the trends perceived in a team. A coach often facilitates about 45 teams and develops expertise to be shared when coaching other teams. He can share what has been a good practice somewhere else without proposing a specific approach as teams have their autonomy in developing approaches for their specific context.
- Discuss any deviances in regard to arrangements that have been agreed within a team, if there are deviances in team practices considering where policy and norms have been agreed upon in the whole organization.

2.4 Organizing Structure and Some Facts

Buurtzorg has a flat organization structure as illustrated in Fig. 2.2. For the governance a Supervisory Board has been appointed. The staff at the Headquarters supports the coaches, the teams and the Board of Management. Informally, Ard

Fig. 2.2 Organizational
structure at Buurtzorg

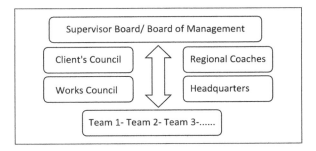

Leferink, Ecare and IVS are important partners of Buurtzorg and often act as the sounding board for the management.

The extensive growth in the past 7 years is obvious.[3] At the end of 2007 there were 300 clients with Buurtzorg. By the end of 2013 there were 55,000 clients served by 698 teams spread across the country. The latest growth is about 100 new locations in the period of 2012–2013.

The teams were supported by a small Headquarters comprising of 39.44 Full Time Equivalent (FTE) staff, 12.72 FTE regional coaches and 6.77 FTE working on projects. By the end of 2013, the total number of employees was 7,188 and the turnover was 220 million Euros.

Based on the Consumer (Client) Quality Index it can be concluded that the clients' satisfaction is high with a score of 9.1. The employee satisfaction score of 8.9 in 2013, is high as well, based on the study by Effectory, an independent market research institute.

---

[3] The numbers on 2013 are based on the Buurtzorg Annual Report 2013.

Theory of Integrating Simplification

3

Abstract

In this chapter the theoretical assumptions of the research approach and the framework that has been induced by applying the Classic Grounded Theory methodology is being presented. Integrating Simplification has emerged as the core category or in ordinary terms, the concept that answers the main concern or the main question of the research. The main concern in the study was: 'What does an organization (such as Buurtzorg) do, to deliver services that are fulfilling the client's or customer's needs and how does it design and organize its activities for realizing a client (customer) focused service?'

At Buurtzorg the underlying assumption is that a client focus is the best approach to serve the client's needs. The main concern of the study includes both the individual professional level and the organizational level of a client focused service.

3.1 Theoretical Assumptions

3.1.1 Theoretical Approach to the Model of Man

Designing and organizing usually follows a few assumptions on man. An interesting debate in management has been going on between Herbert Simon (1973) and Chris Argyris (1973). While this took place a few decades ago, regarding the model of man, it still seems to be relevant (Lovrich 1989; Davis et al. 1997; Hernandez 2012). Both theorists have different views on man and accordingly they propose what researchers on organizational theory should do and how organizations could be built. Simon's standpoint is that this scientific field could be developed if we focus on two kinds of research. First, research which serves to explain why organizations take the form they do and why people act as they do in organizations. Second, research which demonstrates how organizational performance can be improved. For Argyris, however, a focus upon how man typically acts in the

© Springer International Publishing Switzerland 2015
S.S. Nandram, *Organizational Innovation by Integrating Simplification*,
Management for Professionals, DOI 10.1007/978-3-319-11725-6_3

organizational setting serves as a faulty foundation for how organizations should be structured. He thinks the more appropriate starting point for organization theory is that of man's potential capabilities. Hence, according to him, the proper model of administrative man is one which reflects an appropriate vision of human potentialities in the organizational setting (Argyris 1973, pp. 264–265).

These different viewpoints are important in social scientific research. The view of Simon follows a more descriptive approach without room for subjective and normative views on man, while the view of Argyris provides the space for subjective and normative perspectives. In his own words: "Man shows profound capacity to learn to behave is many different ways. Our social science universe is not like the physical science universe which is 'out there' waiting to be understood, while, in the process of being understood will not change its makeup, or which will not play tricks by permitting two quite different views of man to be valid. If the social science universe can be what we make it to be, then what is needed is a concept, a view, or an image of what the world ought to be. As this view develops it should be studied and explored systematically (Argyris 1973, pp. 264–265)". Such a view opens the door to more constructivists' perspectives on studies of organizational innovation for understanding the role of employees, entrepreneurs and managers in implementing such innovations.

Now a few decades later, one could notice the increased interest in management studies on the 'how' to develop practices while missing the 'why and what it leads to'. Incorporating these two questions creates possibilities for normative views on mankind and for incorporating human potentialities and thus an evolutionary perspective on development. At the same time we notice the urgency to focus on sustainable solutions for behaviors of economic stakeholders, under the themes of sustainable organizations, corporate social responsibility and behavioral economics as examples of such a normative view. Such a view has evolutionary features and creates space for developing the world to a higher plane of existence. Philosophical perspectives always depart from such evolutionary standpoints as the main human aspiration. So then, why don't we integrate them into the management practices? Why do we keep such normative or philosophical views only for our private lives and not for the management practices? If nobody questions the current mainstream management assumptions, there will be hardly any management innovation?

Worthy to mention that in the last decade, more management scholars have started, to re-think existing management models which are mainly driven by the economic-based transaction cost theories. They are also re-thinking the position of managers as individuals that are striving for maximizing profit and serving self-interests while ignoring the costs of serving the common interests. They are submitting alternative approaches by introducing more human concepts, psychological theories and interpretative methodologies to study and implement more meaningful workplaces. This book provides another alternative, essentially bridging the gap between economic and psychological thinking by integrating views on control, coordination and decision making, strategic management, market development and human resources. This book serves these scholarly discussions aiming to contribute to the new management paradigm. Interestingly to note here is that the research approach chosen does not position the study fully in the camp of Simon nor in that of Argyris. Simon's critique on Argyris is that the realm of' human potentialities' is a difficult topic for the social scientist. He argues that since potentialities by definition have not yet materialized, it is not possible to observe or document them in any convincing way. In research such transparency to be able to replicate studies, is one of the main scientific criteria. Simon raised many question in the debate (Lovrich 1989): Where should the normative view that Argyris proposes come from? How does one develop a view that is acceptable to most people? He argued that one reply would be that the normative view should be based upon the *desired* potentialities of man. And if we do that, then man should be studied in terms of what he is capable of, not only how he actually behaves. Simon proposes further in the debate that in such a case, we should take the best examples that we have of human beings striving to achieve these qualities, study them and their environment in order to produce generalizations that help us to understand and increase the behavior that is preferred. In this book, that is exactly what is being done. Buurtzorg has been acknowledged as an example of best practices by several types of stakeholders. Studying Buurtzorg will reveal interesting insights to generalize and inspire other organizations in the healthcare and more specific in the community care industries, but it also generates knowledge and insights for other organizations.

The approach that has been followed in the research for this book is grounded in how people behave and how they think. So next to Simon's suggestion of studying a desired behavior, one could say that here Simon's view on how people behave, is being followed. But while focusing on the actual behavior, it also gives room to respondents for sharing subjective experiences which does not easily fit in Simon's approach, unless they can be registered objectively. The Classic Grounded Theory methodology provides such possibility, while leaving space for enhancing the researcher's creative capacity in inducing relevant concepts and relationships between concepts. In the appendices the detailed procedure that has been followed here, can be studied. The Classic Grounded Theory approach gives the possibility to the emergence of several psychological concepts which fits the approach of Argyris as well.

3.1.2 Usefulness of Classic Grounded Theory

The Classic Grounded Theory (CGT) has not been applied very often to the management science. Based on my experience with the current research I think it is a methodology that fits management science very well. The originator of this methodology, Barney Glaser explained a few pitfalls for researchers during a recently held workshop (April 16th, 2014 at Neoma Business School). A few of his notes, taken during the sessions, are quoted here to illustrate what CGT is about and why the CGT approach fits the current study:

- *"CGT is not for everybody. If people use 500 codes they can't conceptualize. CGT is an elite method. Most of the people can't conceptualize. You need to be able to conceptualize. Some people are not good at it; some are very good at it"*.
- Another thing he stressed was that, *"all is data, we do not need to search for complex ways for collecting data. We use just what we see and all that we see that helps to explain the main concern of the study that you are trying to solve. Everything could be used"*. This message is a very interesting contribution to the scientific approaches in management because we study social phenomenon including behavior. In daily practices we behave based on what we perceive around us, including dealing with complex issues. Why don't we use the same natural habits to analyze management phenomenon? This attitude is very close to what has been found as one of the main principles of the Theory of Integrating Simplification, which is using 'common sense'.
- Yet another thing that he emphasized was the message he has provided the experts on CGT. *"Do not make it all so complex, it is all simple"*. It is all very simple he kept saying and was warning the experts not to get stuck in lofty talks but to bring it back to its simplicity.
- Glaser also recommended to keep about 5 core concepts and to document your discovered new properties. *"Show it to people when your working paper is finalized, otherwise they will come out with opinions and start with questions, such as: 'Why did you do this and that'. They do this because of their pre-conceived notions. Shut them up with the why"*.
- Glaser talked about theoretical capitalism and suggested: *"Let the theorist think from their theoretical capitalism. They did not use data for it but have made it up based on their preconceived ideas and work of others. If you want to do away with such capitalism then you have to trust the Grounded Theory Approach. If you cannot show the data, it is useless. Grounded Theory is based on data"*.
- Another interesting message he gave was: *"You do not need years, to do a CGT study, you may do it in a few months. You just observe, interview and follow the steps and also stop at a certain moment just to write up what you have found. You can't do it all. Don't overload yourself, do mention in the implications of your paper what needs to be done in future research"*.
- Glaser stressed the richness of Grounded Theory. *"If you move from one substantive area to another, you may modify what you have found. But its central concept, the core category, will be the same, but it may have new properties in other areas"*. Furthermore he said: *"Grounded Theory is a rich vocabulary. If you get stuck with the question: how do we know, just go back to your data and it will tell you the answer"*.
- He suggested: *"Make field notes. Do not waste your time in recording and transcribing everything from the interviews. Who will tell the truth when they are being recorded. Start with open coding, then selective coding"*.
- Another remark that he gave us during the workshop was: *"The Grounded Theory taps naturalism in all of us"*.

When I attended the workshop, I had already completed a draft version of all but the final three chapters of this book. The experts, including Barney Glaser, have confirmed many of the principles that I have introduced. It also confirmed that this approach was the ideal choice to study Buurtzorg as it is an innovative practice and therefore, gives room for scientists to discover new concepts instead of fitting their practices into existing theories or management models.

3.2 Explaining the Integrating Simplification Theory (IST)

Integrating Simplification emerged as the core category consisting of a process of three principles. It also turned out that these principles are present in different dimensions. Each dimension has its own properties and lower level concepts. More details about the terms that are used to explain the methodology can be found in the Appendices A.1 and A.2. A brief overview of the main steps of the research approach is presented in Fig. 3.1. The building blocks of Integrating Simplification are presented in this chapter and the main relationships are explained as well. Developing a theory rather than just providing a description has been at the core of writing this book because it gives more space for inspiring others and implementing insights, either in the Healthcare Industry or outside this sector. Grounded Theory provides insights that are grounded in the empirical data. This data is being labeled at different levels of abstract and conceptualized around a main concern of the study. Therefore, Grounded Theory is a more 'within' approach than the traditional approaches where scholars try to formulate hypotheses by reasoning from existing theoretical frameworks being tested. Such a procedure does not produce novel ideas or novel concepts as the scholar is trying to verify or falsify what is already known based on other research. If new concepts are introduced to be studied these are always deduced from prior existing frameworks.

The concept of Buurtzorg has already been labeled as a good practice in several contexts. To provide the possibility for a detailed explanation of how Buurtzorg is being organized as a good practice, it seems evident to avoid existing frameworks in first instance. Hence the main drive in the current research has been openness for new concepts to emerge from the practice of Buurtzorg rather than using fixed frameworks. At a later stage, existing literature and frameworks have been examined to position the findings. A reflection of this process has been given in Chaps. 9–11. Furthermore, a new theoretical approach provides the building blocks while leaving sufficient space to complete the context specifics during the implementation of aspects of the good practices of Buurtzorg.

Several sources were used for the input: face to face interviews with founders, Headquarters employees, nurses and nurse assistants in team sessions; interviews with clients and clients' visits; as well as observations during internal meetings, internet conversations, media exposure, company documents, and write ups of the case in other books. A detailed description of the scientific approach of the Classic Grounded Theory followed here, has been described in the Appendices of this book.

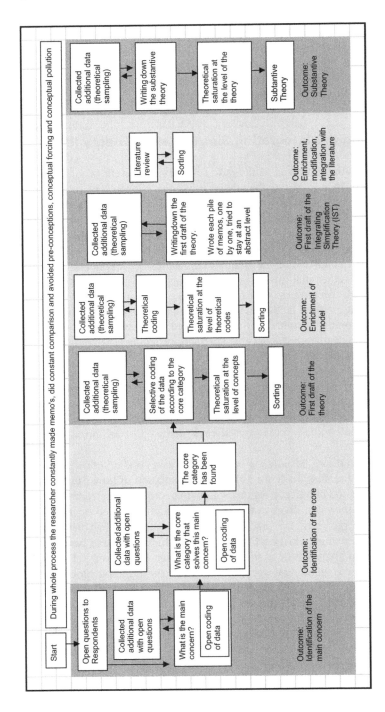

Fig. 3.1 Overview of the research methodology

3.2.1 Main Processes of Integrating Simplification Theory (IST)

Integrating Simplification has emerged as a process of engaging in simplicity and refraining from complexity to avoid organizational disintegration. Disintegration refers to all kinds of wastage due to imbalance, for example: in time and other resources that are required for a task, imbalance between personal and organizational motives, or between personal and organizational values. For example, an expression of disintegration is a situation where employees feel alienated from their workplaces or when clients feel the services they receive do not satisfy their needs or do not fit their belief systems. Disintegration also exists when primary processes in organizations are ignored or get less space to develop due to bureaucratic structures or if control mechanisms dominate over basic humane values such as trust and meaningfulness in organizations. In addition, disintegration can be found when there is a decline in ethical values leading to several kinds of misconduct in organizations. Integrating refers to the opposite of disintegrating. It implies harmonizing towards a whole, a unity or a common goal or higher purpose. Integrating requires being aware of the existing interests of members, of existing resources, beliefs and value systems and the control power of the organization and then bringing these different aspects together in alignment. In this case it is about aligning toward the vision of simplification. Simplifying practices then becomes the united, whole, common or higher purpose.

Integrating Simplification is a form of organizational innovation that enables an organization to operate according to a client focus. Serving the client according to his needs is the main driving force for this type of organizing. There are three organizing principles that form the process of Integrating Simplification (See Fig. 3.2):

1. The process of systematically identifying and assessing what is needed by asking the questions:

   - what are the needs of the client?
   - why do we do things as we always do?
   - how does it help the client?

This process is labeled as the *Needing Principle* as it requires a reflection on the actual needs and practices. It can lead to *resetting habitual patterns*.

2. Continuously connecting to different types and sources of information and cues and reconstructing the perception of reality:

   - what is really going on?
   - are we doing the right things?
   - is there a simpler way of doing things?

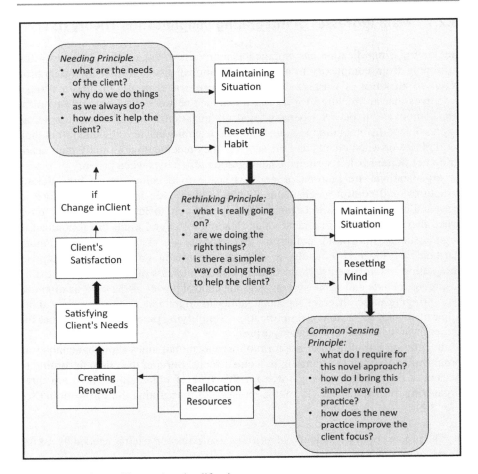

Fig. 3.2 Principles of integrating simplification

This process is labeled as the *Rethinking Principle* as it requires a reflection on existing perceptions. It may result in *resetting the mind* to let novel ideas be born.

3. Designing and implementing tasks according to the current circumstances or new perceived reality until this doesn't work because the context has changed again or someone has a better alternative:

   – what do I require for this novel approach?
   – how do I bring this simpler way into practice?
   – how does the new practice improve the client focus?

This process is labeled as the *Common Sensing Principle* as it requires a reflection on resources and acting in a pragmatic way. It may result in *reallocating resources* (mobilizing several types of resources) *and creating renewal* (for example: empowering client to find solutions for problems).

Each of these three main steps could lead to the conclusion of simply to: continue with the way of working, thus keeping the status-quo or exploring further improvements with the additional steps until the clients' needs are met. Clients then feel highly gratified which leads to a feeling of fulfillment among the employees.

The process starts again and the professionals ask the same questions, each time the client's situation changes. Nurses and nurse assistants actually tell how each client is different and how client's behavior can differ over the course of time. Based on the data, it occurred as if change is the only constant in the context of the healthcare. Clients come and go, and their capabilities can change during the course as well.

3.2.2 Outcomes of IST

Integrating Simplification aims to avoid what could lead to disintegration in the primary organizational process of serving the client and avoiding wastage of any kind in realizing organizational goals. Wastage can be considered in terms of resources (time spent, money and material), unnecessary institutional complexity, mental overburdening and communication based on hidden agendas. The outcomes thus could be looked at directly in terms of client focus leading to client satisfaction and a sense of meaningfulness among employees, low sick leave and high productivity at team and organizational levels collectively. Indirectly, it leads to word of mouth advertising by the satisfied clients and their families resulting in a growth in client numbers and subsequently a growth in the number of employees. Buurtzorg does not spend time and money in advertisement. The work by teams at local level generates the attention required to attract new clients. The Buurtzorg policy is empowering clients to make them independent as soon as possible, as a result clients needing services again return to Buurtzorg based on their previous positive experience.

It is obvious that while the focus is on the client at Buurtzorg, this seems to influence all other relevant performance indicators in a positive way. Controlling on productivity then does not become the main objective of the founder but trusting that teams are able to focus on the client's needs, based on their professionalism and consequently able to take decisions that ensure the organizational goal of productivity as well. Furthermore building the facilities so that team members can focus on the primary process then becomes a concrete managing tool which at Buurtzorg is expressed as all kinds of support from the Headquarters. Integrating Simplification principles are not only present in the relationship between the professional and the client, but also in the managing relationship between the Buurtzorg Headquarters and the employees. This will become clear when explaining the dimensions of Integrating Simplification.

Fig. 3.3 Primary process and integrating simplification

3.2.3   The Primary Process and Dimensions of IST

Organizing the primary process as the main process and aligning all activities of the so called secondary process to the primary process at all levels in the whole organization is a key feature at Buurtzorg. Figure 3.3 describes the relevant steps in the primary process.

When nurses and nurse assistants work at Buurtzorg they easily attune to the Buurtzorg vision which is about a client care focus. It appears that this vision is being perceived in the organization as a higher cause, a noble cause to revitalize the healthcare system. The vision is clear to everyone as it is conveyed as a message when a person is appointed. There are sessions where newly appointed nurses and nurse assistants can meet colleagues and the founder to hear about the vision, ask questions and share their views and experiences. It is important that the nurses and nurse assistants become aware of it and accept it as a working goal which in practice turns out to be 'helping the client as a whole person'.

When a nurse or nurse assistant starts at a client's home this notion is important (See Fig. 3.3). It requires a holistic understanding of the client by assessing their needs, the resources available, the current physical and emotional capabilities, the engaging stakeholders in the professional and social structure of the client and approaching other persons with whom they have social ties such as family members. Based on the collected information, the team could start assessing the current practices the client deals with and simplify circumstances to meet the needs of the client through Craftsmanship abilities. If needed, she will redesign and put into practice what she has thought of as a new solution by using the capabilities, networks and resources that are available. Subsequently this results in value creation of various kinds, tangible and intangible. We can think of satisfaction, productivity, creating community networks and stakeholders engagement to be used in the future as well. This results in the experience of meaningfulness and it strengthens the dedication toward the purpose. Eventually the nurse or nurse assistant may need to cope with new clients as former clients exit or due to new clients created by a new composition of teams causing the schedule of care delivery needs to be adapted as well. This adjustment requires the whole process to renew again starting with attuning to the client.

As stated earlier managing at Buurtzorg is about simplification by building trust and building facilities that support the primary process in the organization. Managing by trust emerged in two different dimensions: attunement to the client and Craftsmanship. At a more abstract level we could label both as the vital level of the organization.

Managing by supporting facilities emerged in two other dimensions, representing the secondary process mainly: Intrapreneurial Freedom in teams and Pragmatic Will by ICT facilities. At a more abstract level both has physical and mental elements. The physical represents the concrete facilities and the mental represents the mental abilities when using these facilities. These supporting facilities have certain conditions such as, agreeing on productivity as a safeguard (Chap. 6) to ensure the business objective. This is not a dominating goal, it is one of the necessary goals to exist, but it is integrated with other goals and conditions. The secondary process exists along with the steps in the primary process but it is up to the nurse or nurse assistant whether he or she makes use of Intrapreneurial Team Freedom or the ICT facilities to enhance each step in the primary process.

Furthermore it emerged that serving the client in the best possible way and aiming for a client focus, is being experienced as a higher purpose by employees at the Headquarters, nurses, nurse assistants and the founder, co-founder, creative thinker and all other experts who are actively involved in Buurtzorg. Such a higher purpose avoids making the distinction that often occurs in organizations in terms of personal versus organizational interests. If a goal is being experienced as a higher purpose, everyone agrees that it needs to be strived for and automatically everyone who appreciates it as a higher purpose will invest all possible effort to achieve it. The higher purpose then becomes a leading principle in the organization which does not have a single but multiple owners in the organization. At Buurtzorg it acts as the binding factor in the organization, by integrating the primary and the secondary processes. Such a higher purpose as main motivation occurs if belief systems of a group of individuals synthesize. This happens more easily if people

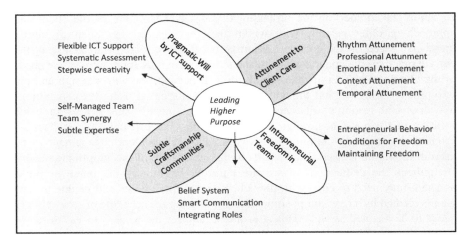

Fig. 3.4 Dimensions of integrating simplification

have the same background, history, value system or a common enemy in opposition.

We could label the vital levels containing the two dimensions: Client Attunement and Craftsmanship as relevant drivers of the primary process at Buurtzorg. We could label the physical and mental level containing the two dimensions, Intrapreneurial Freedom and Pragmatic Will with ICT as the relevant drivers for the secondary process at Buurtzorg. Both are required and act in synergy through the leading dimension of the higher purpose. This dimension could be labeled as the psychic or higher mental level of the organization. Integrating Simplification relevantly occurs at the vital, physical, mental and psychic or higher mental levels of the organization resulting in approaches that are meaningful to the client and the employees and which generates sustainable business results.

The three principles occur in each of the five dimensions. We could state that *Integrating Simplification occurs through a Pragmatic Will, Intrapreneurial Team Freedom, Subtle Craftsmanship and Attunement to the Client (a mindful assessment and adjustment to the needs and capabilities of the client (as a whole person)), as well as the dedication of the leader to a higher purpose and his willingness to serve this purpose rather than to lead an organization.* Figure 3.4 presents these dimensions and their properties which will be explained in detail in the Chaps. 4–8.

These 17 properties consist of lower-level concepts to be discussed in the following chapters as well. Pragmatic Will by ICT support has three important properties. Because of the flexibility offer of the ICT support the tendency to explore ICT increases. Another feature is the need to conduct systematic assessment in order to improve the quality of the support for realizing a client care focus. Furthermore, it emerged from the data that the introduction of creative ideas in a step by step approach is the best pragmatic approach so that employers get used to it.

The dimension of Subtle Craftsmanship in communities contains the following properties: Self-Managed Team, Team Synergy and Subtle Expertise. So far, the Self-Managed Team has occurred as an important element in all Buurtzorg's good practice descriptions. It is also one of the highly attractive features for nurses and nurse assistants as they have expressed in employee studies. Synergy in teams based on roles is another important property of Craftsmanship. Nurses and nurse assistants express how next to their professional competencies, more personal competences where they are open to subtle cues, help them in their Craftsmanship. They state that professionalism is not enough; it should always be a balance between professionalism and personal expertise. In Chap. 5 a more detailed explanation will be provided about the Subtle Expertise. All of these properties contribute to the necessary Craftsmanship for realizing a client care focus.

The dimension of Leading a Higher Purpose also contains three main properties. Due to a certain set of beliefs a higher purpose occurs. A belief system is something that could sustain for a while and it could work as a 'golden rule or DNA' in an organization. A remarkable feature at Buurtzorg is the importance given to the virtual communication style to reach out to employees and colleagues who are spread all over the country.

The Intrapreneurial Team Freedom dimension emerged with the following properties: Entrepreneurial Behavior, Creating Conditions for Freedom and Maintaining the Freedom to create opportunities and do the needful in order to deliver a client care focus.

Based on the study five different kinds of attunement occurred as important properties of the dimension of Attunement to the Client Care. These are attunement to rhythm, professionalism, emotion, context and the temporal character of the relationship between the professionals and the clients.

3.3 The Concepts and Their Relationships

Figure 3.5 gives the overview of all relevant elements of Integrating Simplification. Managing by trust at the level of client and Craftsmanship gives the aspect of building trust as a key feature in the organization. Managing by supporting facilities gives the aspect of striving for effectiveness in the whole organization. Everyone develops a capacity to judge what is really going on, what is the right thing to do, what are the possibilities to simplify actions and what are the best actions to renew a practice or a situation. It seems that terms such as management and leadership do not resonate in the organization. Employees expressed that they do not consider the founder or the coaches as managers. They know their own responsibilities. While the founders and coaches may give suggestions and tools for making the decision, what to do with them is theirs. At Buurtzorg the terms management and leadership do not have a place. Some employees expressed their need to be led or coordinated especially when they started to work for Buurtzorg. However, after a while they became familiar to the concept that one needs to lead oneself and manages his work by knowing his responsibilities and seeking the connection and collaboration with

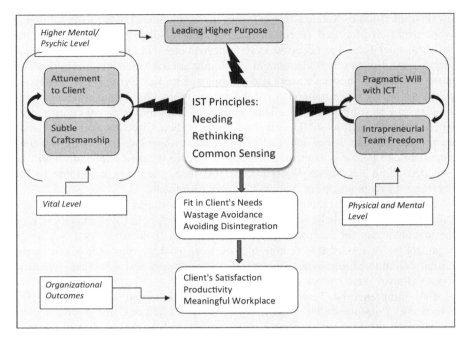

Fig. 3.5 Building blocks of integrating simplification theory (IST)

other colleagues but mainly with the vision of the organization, which is helping the client in the best possible way. A connection to such a higher purpose results in the expression of detachment from being managed, led, coordinated or controlled.

While employees acknowledge that the founder is an important driving force (Chap. 8) the good thing here is that they do not feel they are dependent on him for getting the work done, nor does he think employees should be dependent on him. Such a detachment expression ensures a sustainable existence of the organization. A side effect is that whenever the founder is conveying a message or opinion through the virtual platform or at a meeting, the messages and opinions are taken very seriously and become even internalized in the belief systems of the employees. They become a shared value. One could state that because of the implicit leadership, when this becomes explicit or visible, its strength can be dominant.

The main approach at Buurtzorg Nederland is to deliver care that is client focused. In daily practice it is being labeled as a client focused approach towards care. Integrating Simplification defines how the process of helping the client in the best possible way is being conducted in practice. What is the best possible service to the client? The Buurtzorg DNA (09-07-2011 version 7) describes a few quality indicators for helping the client. These are:

- To offer solutions to clients while keeping them from becoming 'addicted to' or dependent on the support care they receive. When clients do need a lot of care and support, the best possible help comes from empowering them to become independent as soon as possible by focusing on their capabilities.
- To offer solutions to clients to enhance their quality of life or to maintain the current level of quality as long as possible.

These have been confirmed in the interviews that have been conducted. Based on the main concern, Integrating Simplification helps the organization to gain market position, to easily adapt to new situations, innovate new services and to operate successfully with high productivity and employees' commitment. The various activities that comprise Integrating Simplification have been categorized in main principles, dimensions, properties and lower-level concepts.

Client's Integrated Attunement
It tells us what needs to be done to get an overview of the client from a holistic perspective and what actions are required to implement for serving the holistic needs. In this process it is important to know how to stay attuned to the client's needs and capabilities and how to keep his or her independency as long as possible. It is also necessary to know, what style of communication with the client and his or her significant others is required to serve their needs, what interactions are essential to mobilize and foster sustainable networks for ensuring good care, empowering independency and gaining insights in the available additional resources and capabilities. Given the client's current medical and social, demographic and geographic conditions we ask the following questions: What are possible predictions for the intensity of care and support for the near future? What are the things to be taken care of now to maintain the current level of quality and to prevent a decrease in quality in life? What are communication strategies to stay attuned to the future condition and needs of the client?

While a holistic view asks for insights at different levels thus making the picture more complex for the nurse or nurse assistant as she has to gather and cope with more information, for the client it is a simplification. They entrust their 'problems' to the professionals. Among many clients this arouses a feeling of being relaxed. Subsequently this may contribute to a feeling of a higher quality of life. It may also contribute to a faster recovery or an easy coping with their deprived situation.

Craftsmanship
Integrated attunement can be realized through Craftsmanship. Community nurses are trained with expertise to get a holistic view of the needs and capabilities of the client. They are trained to visit clients in their private environment and therefore know how to relate to privacy issues, how to develop a personal approach while still keeping a professional distance. They are trained to offer different kinds of solutions: medical related, psychological and socially structured. They are also trained in communication skills to discuss various types of issues with clients. They attain, practice and master skills of different kinds. This means that they possess a

deep understanding and maturity. They gain a holistic view and develop holistic approaches to solutions. They build a network, and know relevant stakeholders in the neighborhoods of their clients. They develop additional insights of the whole chain of care while dealing with these networks and stakeholders. Therefore they are able to tap from these resources when solving various queries, also in the future. Due to their expertise they can anticipate on the future needs of the client as well. This chain perspective resembles Craftsmanship. Through their Craftsmanship they help the client in the best possible way, they foster sustainable networks, use available but often untapped resources and they help the client in a personal and professional manner.

Teams are provided with frameworks for self-management. These are booklets with simplified structures for conducting meetings; a few basic principles of team dynamics and examples to help employees create awareness of what can go wrong. Furthermore teams can get guidance from experts from an education facility which is available for 1.5 days each week for enquiries. Every start up team receives training from this facility. Coaches are provided advice in team dynamics as well.

These smart simplifications have direct impact on the time spent by nurses and nurse assistants. The saved time is used for extra care and activities which enhances the clients' satisfaction and a holistic view on their needs. There are other kinds of simplification that indirectly contribute to the main concern. However, they directly influence the organizational performance. For example, a flat organizational structure to avoid wasting time for administration or management control tasks. The structure therefore is very flat consisting of a managing director and a strategic corporate director. In addition, there are coaches who facilitate the processes of Craftsmanship. A small back office facilitates other business tasks such as Human Resources, Finance, Service, Administration, and Management Assistance. Job positions are also simplified into a few classifications only: project employees at the Headquarters, nurses, nurse assistants, coaches and directors.

The care and support are organized in such a way that the client receives help from a small team of nurses and nurse assistants. This number varies per team but a team usually has a maximum number of 12 nurses and nurse assistants. Usually a client receives help from 3 to 4 team members. The rationale behind a small team is building trust with the client, maintaining their privacy as much as possible and enhancing a deep understanding of the client's needs. Getting a holistic view of the client's needs and capabilities and gaining a good overview of the resources of the client to improve their quality of life is essential. Due to this overview, significant others including family, friends and neighbors can be approached for additional support in whatever beneficial way when needed. Becoming familiar with a small team, clients are able to build warm relationships with the nurses and nurse assistants and are more comfortable to address different kinds of needs or issues they face. They only need to share with a few nurses and nurse assistants rather than explaining about their needs to many.

Nurses and nurse assistants work in Self-Managed Teams. This facilitates a faster decision making process to serve the client in the best possible way. Team members do not need to wait for a manager's approval when facing a query from a client, when experiencing that a certain approach does not work or can be improved to serve the client better. Instead they apply peer supervising and mentoring to do the needful. If queries are related to governmental regulations or rules of insurance companies and they do not have a solution or response, they approach their coach, post their query on the website or they enquire with the Headquarters for support and answers. Types of queries related to their clients are generally solved by themselves. It is the team that is important in handling the day to day issues to take care of the client's needs.

Craftsmanship facilitates an attunement to the client in an integrated way. It simplifies the process of exploring networks, building trust, effective communication and the development of insight of the whole picture. It contributes to employee satisfaction and commitment, as well as the organization's outcomes such as productivity and growth in number of clients, through the networks that are built. It contributes to client satisfaction and sincere loyalty. This produces word of mouth marketing leading to new clients. Therefore marketing costs for attracting new clients are extremely low.

Running the activities in a small team themselves means that they also need to find an office, get clients, build networks with relevant stakeholders in that particular area including hospitals, doctors and other professional caregiving institutions. In practice they continuously need to refresh their roles, tasks and ideas in order to cope with the needs and the features of the particular community they serve. They need to attune with the present reality in order to get things done as they are responsible for their own output. They must be adaptable when the demand for care increases. They need to be able to improvise if unexpected events happen with their current clients or if new clients knock on their door. There is a policy that if terminally ill patients approach a team, they cannot refuse them. They have a priority for assistance.

Team members can turn to a coach or the training institute for advice and support when they encounter issues that they cannot deal with internally in the team. They mobilize resources themselves, such as expertise that they are lacking or a particular service such as night care. They are responsible for recruiting and hiring team members as well as for the administrative tasks. The internet facilities support them in these tasks. Output such as productivity and rate of sick leave become transparent due to the internet facilities. They can also seek support from other neighboring teams.

Pragmatic Will

While Craftsmanship comprises the primary process of nursing and caring, an attitude of Pragmatic Will enables the Craftsmanship process and the process of integrated attunement of the client. Pragmatic Will refers to the discipline of designing arrangements in the organizational architecture or designing the physical features of the organization to stay focused on serving the client in the best possible way. It is about simplification in the architecture and integrating this simplification through Craftsmanship and directly through integrated attunement of the client, which contributes to a client focus. Pragmatic Will is about organizing and functioning in a specific way to ensure integrated concrete results at several levels: from a client perspective, Craftsmanship perspective and a business point of view. Several activities comprise the Pragmatic Will. Each of these is related to one or more of the other core concepts of Integrating Simplification.

There are ICT facilities at several levels: an internal virtual community to communicate and share experiences; facilities to make productivity transparent on the virtual platform; facilities for quality control, reducing various printed forms by digitalizing them; digitalizing processes to reduce workload and increase flexibility. They are all aiming to reduce the complexity and therefore create more time for serving the client in the best possible way.

There is a limited administrative reporting. The numbers of forms to be filled in at the client's visits are kept as low as possible. There is an attitude of doing only what is necessary. Forms that are commonly used in the industry for quality control have been simplified to avoid spending too much time for producing administrative reports. Also the number of forms and ways of reporting to the Headquarters are significantly lower compared to the industry standard.

Overall we can state that Pragmatic Will leads to outcomes that directly enable Craftsmanship to serve the client's needs in the best possible way. Furthermore it results in low overhead costs and low complexity. It also offers a path, guideline or framework that is found systematically throughout the organization. It serves as a culture to which everyone in the organization abides. Because of its simplicity it is known to everyone in the organization and easily assessed and applied. At times of conflicts, confusion or uncertainty this systematic path is often being assessed mindfully leading to solutions. Having such a systematic path helps to get a detached view, apart from emotionally infused points of views, especially when conflicts occur in teams.

Intrapreneurial Team Freedom
Furthermore the process of Craftsmanship is being facilitated by an attitude of nourishing an Intrapreneurial Freedom in the team. At the team level, individuals experience freedom to express their ideas for improving the client focus approach, the freedom to explore with different tasks such as planning, coordination, recruitment interviews, chairing meetings for enhancing entrepreneurial skills in addition to their professional Craftsmanship skills. Teams take responsibility and act like intrapreneurs. Teams formulate themselves, either as a new team because they have noticed a need in a particular geographical area or as a second team. The maximum number per team is 12. Teams that have grown beyond this number need to split and create a second team. There are areas with a single team but there are also areas with more than two teams. They receive some guidelines, are aware of the mission of the organization, make sure they possess the skills to serve the client and to run a team with mates. Team members are also responsible for exploring possibilities; to get new clients in the future, to search new innovative approaches, develop new expertise and knowledge to serve the clients in the best possible way.

In employee surveys the entrepreneurial space is valued highly by many of the nurses. During face to face interviews with nurses the opportunity to manage the own work, the freedom to experiment with new approaches and serving the client as a whole person are often mentioned as main motivators. They value the small teams, the autonomy to organize their work, the possibility to discover, explore and develop new skills when setting up the team and running the activities themselves. This improves their self-esteem. Some of them stated that in previous workplaces they would never discover their hidden talents. The ICT facilities enable their entrepreneurial attitude of taking initiative, being autonomous, frugal, innovating and pro-actively exploring the future. They also experience the flat organizational structure as a very positive framework because it creates the possibility to reach out the Headquarters quickly for any type of query. Due to all these entrepreneurial features their Craftsmanship as nurses and nurse assistants has been revitalized, the workload that does not serve the primary process has been simplified and reduced and therefore they have more time to practice their entrepreneurial skills. Furthermore they feel due to the entrepreneurial space that they are able to serve the client in the best possible way which gives meaningful lives to the clients and meaningful workplaces to themselves.

Leading Higher Purpose
Buurtzorg Nederland has been established as an alternative to the home care industry by revitalizing the practice of community care which was present a few decades ago. The main motivation was to increase the quality of care by reducing the complexity which was often the result of a more business approach to care. This business approach comprises mainly of management practices for control to increase the efficiency and deep specialization of tasks resulting in a loss of the overview when serving the client. Buurtzorg claimed that this business approach was a rather bad practice which did not lead to the targeted quality and efficiency. Such a claim resonated with many employees already working in the home care industry. What Buurtzorg did by starting up the organization was felt as a higher purpose worth striving for. Through this higher purpose Buurtzorg could mobilize a large number of nurses to follow its mission and approach. In the interviews, employees expressed a feeling of ownership of Buurtzorg Nederland. Some feel they have contributed in building the organization and express a feeling of pride. Many employees expressed that serving the client in the best possible way is what gives them fulfillment, something that they have not felt for years but what was their occupational calling when they choose the nursing profession. The way Buurtzorg is organized gives them this possibility. Many employees also shared the opinion that the mission and strategies at Buurtzorg fully resonate with their own mission and strategies. They often address to it as an ideal or noble cause to strive for. Some refer to the founder as a person with high ideals aiming to change and transform the industry. The higher purpose also resonates with clients and other stakeholders who are not direct competitors. This higher purpose thus resonates at several levels within and outside the organization and results in a sense of belongingness and commitment to the activities of Buurtzorg which can be seen as a way of simplifying the value proposition of the organization.

Integral fees for several nursing and caring activities are standardized. There are no separate fees for several tasks (nursing, caregiving, supervising) but a general fee which is the estimated average for the various activities that clients need. This enables Craftsmanship as the employees do not need to justify the time spent at a client for the separate tasks but for the whole task of serving the client. Clients experience this very positively. They are treated as a whole person rather than as a person with several types of needs. This makes their lives much simpler.

The first founder initially may be invisible as a leader because of lack of management layers, but such a flat structure enables the process of easy approachability. Eventually he becomes visible because he systematically conveys his message of striving to serve a common purpose. His powerful source to work for a common purpose is being fueled by his own life ambitions. This common purpose resonates with values of employees, clients and other stakeholders. The common purpose of the founder acts like charisma of purpose rather than charisma of the leader. He has dedicated himself to a compelling and deeply held common purpose to contribute to renewing the Healthcare Industry in order to uphold humane values of caring for clients. His original mission, due to the high and fast growth of the organization has become a profound mission. A profound mission naturally has the features of simplification and integrating. The more he resonates with people around him the more it gives him a sense of destiny or calling in his life. This subsequently fuels, because of the charisma of purpose, the whole organization. This leads to a 'never give up' attitude towards realizing the profound mission of the organization, yet a 'willing to let go of fixed approaches' to ensure openness to new approaches in realizing the profound mission and for adapting to new situations. Because of the self-management structure of teams a lot is taken care of by the teams themselves. The first founder acts at the strategic level and for external relations, has flexible working hours and thus spends a lot of time working outside the Headquarters often at irregular hours. He makes himself visible as a leader to the employees if they address him like a leader by asking for his opinion or in conflict issues at a team level or between coach and teams or for new policy or for signing contracts and meeting new employees. This also implies that his visibility as leader is irregular and employees are not dependent on it. They can operate in a detached way from having a visible leader around.

He adjusts himself to several roles that he has to play outside the organization as well as a change agent in the industry. Here he has to detach himself from one specific role as a leader. Concepts that are induced from the research data feature a leadership style which consists of four main roles. The way the founder reaches out to the employees, who are based all over the country, as the leader or manager of the organization is one feature. Communicating through the internal virtual network has been an effective way to reach out to the whole organization. Another feature comes from how he takes the role as a change agent in the industry. This helps to continuously remain attuned to the dynamics in the market and it gives possibilities to change the course of discussions that are taking place in the industry. By being a community nurse himself the founder resonates well with the employees. He occasionally performs duties as a nurse also during holiday seasons and therefore stays connected to the heart of the operational activities of his organization. And finally he has an integrating role which will be explained in detail in Chaps. 8 and 9. This role occurs as an enabler for holding the Integrating Simplification process together. The term that will be used in those chapters is Yogic Leadership.

Contrary to the first founder, the second founder forms the internal backbone of the organization. She takes care of the day to day management tasks. In contrast she is visible all day, usually from early morning until evening. Her fixed pattern of availability creates a sense of order and solves day to day issues. She may not be the expert on each nursing related topics since she does not have a nursing background, but she serves as a sounding board for all kinds of topics to be dealt with including governmental and insurance rules and regulations, and other practical related issues such as recruiting and hiring personnel. Topics that require a strategic view will be discussed between her and the first founder either face to face or at organized meetings where coaches also participate. These coaches serve as leaders at another level as well. The coaches are supporting the teams and face several issues regularly which they bring to the attention of the founders in monthly meetings. At these meetings decisions are taken regarding new policy or new approaches. New ideas, conflicts and frustrations are shared. Coaches also work according to a flexible working pattern and approach. They make themselves visible when needed or when invited by teams. Coaching explicitly does not comprise of managing and controlling. Moreover they facilitate the processes in teams so that teams can serve the client in the best possible way.

Higher purpose and leadership act as fuels in the coordination of the several components in the organization. They influence serving the client indirectly through other components such as; integrated and attuned client focus, Craftsmanship, Pragmatic Will and Intrapreneurial Team Freedom. They foster simplicity throughout the organization.

Attuning to Clients

4

Abstract

In this chapter we will explain how attunement to the client occurs at Buurtzorg. A main enabling process in the approach to the clients is the assessment of their capabilities while trying to empower them to become independent as soon as possible. The client's context is being assessed as well by considering the roles played by significant others such as family members, friends, neighbors and volunteers. In cases where social ties (significant others such as family, partner, neighbor) could be involved to realize a speedy recovery of the client, yet with low complexity, they are integrated as important stakeholders. Just intending a client focus by considering the whole situation of the client is not enough. It should be perceived as the main purpose at all levels of the organization. Rather than considering the client as a sick person or a person who needs help, the client is perceived as a person with capabilities; as a person, with significant others around him; and as a person with certain belief systems. Figure 4.1 gives an overview of the main stakeholders in the process of attuning to the client.

4.1 Attunement

One concept that emerged from the data is Attunement to the Client as one of the core concepts of Integrating Simplification. We found the following lower level concepts of attunement (Fig. 4.2):

- The client is occurring as dominating party to whom nurses and nurse assistants attune to in the sense of *timing* (rhythm) of delivery of care and the ability to be flexible if the client's needs change. We label this as the **Client as Zeitgeber** or the dominant actor.
- We also found an *interactive* process of attunement. Client and nurses and nurse assistants interact with each other and mutually build a relationship of care. In this relationship of care, caregiver team's professionalism is an important

© Springer International Publishing Switzerland 2015
S.S. Nandram, *Organizational Innovation by Integrating Simplification*,
Management for Professionals, DOI 10.1007/978-3-319-11725-6_4

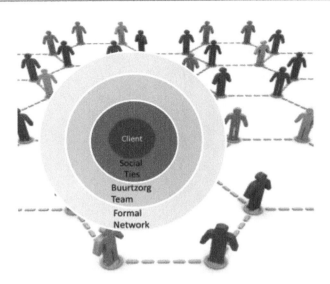

Fig. 4.1 Relevant stakeholders in attunement process

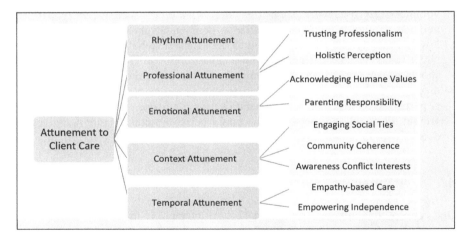

Fig. 4.2 Client attunement

guiding principle which is labeled as **Trusting their Professionalism**. Interaction induces a constant process of gaining new information as a source for actions. Nurses and nurse assistants at Buurtzorg perceive their client as a whole person in a process of interactions. An aspect of this interaction is a **Holistic Perception** of the client.

• Another type of attunement which occurred in the data seems to be more on the *emotional* level. It occurred that nurses and nurse assistants take more responsibilities than professionally would be expected from them. This is not incidentally happening but is rather a pattern that is being realized and which is almost a culture at Buurtzorg. In the data we identified a concept that we could label with incorporating **Humane Values** as a central aspect in the way of working. Another concept is **Parenting Responsibility**. If necessary, based on their feelings, nurses and nurse assistants act as 'parents' for their clients.

- A fourth form of attunement occurred, which is attunement to the *context,* where the care is based because this context is important for the client. In delivering the care from the perspective of the client the main context is often his home but from the Buurtzorg perspective this context is broader. We found the following concepts: it includes the social structure of the client which is labeled as **Engaging Social Ties**. Furthermore the nurses and nurse assistants interact with other stakeholders in the professional community structure which is labeled as **Community Coherence**. Yet another concept that occurred in being aware of conflicting interests of stakeholders in this professional community structure which is labeled as **Awareness Conflicting Interests.**

- A fifth form of attunement occurred in relation to *temporal* conditions due to change in client's portfolio. Two aspects that fit this concept are **Empowering Independence** of clients and **Experience Based Care.**

In the following paragraphs these concepts and their properties will be described and illustrated with citations followed by a reflection of how Integrating Simplification occurs when attuning to the client. As the Classic Grounded Theory forms our methodology of this study, relevant literature was studied as well to see how the findings contribute to or are aligned with existing concepts. It can be noticed that the concepts that are mentioned as lower level concepts of attunement resembles the concept of entrainment. Entrainment is perhaps not a very well-known concept in management or organizational studies, but it is relevant in this case. Without aiming an extensive description of this concept and the state of its art in academics in the next section we will define and refer to insights on entrainment to understand the process of attunement to the client. In simple words for daily use the concept of entrainment is about alignment.

4.2   Client as *"Zeitgeber"*

Respondents mentioned how important it is to make sure that a team comprises a few nurses who are able to deliver service during flexible hours, because there are always clients who prefer or due to circumstances require flexibility. In several interviews nurses and nurse assistants tell how their private life is totally aligned to the needs and preferences of the client. The concept of entrainment will be described briefly to explain how the client becomes the dominant rhythm (the Zeitgeber).

The term entrainment was first coined by the Dutch mathematician, Christiaan Huygens (1629–1695). He identified the phenomenon of *entrainment* when he noticed that two pendulum clocks, when placed on a common support, would synchronize with each other, even after being deliberately disturbed. This phenomenon has also been described in a wide variety of other systems, such as fireflies illuminating in synchrony, adjustment of speech rhythms during conversation or sleep-wake cycles synchronizing to the 24-h cycle of light and dark. It has mainly been used in physics and in the last decade the phenomena of entrainment has been introduced to the field of human behavior and management.

How can we define this concept? Sandra and Nandram (2013) define entrainment as a synchronization process over time whereby two or more naturally occurring rhythms interact with each other in such a way that they adjust towards and eventually lock-in to a common phase and/or periodicity, most often to the rhythm being more powerful or dominant, and finally maintain a consistent relationship.

At Buurtzorg natural rhythms occur as often as possible. Entrainment therefore could be an interesting phenomenon to understand how attunement to the client happens. Let us examine its properties. First of all, entrainment involves *rhythms* or cycles that can repeat themselves at regular or irregular frequencies. Several researchers refer to this property, using words such as cycle, rhythm, oscillating bodies, and rhythmic process.

The second property is *adjustment*, also expressed by synchronization or modification (McGrath and Rotchford 1983; McGrath et al. 1984; Jones and Boltz 1989; Ancona and Chong 1996; Bluedorn 2002; Pérez-Nordtvedt et al. 2008). So, entrainment is an adjustment, but of what? According to most definitions, it is an adjustment of *phase* (McGrath et al. 1984; Jones and Boltz 1989; Ancona and Chong 1996; Bluedorn 2002; Letiche and Hagemeijer 2004; Pérez-Nordtvedt et al. 2008) and/or *period* of a rhythm (McGrath et al. 1984; Jones and Boltz 1989; Ancona and Chong 1996; Bluedorn 2002; Pérez-Nordtvedt et al. 2008) to an external rhythm or *pacer* (McGrath and Rotchford 1983; McGrath et al. 1984; Jones and Boltz 1989; Ancona and Chong 1996; Pérez-Nordtvedt et al. 2008). The pacer to which weaker cycles entrain is called the "Zeitgeber" or dominant cycle (McGrath et al. 1984). At Buurtzorg nurses and nurse assistants are the weaker cycles and they entrain to the client who acts as pacer or Zeitgeber.

The following quotes were expressed in a group interview with a team and give an impression on how the client works as a Zeitgeber or a dominant rhythm:

• *Your partner and children should be able to cope with it when you work at Buurtzorg. It is not just a workplace. Your clients' preferences are the starting point of your planning. Usually you adjust your schedule to the clients you have agreed upon with your teammates, also if their preferences change due to a decrease or even improvement in their medical condition. In practice this means that you should be available to take extra or flexible hours to serve your clients. We try to schedule a few 'fixed' nurses per client so especially if someone's condition changes we do not want to send a 'new face' to the client* (Team interview).

- *Sometimes suddenly you need to leave while you were preparing the dinner for your family or while you are doing your groceries. It is not that only I am flexible, during such a circumstance, but also my family members: I need their support and understanding and they need to be able to cope with it as well* (Team interview).
- *Of course when you are not on duty you can switch off your phone but I do not mind keeping it on. If someone from Buurtzorg phones I am available. I am then the person who decides whether to take the phone or not. I can decide to refer to another colleague who is familiar with the client or solve the issue myself. I feel more convenient if I can decide what to do instead of ignoring any query by just turning off my phone in my spare time* (Team interview).

A client tells: *"I was very ill, I could have died and I was kept in the hospital. There were protocols about visiting hours but in such circumstances you are not willing to abide to these protocols. Your family would love to visit you anytime. Having the possibility to get nursing at home is the best option. As soon as I had the possibility to get back to my home I asked for Buurtzorg. At Buurtzorg they are very flexible towards my own needs and they try to attune as much as possible to my preferences regarding timings and number of nurses"* (Respondent 2).

4.3   Properties of Entrainment

Beside studying the dominant rhythm there are other properties of entrainment that fit the concept of attunement to the client. It is mentioned that the rhythms *interact* (McGrath et al. 1984; Jones and Boltz 1989) and *lock-in* to each other (Letiche and Hagemeijer 2004), also expressed as a *consistent relationship* (Bluedorn 2002). This means that there needs to be an *interaction* between the rhythms. There are many forms of interaction possible, from weak to strong coupling. Typically, the interaction is weak, otherwise they would lose their independence or autonomy and form a new coupled system. To lock-in to a common phase and/or periodicity, and as a result maintain a consistent relationship, the periodicities of the rhythms need to be in close proximity to each other (Aschoff 1979). If there is no interaction, the rhythms are still active without any adjustment to the other. Sometimes rhythms that do behave synchronized do not necessarily imply entrainment. Entrainment always involves synchronization of two rhythms based on an interaction.

At Buurtzorg such a consistent relationship occurs in the professional context between the client, his family and the nurses or nurse assistants. The main interactions then occur in the direct process of care delivery. We label these as Professional Attunement and it emerged as trusting professionalism and a holistic perception of the client (4.3).

Another attunement resulting in a consistent relationship based on interaction, occur at the emotional level. Such an entrainment was not found in the academic literature but from our data it emerged that in interaction the emotional dimension is relevant as well. It occurred as acknowledging values and parenting responsibilities (4.4).

Another property of entrainment is its *temporal* character which means that with new interactions a new stage of entrainment can occur (McGrath et al. 1984; Ancona and Chong 1996; Pérez-Nordtvedt et al. 2008). For example, when a new team starts, the team members attunes to the new situation and the new clients. From the data it emerged that at Buurtzorg an experience based care approach and empowering independence facilitate such temporal entrainment. Teams are often temporary as they get more clients. When a team exceeds 12 members, it is required to split and start a new team. Temporary entrainment also occurs due to change in the client portfolio: clients come and go so the situation is continuously changing. Ancona and Chong (1996) mention an entrained rhythm may initially seem to be resistant to a change in cycle and will persist even when the external pacers are removed. However, McGrath et al. (1984) assumed that once the entrainment is established, it "persits to some degree even when surrounding temporal conditions have changed" (p. 31). If we follow the developments of newly started teams at Buurtzorg we conclude that such external occuring rhythms become entrained eventually. A clear vision and simplicity in rules and regulations then help to get a swifter entrainment condition (4.5).

Yet another property of entrainment is that *rhythms that are endogenous or naturally occurring* (McGrath et al. 1984; Pérez-Nordtvedt et al. 2008), will mutually entrain to each other and subsequently, they become collectively entrained to powerful external pacers (McGrath et al. 1984; Ancona and Chong 1996; Pérez-Nordtvedt et al. 2008). At Buurtzorg it seems that such a collective entrainment happens in regard to the context. We label it as Context Attunement and it comprises engaging the social ties of the client; realizing community coherence, being aware and coping with conflicting interests (Sect. 4.6).

If the entraining rhythm cannot be influenced (e.g. the daily cycle of light and dark), then we talk about asymmetrical entrainment. Most entrainment researchers look at this type of entrainment with the external environment as the origin of the dominant rhythm (Zellmer-Bruhn et al. 2004; Standifer and Bluedorn 2006). However, both external and internal rhythms can act as the dominant rhythm. Symmetrical or mutual entrainment is the case when rhythms do influence each other, such as the crickets chirping in unison and fireflies flashing synchronously (Ancona and Chong 1996; Strogatz and Stewart 1993). Typically, those rhythms are internal rhythms.

Sandra and Nandram (2013) define two general types of entrainment: inner and outer entrainment. Inner entrainment occurs when rhythms within a system become synchronized. Synchronization between the heart and the brain in a human body (McCraty et al. 2009) or between a firm's acquisition and alliance activities within the same firm (Pérez-Nordtvedt et al. 2008) are examples of inner symmetrical entrainment, also called intra-entrainment (Shi and Prescott 2012). The synchronization of a firm's activity with an external, environmental cue is an example of inner asymmetrical entrainment, also called extra-entrainment (Shi and Prescott 2012). The several types of attunement, labeled, fall into the inner entrainment. Professional attunement is about interaction within the same system which is care delivery. Emotional attunement may also occur in this same system. This holds for temporal attunement as well.

Outer entrainment occurs when rhythms between systems become synchronized. Synchronization between a firm's acquisition activities and the acquisition activities of their competitor (Pérez-Nordtvedt et al. 2008) is an example of outer symmetrical entrainment. People entrained to the environmental cue of the day and night cycle is an example of outer asymmetrical entrainment, as well as a firm's quarterly reporting. In the next paragraphs the several types of attunement will be described mainly with the help of quotes from interviews.

4.4 Professional Attunement

4.4.1 Trusting Professionalism

The professionalism of the nurses and nurse assistants is being characterized by a combination of cure, care, nursing, washing, case management, monitoring and risk management aiming to improve the health and quality of life of the individual, his family and the community he lives in (Pool et al. 2011, p. 37). And health is a process that comprises physical, psychic and social functioning while illness is defined as being out of balance. The community nurses and nurse assistants at Buurtzorg are not fixed to a specific work setting. Each setting requires a specific working approach and embodies relevant methods and competences. Within these settings there is an interaction between societal relationships, social structures and cultures around clients and patients with specific needs and problems. Buurtzorg works according to a community health nursing approach (Pool et al. 2011, p. 39). The services are embedded in the social structure of the individual client and his caretakers, usually life partner or children. The nurses and nurse assistants are engaged with insights, knowledge, a flexible attitude, and alertness. No client or situation is the same as previous ones. Problems are often very complex and therefore the nurse needs to be able to understand each specific circumstance and find solutions, most often these are unique solutions.

There is a client care relationship at the core of every activity that is being delivered by nurses and nurse assistants. In this relationship the interaction plays an important role between the client and the professional providing care. According to Pool et al. (2011) it is not a family relationship but a special one, having humane features and social aspects while at the same time bearing the professionalism of the nursing practice. The client in a way is dependent on this professionalism and its impact grows if the relationship is based on trust. The client should not worry about the professionalism of the nurse or nurse assistant. He should trust that all relevant competences are present and can build a valuable client-nurse relationship. His experiences with the nurse or nurse assistant, their availability, and their proven capability to deal with his problems will nourish this relationship. At Buurtzorg the term client is preferred instead of a patient or a customer. Because a patient only recalls illness while a customer recalls a business like relationship which is not the case in the community healthcare environment. Trust is a key driver and therefore 'client' suits better as a term.

A client expresses: The most important thing about Buurtzorg is that you can count on their expertise, you can fully trust them on that. And they bring in something extra which others do not bring. Usually if a person gets old like me and becomes ill you need people you can count on. My husband passed away and I do not have children around who can take care of me. I have become very dependent on what I call these 'second-hand-institutes'. Because, we as old people are now perceived as 'second hand things' and we are therefore less attractive. According to my experiences with a few of them I can tell you that those nurses of these second-hand-institutes do not care at all about the wellbeing of the client. They do not treat you as a human being but as a number, as a second hand thing. I even do not have neighbors or other relatives who can help me so I need help at home and I prefer to experience warm and humane relationships with those who take care for me. I was glad to find out that Buurtzorg is the best alternative to these second-hand–institutes. Imagine how it is to be treated by nurses who do not treat you as a human being, what should then be the reason to keep yourself alive? (Respondent 23).

4.4.2 Holistic Perception Client

From the data it emerges that at Buurtzorg the client is being perceived in a holistic way. The client is not just a sick person who requires a medical diagnosis and subsequently a treatment. They follow a community health nursing approach while including a broader—holistic—perception of the client.

This is one of the aspects what makes Buurtzorg different and which facilitates the main concern. The main concern in the study was: 'What does an organization such as Buurtzorg do, to deliver services that are fulfilling the client's needs and how does it design and organize its activities for realizing a client focused service'.

The underlying assumption at Buurtzorg is that a client focus is the best approach to serve the client's needs in the best possible way.

The following quotes show how holistic perceptions are put in daily practices.

In some circumstances I am the only person who comes to the client's home during the day and sometimes a client only meets us during the whole week. Because they do not have many relatives or the relatives do not live nearby. Then we almost become a family member. I have experienced that the client is waiting for me. In such cases I try to schedule a few minutes to drink a cup of coffee or tea with him after I complete the tasks. My role is then a bit different than a nurse but usually during those moments additional issues pop up. We give the client personal attention. We therefore say our service is professional and personal (Respondent 20).

When I compare this job with my previous job then here I do everything for the client. You need to act like a jack of all trades and be willing to take on several roles. This is only possible if you sincerely pay attention to the client as a human being and not by perceiving him as a sick person with certain symptoms that need to be treated (Respondent 38).

We have this saying amongst each other: you serve the client as if she is your own Mom or Dad. When your own family member complaints about pain or any form of discomfort you automatically perceive the whole situation and you compare all the signals you get from her and you try to make a logic interpretation out of it. Concluding what is going on is then not a pure technical process but you look at the whole picture of how the person usually behaves etc. You have the personal history of your family member and you may even include subjective analysis. But also if you do not have the whole history of your client, by being around such a person and having chats while you are helping her, and showing sincere interests in her life you get information that helps you to come up with a better holistic judgment. The clients feel it as well, whether you just do your job, or whether you really show interest (Respondent 37).

A client said: In other home care organizations the nurses back up the errors that are made by their management and spend a lot of time in politics while they should be there for the client. And because there are so many different nurses for one client they need to spend a lot of time for transferring the information about the client. There is no respect for the needs of the client, only their own concern prevails. I feel at Buurtzorg things are different: the nurses are there for the clients. You can always ask them all types of help. They will not solve everything immediately but at least they can help tracing who you need to call upon. They do not mind if they need to spend a few more minutes during a visit. They give you the feeling as if they want to make sure your needs are taken care of (Respondent 2).

4.5   Emotional Attunement

4.5.1   Acknowledging Humane Values

A client care relationship requires a certain type of ethical behavior from both the professional and the client. The professional does not sell products or services to the client, he delivers service based on a responsibility he has for the client. This responsibility he derives from his craft. At Buurtzorg this responsibility supports a broader boundary as has been expressed by nurses, nurse assistants and clients. This responsibility does not flow only one way. It is based on interaction and both parties attune to each other in the course of time. Clients adjust to the nurses and nurse assistant and they also adjust to the clients. In their client care relationship they build a special bond which is not a family bond but a humane bond. This seems more than logical but in reality, humane values in healthcare practices has declined.

From the interview data and the weekly diaries and examples in the books that have been written about Buurtzorg it becomes obvious that humane values are at the top of all professional activities. There are automatically considered in each step of serving the client. There are so many expressions of these values and it is not the intent to describe them all here. To explain what is done differently at Buurtzorg the following two quotes may be helpful. Here two nurses are referring to experiences in their previous jobs where there was hardly any room for humane values:

> *Over the last couple of years, I had been responsible for over 80 patients I never visited. My job as District Nurse had been made redundant and I was expected to work on solving routes for which no staff was available. The planning was made somewhere else by someone who didn't know the patients. This went wrong so often, that at a certain point; I could no longer explain to patients why nobody was available or only at a time other than what had been agreed on. I had 14 managers in seven years, and was fed up with that as well. The organization had become too large and elusive and no one felt responsible for our care. There were complaints and issues amongst colleagues every single day (Quote of Marja Feenstra from Amersfoort, source: De Blok and Pool 2010, p. 10).*

> *I had left the homecare organization because all I did was close the holes in client care planning. I did the intake with the intention of offering good healthcare, but I could not achieve this because so many people were involved in daily practice. Sometimes a person wasn't even planned in at all. Due to the new planning system that had been implemented, I didn't find out until the next morning that someone had not received any evening care the night before. The worst thing was that people couldn't call and therefore had been forced to remain seated in a chair the whole night. I found that unworthy (Quote of Ellis Heijblom from Breda, source: De Blok and Pool 2010, p. 11).*

4.5.2 Parenting Responsibility

Taking the responsibility based on certain ethics which is the norm in community healthcare is not enough at Buurtzorg. It has been observed that the responsibility goes further and adapts the feature of parenting responsibility. An entrepreneur usually has more success if he is able to be passionate about his products and services and if he really cares for the needs of the customer. Here a nurse or nurse assistant does not only take care of the needs but obviously loves his clients. Frequently a sincere humane interest in the client has been expressed as the most fulfilling aspect of the job. A few quotes and letters of clients will illustrate this parenting responsibility.

> **Box 4.1 Letter from a client who shared this pleasant unexpected surprises: nurses dressed up on the Dutch festival Sinterklaas' eve and on Christmas 25/12**
>
> *Dear Jos and Gonnie,*
>
> *I am very satisfied about the staff. They are visiting me now for 1 ½ years already. I really feel at home with them.*
>
> *A good 2014!*
>
> *Client*
>
> *Photo: example how they surprised me at Christmas. Where on earth to they find the time to play Santa Claus! Thank you very much for your wonderful staff.*

It is said that about 80 % of those who have chosen for this profession are being fuelled by the humane, social, and warm features of the profession. Not every institution however provides feasibility for these features to be fulfilled.

The client's representative had an interview appointment with me for the research interview and when I arrived at his residence, there was a nurse present who was not on duty but who just came over to make sure the client was well and to discuss another issue related to his work as client representative with her. When I asked the client if this was a regular pattern, he told me that the nurses have become part of his family. So if he doesn't feel well one of the nurses will give him extra attention by giving a call or dropping by with some soup or fruits etc. A few minutes later the scheduled nurse arrived and it was like normal to see another colleague drinking a cup of coffee with the client.

> **Box 4.2 Client's letter who has received a Christmas present from a team**
>
> *Buurtzorg Nederland*
>
> *Attn. mr. J de Blok*
>
> *Rotterdam, December 17, 2013*
>
> *Dear Mr. de Blok,*
>
> *Last week I was pleasantly surprised by one of the workers of the team Buurtzorg Vreewijk in Rotterdam-South with a Christmas package. It contained all kinds of useful utensils.*
>
> *By means of this letter I would like to express my gratitude for the excellent work that is done by the team. Always ready to help, day and night for young, old, ill or handicapped, under all circumstances. Also a friendly chat is part of their capabilities and many lonely people feel strengthened by such a chat, in order to go to bed with a peace of mind.*
>
> *Finally, dear Mr. de Blok, I would like to wish you and everybody that is part of Buurtzorg Nederland a Merry Christmas and a prosperous and healthy 2014, and that your organization will settle solidly in our society.*
>
> *Kind regards,*
>
> *Client*

In a team meeting in another region it occurred to the researcher that this was not an exception. This pattern does occur in other teams as well. Nurses were concerned about a client and wondered whether they needed to adjust their schedules a bit to make sure that the client's needs were served. In this particular case the client was awaiting the results of a medical examination which could turn out to have a negative result.

Box 4.3 Letter from a client who has received a CD from a team

Dear Jos and Gonnie,

A few weeks ago we received the Buurtzorg CD from one of your staff, for which we would like to thank you very much. We played it immediately, but only listened superficially because we did not have so much time. These days, as you probably know, are flying by when you are old, while it seems as if you are doing nothing, as a matter of fact you are doing only half of what you did in the past!

This was a very nice present, what a nice initiative and it shows that you enjoy accomplishing it. This enjoyment is what gives you the power and it shows in your staff; they are without exceptions all angels. They really take care of their customers, are compassionate, and are friendly, flexible and well organized. We are very happy with them! This is why we are so thankful that you started this organization!

I hope all goes well with you,

With kind regards,

Client

As they knew that the client's family does not live close by, the nurse wanted to be sure that there was a person around who could emotionally support her. Such a client relationship may be acceptable in this specific industry but may not be an acceptable pattern in other industries. The nurses sometimes take the role of a family member or a 'parent'.

4.6   Context Attunement

4.6.1   Engaging Social Ties

One of the emerging aspects is the strength of engaging significant others from the social structure of the client. Nurses and nurse assistants who initially saw their jobs as a professional activity only, express how in the beginning they felt uneasy about it because they wanted to avoid reactions such as 'mind your own business' from the family members. But after witnessing how other teammates do it and just knowing that it fits the Buurtzorg way of working they eventually tried it and realized that it works. When they are uncertain about whether they are crossing a sensitive line they discuss this with colleagues.

The following quotes illustrate how engaging social ties is part of the client focus approach.

At Buurtzorg I organize things in attunement with the client, his families and my teammates. It is very different compared to what I was used to when I was working in the hospital. But actually I realize that it is more natural to include the social structure of the client to be able to put a client focus into practice. This provides me the possibility to develop several of my hidden talents. I act more responsible and feel I have much influence and control on the way I do my job (Respondent 21).

We try to find out how the client's social network looks like to see if someone from his network could be engaged to solve the problem of the client. In some cases help from his neighbors, such as a short visit to check if the client is well, solves a lot (Respondent 3).

4.6.2 Community Coherence

Attunement to the context can be realized by coherence in the community by engaging the other stakeholders or by simply being a member of the community.

The following quotes and letters illustrate this.

Ellis Heijblom from Breda explains how this works in her team: At Buurtzorg, we need to find our own solutions. This can be tough, for example when we've decided not to accept any new patients, but we are called upon by a terminally ill patient. So far we have all decided to make an extra mile to give someone good final care. This does mean we have to find a solution for the overtime. But the atmosphere in the team is so good we can safely say 'share' when it becomes too much (source: De Blok and Pool 2010, pp. 32–33).

Box 4.4 Letter from a client to Buurtzorg Nederland
Ladies Buurtzorg Veenendaal-West
Veenendaal, December 14, 2013
Dear people,
After ending your common daily medical care for my wife Gerda, we would like to let you know the following.
We took the advice of our family doctor, Dr. Huizinga to call upon your organization. In our experience, the necessary personal care for my wife Gerda has been handled in a professional, but also much appreciated, loving way.

(continued)

Box 4.4 (continued)

On a daily basis, without exception, we experienced that your cooperation is based on mutual trust, a great team spirit, mutual respect and the willingness to learn. Agreements with us were always followed up consequently and because of your willingness to immediately take action in unexpected situations we felt assured of trustworthy support.

These experiences made a big impression, helped us and contributed significantly to a further recovery of Gerda. We are very grateful to you and will share this with others when this is applicable.

We wish you a Merry Christmas and a prosperous and New Year full of love.

Clients (Mrs. and Mr.)

c.c. dr. C.E. Huizinga (Veendendaal), director and Mr. A.J. Zwart "Buurtzorg Nederland" (Almelo)

Box 4.5 Letter from a client to Buurtzorg Nederland

To Insurance Agency AGIS

Amersfoort, March 23, 2014

Dear AGIS,

I would like to let you know that I am very satisfied about Buurtzorg Amersfoort! I am approached and treated in a very friendly and respectful way!

I would like to be cared for by them forever! In week 12 and 13 of 2014 I contacted them because I was confronted with type 2 diabetes from one week to the other.

I hope this type of care continues to exist, and that you are doing everything possible to make sure it does, in case this type of care seizes to exist.

Kind regards,

Client

P.S. I have type 2 diabetes and have to take blood samples 4 times a day and inject insulin 2 times per day, Nova mix.

During a group interview team members express: *"We meet each other very frequently, also during non-office times as many of us live in the same neighborhood. We also meet family members or neighbors of former or current clients when we do our groceries or if we go for a walk and then we usually have a quick chat and get to know about the latest news and specific client's conditions. It helps you to keep an eye on your clients"*.

4.6.3 Awareness Conflicting Interest

Several interviewees expressed their alertness towards other stakeholders and how being aware of possible conflicting interest can facilitate decisions regarding serving a client. Often in the literature the entrainment occurring from external 'forces' produces the dominant interactions. Here at Buurtzorg even these external forces are becoming part of the interaction and gain the potential of being synchronized just by following the first step of becoming aware of how external cues deriving from conflicting interest influence the process of a client care focus.

> *In the Healthcare Industry there are different parties involved, each having their own interests. We should be continuously aware of what is good for the client when we deal with the insurance, hospitals or suppliers of medical products. We must know what the interests of all the main stakeholders are. Because it is rather an exception than a rule that: what is best for the client, is the main interest of such stakeholders. Sometimes I wonder why this happens. Oftentimes they don't care about the client at all and their only aim is to serve their own interests. Sometimes they do not even know what is really going on. They are alienated from what happens at the grass root level. How can such institutions have such a big role on client's who are in the last stages of their lives and vulnerable, not able to 'fight' against these institutions? Every little thing to improve the quality of life from our side then has priority. We do not worry about these conflicting interests all the time but we try to be aware of them in order to proactively prevent or take certain steps when needed (Respondent 6).*

> *The approach at Buurtzorg allows you to directly communicate with the family doctors and other professionals. It allows you to get clarity of what is happening and what is possible. You need to be aware of possible conflicts, their interest etc. (Respondent 5).*

During a meeting there was a discussion about a particular issue and one of the participants argued as follows: "*There is not such a thing as a personal interest which is different than the Buurtzorg interest. If that is perceived and experienced then we should talk about this*" (Respondent 39). The discussion continued about keeping the responsibility clear and there where it fits, for example: "*the responsibilities regarding the productivity of teams lie at the team level. They know what type of clients they have, what types they can get and what they need. If they need to split up because they have too many clients they should do that. They know the available support and guidance they can get. If they need to acquire clients because they do not reach their targeted productivity, then they themselves know what strategies are best*" (Respondent 24, interview 1).

An employee stressed that sometimes there are 'hidden' rules or approaches in terms of 'this is the way we do things at Buurtzorg'. If you do not try to understand what Buurtzorg is about, you may miss a few of these insights and sometimes by chance you encounter them. Therefore it is very important, she says, to stay attuned to the founders and those working at the Headquarters, even if your focus is serving the client.

In several cases it seems that there is a kind of attitude that everything is fine. For example when employees express that there are certain ways how things at Buurtzorg are done, expressed as a certain Buurtzorg culture, but at the same time they believe that if you do not want to follow these, it is fine as well. However, you must be aware of them and if you have a better way of doing this and you prove it works, it is accepted.

ICT experts express that the services they provide should be facilitating the primary process. *"We can provide these services to several other institutions but we have learned that we need to be aware of the various interests that may be active in an organization. At Buurtzorg you should be aware of not dictating or standardizing too much because that would be against the Buurtzorg principles. There should always be room for own decision making on when and how the given ICT context could be applied within a certain range of rules. People should experience for themselves that a certain way works for them. A main consideration therefore for us when developing the facilities is to keep it all simple, making sure that the needful is being done and still be alert that there is space for flexible application whenever possible"* (Respondent 29).

4.7   Temporal Attunement

4.7.1   Empathy-Based Care

An empathy-based care is important to sustain professionalism with a client care relationship which is an important starting point for all activities at Buurtzorg. These activities facilitate the primary process of the care delivery.

An empathy-based care is part of the temporal attunement process. Nurses and nurse assistants continuously stay attuned to the client's needs and circumstances. Based on interactions they know what is really going on and actually realize that the only constant is change. Client's situations change every day and it requires a certain attitude to cope with it effectively. By using one's empathy it enables coping with the changes. Pool et al. (2011) stress how important such an interaction is and label the dialogue as an important feature of the empathy-based care. The dialogue leads to a new status quo but this status quo is also temporary. Through the dialogue the nurses and nurse assistants come to know which meaning clients and their families give to certain words, situations and experiences. They stay attuned to each other.

Pool et al. (2011) describe how the meaning given to a circumstance can differ between a nurse and the client. A client may say they feel sick, while objectively speaking the client may have social constrains that give rise to stress and subsequently influence their feeling of wellbeing. The nurse and nurse assistant try to really listen to the story as is being told by the client and they even try to observe subtle physical reactions to get a whole picture of what is going on. This empathy-based care is being practiced at Buurtzorg by applying the following four values: equality, completeness, eligibility and autonomy (Pool et al. 2011, pp. 55–56). The way Pool et al. define these values based on their research will be described here.

- Equality refers to the understanding that professional expertise is not better or higher in the hierarchy compared to insights that are derived from experience when making decisions. A client and his family, nurse or nurse assistant all have an equal contribution in decisions while a client is dependent and trusts the professionalism of the nurse and the nurse assistant. The decisions are thus a product of interaction. The outcome of interaction can vary due to the complexity of each circumstance and thus reaches temporal attunement.
- Completeness refers to the understanding that caring is an assignment for all stakeholders who are involved in the care delivery process and only by sharing perspectives, then working jointly on the tasks that are discovered from sharing, the intended results will be achieved. The nurse and nurse assistant, family member or any volunteers involved with a client of course has their own responsibilities in this process. Each circumstance is different and thus will have a different interaction outcome and temporal attunements.
- Eligibility refers to the understanding that nurses and nurse assistants have to work according to moral and legal duties that are derived from their professional responsibility. They safeguard these roles and the relationship it requires in the care delivery process. Each circumstance may require a different expression of these duties and thus show a temporal attunement.
- Autonomy refers to the situation that a client is allowed to develop and maintain his beliefs on the situation, his physical condition and his life. Autonomy occurs in interaction with an environment which of course can change and consequently show a temporal attunement.

4.7.2 Empowering Independency

At Buurtzorg encouraging clients to operate autonomously as soon as possible, is one of the core values as stated in its vision. This is also a feature of temporal attunement which requires the so called dialogue.

The following quotes explain how this works in practice.

I always ask the client to define his problems or needs, himself. Then I come to know what he is capable of doing for himself. It also makes him aware of his current situation, his fears or other issues. It is a way for me to attune to his situation. Of course sometimes a client can't express his situation precisely enough but then a family member such as the partner or a son or daughter operates as a contact person with whom I discuss more details about medicine and preferences regarding washing schedule or type of breakfast. But even then I try to get the client involved in the conversation regarding the care and service that I and my colleagues provide (Respondent 22).

In our team meetings we discuss every client's needs, situation and his capabilities to become independent again. In simple situations such as a client with one single problem such as a wound, we will stop with our services the moment the client starts doing well again. We discuss this with the client, family doctor and family members. If the need is more complex because it concerns more than medical related care, usually we gradually change our schedule for example from a few times a day to one time a day to a few times a week so that the client can adjust to the situation where he can continue with his life without us. Usually it is a fear they need to deal with. And a few conversations are helpful to activate the client again (Respondent 5).

I find it very important to encourage the client to be as independent as soon as possible and to be able to decide with the client what this takes, because you need to involve the client in this process (Respondent 20).

A client expresses: I am dependent of Buurtzorg but it is a dependency with gratitude not with frustrations which I had in the past when I received care from other institutes.

4.8   Integrating Simplification in Attunement to the Client

The three main aspects of the Theory of Integrating Simplification are the needing principle, rethinking reality and using common sense to put things into practice to solve an issue. In each of the attunement concepts these three principles are inherently present. In order to become attuned you should know what is needed. In order to solve an issue nurses and nurse assistants continuously rethink the circumstances and resources. They are faced with several issues and are trained to acknowledge each of them as a unique one. Only by putting ideas into practice, creates a value for the client and nurses and nurse assistants who are continuously using their professionalism and common sense to come up with the best solutions. By integrating these principles, which means by applying them at every aspect, the impact becomes sustainable. Simplification is at the core of all these activities.

A letter from a client illustrates how Integrating Simplification is being experienced at the clients' level. Several of the lower level concepts and properties that have been explained in this chapter, are spontaneously mentioned in the following letter (Box 4.6).

Box 4.6 Letter from a client to thank the founders

To the board of Buurtzorg

August 8, 2013

Honorable Directors,

For the first time in my life, I got to meet the organization of case in the Netherlands. In March, I had to undergo two intestinal surgeries in four days' time. During the second surgery, a stoma was placed close to the surgical wound. For my wife and me, this was the reason to call in the help of Buurtzorg Burgh Haamstede: as long as the wound was open we required assistance, given the great risk of infection. After the wound was closed we were capable of doing the care ourselves.

I look back at this period with admiration, especially towards the organization. Just one phone call was enough to get everything going. Even with the help already planned in for March 25, just a phone call was enough to postpone everything because of complications from surgery, which caused the stay at the hospital being longer than expected. I know from my own 'organizational' experience that this seems simple, but for the planning this can have a huge impact. The flexibility and friendliness, where the patient and partner were always number one has made a deep impression on us. The way things are organized should be given a big credit for that. Obviously a minimum of administrative hassle and a maximum care when this happens is necessary. I would like to compliment you on this.

But there is more. The team of Burgh Haamstede made a powerful impression on us. They were always punctual, always cheerful, helpful, never looking at the clock, never stressful or hurried. I like to thank Heleen van den Berge, Nel den Boer, Yvonne de Meij and intern Nienke (who really wasn't an intern but a full staff member with regard to knowledge, capability and cheerfulness) all very much for their care. As a patient and partner it is always a happy moment when these ladies are dancing at the side of your bed because your wound closed another millimeter. It is really very stimulating when there are people around where nothing is a must and everything allowed (and even help with it if necessary) and at the same time stimulate you to find your boundaries which made it possible for me get back on my feet again much faster. I don't usually speak excessively about people that just do their job, but there is just no way to avoid it, because it was much more. Also after the period of care, there were problems with a leaking stoma.

Even though my wife was helping me wonderfully, at some point self-confidence was decreasing. So we called for help from the team a couple of times. Again, this was no problem. The stoma was replaced and my wife was reassured. They left us with our compliments of the ladies and a smile on our faces. And if all that is still not enough, there was something else that stood out for us: the after-care. Also after the period of care, the ladies came over

(continued)

Box 4.6 (continued)

for a cup of coffee. Just a social call, they said. But it was obvious to us that they did this to check on the situation. I don't have insight in their adminis-tration, but I think that they did this without writing these hours. They definitely did this out of sincere compassion.

On behalf of my wife and me, I would like to express my appreciation by means of this letter, that we also copied to the team, and we express the wish that this formula, staffed with these kinds of people, will conquer the Netherlands very quickly.

Thank you very much.

Clients (Mrs. and Ms.)

Acknowledgement The author acknowledges the input that was received from Danny Sandra on the concept of entrainment in composing this chapter.

Subtle Craftsmanship in Communities

5

Abstract

Craftsmanship has been defined in the Oxford Dictionary as the skill in a particular craft. In this chapter we refer to the craft of nursing and caring. From the data the concept of Craftsmanship has emerged as an important factor in describing the client focus approach at Buurtzorg. The Craftsmanship at Buurtzorg involves more than only individual oriented skill to work as a professional. As Self-Managed Teams form an important organizing structure at Buurtzorg the Craftsmanship in the team context will be explained next to the individual skills.

5.1 Properties and Concepts of Craftsmanship

The properties of Craftsmanship, as they have emerged in the study, are presented in Fig. 5.1.

First the Self-Managed Teams approach will be explained as a relevant property. Three lower level concepts will be presented: practical support, small size of teams and community based care.

The second antecedent that appeared in our research is the team synergy consisting of team skill composition by explaining the team roles that are present at Buurtzorg; team role rotation and a harmonious team climate.

The third antecedent is subtle expertise for community care. Here we focus on what it requires at the individual level to accomplish successful Craftsmanship. Three lower level concepts emerged as important. First, in-depth expertise which represents a deep understanding and the maturity required to operate as a professional. The second lower level concept is mindful communication to enhance a positive team spirit. The third is subtle perception of cues in the context of the work.

Stewart et al. (1999) define a team as "...a collection of individuals who exist within a larger social system (...), who can be identified by themselves and other as

© Springer International Publishing Switzerland 2015

S.S. Nandram, *Organizational Innovation by Integrating Simplification*, Management for Professionals, DOI 10.1007/978-3-319-11725-6_5

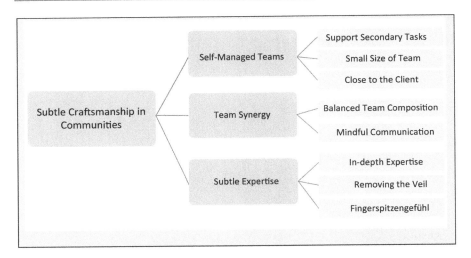

Fig. 5.1 Subtle craftsmanship

a team, who are independent, and who perform tasks that effect other individuals and groups". This definition fits the teams at Buurtzorg.

The organization consists of community care nurses and nurse assistants in communities while being part of the larger system of Buurtzorg Nederland.[1] They operate independently and perform tasks that have an impact on others, in this circumstance, the client. Buurtzorg aims for professional care combined with a personal touch. For each client, a team prescribes a personal nurse. The first objective for this nurse is to get the overall view on the client's medical conditions, identify his social ties and build a trusting relationship. Teams aim to schedule as few nurses as possible per client. Considering the client's care needs and professional judgment, the nurse together with the client, his social ties, such as a partner or child who serves as contact for client, agree on nursing and care required as well as possible outcomes. During the period of care this agreement is re-evaluated and adjusted when required. Different stakeholders are presented in Fig. 5.2.

5.2   Self-Managed Team Structure

Buurtzorg works with Self-Managed Teams of nurses and nurse assistants who schedule their own work, recruit new colleagues for their team and determine the best approach without involvement of a manager or supervisor. The team decides within the team what tasks need to be done and assigns them accordingly, in addition to their professional roles. The teams are supported by regional coaches and the Headquarters of Buurtzorg for client administration, projects, strategic

---

[1] Based on Buurtzorg DNA document, 9th July 2011; Pool et al. (2011) and interviews.

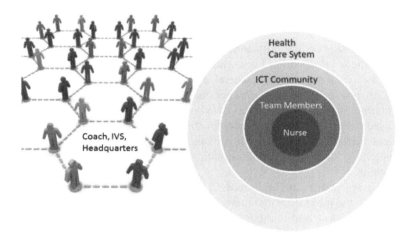

Fig. 5.2 Stakeholders in craftsmanship

queries, contracts, management reporting, staff administration and accounting. Every employee of Buurtzorg is connected through a virtual community called the Buurtzorgweb. Its approach, aims to simplify procedures of control, communication and integrating all internally and external stakeholders in the ambition to deliver the highest quality of nursing and care for the client's needs and avoid wasting time on irrelevant tasks in realizing the ambition.

Teams consist of 12 persons, maximum. The members of the team all work together to achieve the team goals. During this process they learn from each other and they share their insights. On a regular basis teams meet to discuss conditions and progress of their clients, productivity and professional related topics as well as additional issues that occur in their work. Each team designs its own annual plan.

Each team member is aware of her roles, being a professional (nurse or nurse assistant), a team player and contributing to additional tasks. Different kinds of information are disseminated through the virtual network. For professional development and information there are E-training modules, annual congresses (for meeting colleagues from other teams and regions and for researching insights in new developments), introduction sessions (for new colleagues), team visits and expert groups (on specific syndromes). The initiative to use these resources and when, lies with the individual team members or within a team. On the virtual web, additional information regarding policies and forms to be used are available.

Teams can operate autonomous in many ways, have the freedom to ask for support and are responsible for their productivity. In a way they operate as intra-preneurial teams (See Chap. 6).

5.2.1   Practical Support Structure for Secondary Processes

The teams get support digitally from the Buurtzorgweb. This virtual community comprises client information. Furthermore there is the Buurtzorg Square, another part of the virtual platform, where employees share articles, news, share discussions, post questions, share experiences and insights, as well as get inspired by this community. Each team has its own domain in this virtual platform which can be accessed only by the team members for sharing team specific information related to financial updates, experiences with clients, professional oriented information and the productivity of teams. This information serves as reflection on its own team development.

Client assessments are registered in the Buurtzorgweb and therefore made transparent to the other team members. The hours that are spent for clients' services are registered as well and reimbursed based on the specific client arrangement and the possible reimbursing agencies. The administration office at the Headquarters sends the invoices to the clients and other reimbursing agencies. The financial administration unit controls the rest of this process.

Each team has the possibility to apply the Team Compass, an assessment tool on the Buurtzorgweb for their team performance. The following types of information are presented and can be traced by teams: average productivity (called the Housekeeping book), productivity development during the year, development of number of client hours per week, development of number of client hours per month, number of clients, types of target groups and its numbers, transit time of clients, average number of employees per client, client satisfaction, exit interview survey, and average score on team climate. For some indicators the team is presented with a benchmark from the whole organization which makes it possible for teams to compare themselves with the average in the organization. They can use the Team Compass and discuss the findings on a regular basis.

Salaries and expense refunds to team members are paid by the financial administration unit at the Headquarters. This unit also manages other expenses such as rental fees for a team's office space and the purchase of ICT equipment such as phones, tablets, computers, and laptops. The group 'Almelo General' at the Headquarters manages the whole accounting and controlling unit. The 'Personnel Unit' arranges the contracts with all employees including the team members. Each team however decides itself about expansion with new personnel and conducts the recruitment. Only after this process is completed the team announces it to the personnel unit, who then takes charge of all formalities of hiring, creating an ITC account and access to the Buurtzorgweb and other facilities if required. Each team also decides itself about renting office space but they are required to stay within a maximum expense determined by the founder. Each team decides about the content of the work and tasks to be done and about the local arrangements that they need to make. There are guidelines however about roles in a team that they need to arrange amongst themselves.

There are also various standardized forms available on the Buurtzorgweb and digital facilities for client assessment and monitoring, for example, through tablet computer applications. Buurtzorg also supports teams in their local operations by

Table 5.1 Support staff

Support at the headquarters	FTE's
Directors (founder and co-founder)	2
Reception	3.2
Rental office administration	2
Payroll administration	3
Personnel administration	4
Accounting administration	4.4
Client administration	8
Assessment and Intake administration	2
Production	3
Community service administration unit (for household services to clients 'Buurtdiensten')	1
Private nursing and care (PGB and Private track)	0.8
Logistics	2
Coaches	15
TOTAL	**65.4**
Other support available for teams	
Helpdesk Ecare	1
IVS (for training and advice on Self-Management Teams)	0.3

providing promotional material, information about specific client groups, specific stakeholders in the Healthcare Industry such as other care providers and other relevant information that they need to know when a local team starts up. Buurtzorg offers coaches, team start-up, team development support and guidance by IVS, an external training institute. According to the Buurtzorg philosophy many of these guidelines are considered as supportive and not mandatory. We could say that the support facilities therefore have a physical distance to the teams. Mental distance is also created because teams are not obligated to use them, but choose to only if they feel it may contribute to their practices in helping the client. However, due to experiences of trial and error, teams refine their local practices and often rely upon the existing guidelines or are inspired to fine tune a guideline to implement it according to the local constraints. The more they see the benefits, the higher the tendency of making use of available support.

When a team wants to expand with a new team in their neighborhood, coaches are being approached for brainstorming, guiding and deciding about its feasibility. This is not a formalized process as sometimes a team member approaches the Headquarters or the founder directly. The Headquarters has written information on the specific steps and requirements for setting up a team which teams can ask for directly whenever it is required. This procedure has also not be formalized however the moment a new team starts the criteria are clear and need to be followed.

Each unit mentioned in this section comprises of a few persons, often a few FTE's only. The whole of Headquarters' support and overhead consisted of 65.4 FTE's on 1st of April 2014 (See Table 5.1).

Quotes to illustrate the supportive character of the Buurtzorg Headquarters:

At the Headquarters they do a lot for us so that we have enough time to focus on our clients. Working for Buurtzorg is pragmatic and gives overview. Realizing that they facilitate us so much and the approachability of the founders gives me an extra drive to walk an extra mile and act with dedication (Respondent 6).

If we have a question we can easily connect with the Headquarters. If we want to talk to the founder, that is also very easy. We cannot meet him very often but if there is an issue to discuss he will always call back (Respondent 5).

All the supportive units are very responsive. We first try to solve things ourselves but sometimes there are new issues and then we connect with them to see if they have any inspiring solutions. Sometimes it concerns just administrative queries regarding registration of hours or certain expenses such as printing a flyer or invitation card for an anniversary of our team. Then it is good to know if there are certain guidelines to apply (Respondent 5).

5.2.2 Small Size of Teams

In the research data limiting the size of the teams emerged as an important factor for getting the work done which is a client focus approach. While in the academic literature there are many definition of teams it is interesting to note that the small size already appeared in the definition of Katzenbach and Smith's (1993). According to them a team is: *"a small number of people with complementary skills, who are committed to a common purpose, set of performance goals and approach for which they hold themselves mutually accountable"* (p. 112).

At Buurtzorg teams decide themselves when they need to split up. There is a maximum norm of 12 but in practice some teams consist of fewer nurses and nurse assistants. The small size of teams gives the advantage of the possibility to allocate a small number of nurses and nurse assistants to a client. There is a higher chance of effective communication among team members. A client says: *"Because only a few nurses will come to your residence it feels good to have familiar faces. You feel that they treat you like a human being. My previous home care providers did not work like that. The nurses were not engaged in my problems. They were not interested in my preferences as a human being. At times they were very unaffected and if you are sick you are dependent on others, you need warmth and personal attention and the feeling that someone listens to you"* (Respondent 23).

5.2.3 Close to the Client

Because the teams organize themselves in local communities geographically they are close to their clients. Team members often know the history of these communities and have their own social ties there as well which simplifies the enlargement of their networks. Word of mouth works effectively in these local communities which implies little or low marketing costs for finding new clients. Teams usually strategically decide where to start and where to set up their office. Often they choose for a place with 'traffic' related to care such as close to a general practitioner/family doctor's office, office of a local municipality or other community oriented agencies. The community based care focuses on the context of the care and the social dynamics. The context is often at a client's home. Given the character of the community based care, the medical model is not dominating in the diagnosis and intervention but a social model which inherently has the medical character but which incorporates a broader perspective for analysis and solutions. This is done by viewing the client as a whole person rather than a person with a specific medical problem. Such a whole systems view requires a close connection with the social ties of the clients, both formal and informal.

5.2.4 Integrating Simplification in Self-Managed Team

It is obvious that there is a lot of support available from the Headquarters and coaches which can help a team to work efficiently and effectively while meeting the professional standards and still having a warm client relationship. It is the Buurtzorg philosophy that there is a certain minimum requirement to be fulfilled while leaving enough autonomy to the teams to make use of the additional available support and facilities. During the course of the development of Buurtzorg, because of its growth, the volume of procedures that are being written down have increased but these are not meant as control or formal coordination mechanisms but rather as a support network which can be applied and adjusted to the specific context by the teams (reconstructing realities). Even though it has experienced a fast growth, Buurtzorg keeps the philosophy of simplicity alive. It depends on the integrating capacity of teams how they make smart use of the available support. In practice they will keep asking themselves: why are we doing certain things the way we do, how does it help the client and are there better alternatives if they feel something is not smooth enough. Teams encourages themselves of continuously improving their work output and quality. Patterns and habits may develop during the years but they are responsible for their own productivity. Keeping this in mind and the fact that almost every region experiences a growth, teams are naturally regenerated by new employees and thus a re-orientation and refreshment of old patterns and habits. Of course things that work stay alive as long as possible but sometimes just explaining to a new employee how it works at Buurtzorg at the team meetings give enough space for rethinking practices and applying the common sense attitude.

5.3   Team Synergy Through Roles Within a Buurtzorg Team

5.3.1   Balanced Team Composition

At Buurtzorg the Self-Managed Teams comprises seven roles. Everyone has the role of nurse or nurse assistant while the other roles are additional to get the work done in each team (See Table 5.2).

Tasks Roles and Social Emotional Roles
The *nurse and nurse assistant* provide information, encourage healthy behaviors and provide both curative and palliative care. The activities are focused on empowering the ability of the client to cope independently and maintain the quality of life. During the intake of the client, a holistic assessment is carried out comprising all relevant physical, psychic, social and cultural factors and the way the client gives meaning to life in addition to his views on illness and death.

A *housekeeper* ensures that practices in a team comply with contracts constructed with third parties. She makes sure the required instruments, medical devices, housekeeping and office material are present. She has a role as treasurer by giving account information to the other team members regarding expenditures and available budgets.

The *informer* is aware of the hours that are spent for caring and nursing activities. On a regular basis she communicates to the rest of the team about the financial situation and performance level of the team. If she notices misalignments, she does what is required by communicating to the team member or to the client administrator.

The *developer* participates in working groups in Buurtzorg, distributes knowledge in the team, and participates in relevant working groups outside Buurtzorg.

The *planner* ensures continuity of the care provided to the client by preparing a schedule that is as efficient as possible. She incorporates changes in the schedule according to the arrangements with clients and team members and informs the colleagues about these changes.

A *team player* tries to assess what the beliefs, opinions and ambitions of herself and her colleagues are through questions such as: why are we doing things the way we currently do; what are the challenges we face; what are the type of decisions we take? Together with other teammates she tries to find solutions. She encourages finding synergies within the team with the focus on the organizational goals even if it requires her to subjugate her personal goals. The primary belief of a team player is that she cannot be a winner unless she finds the synergy in wholeness with the other teammates and the organization. Therefore the following principle exists: *one for all, all for one*.

A *mentor* serves in coaching new colleagues and provides instructions, advices and feedback to those starting an internship.

A team player and a mentor role represent the social emotional roles while the others are tasks roles.

Table 5.2 Roles in a team

Role	Contribution	Dominating IST principle
Nurse/nurse assistant: Provides the nursing and caring in attunement to the client's needs and his social ties according to the latest professional standards	Organizing and delivering professional care and nursing attuned to the client's need and in agreement with the beliefs on quality and safety of the client, nurse/nurse assistant and Buurtzorg	Needing Rethinking Common Sensing
Housekeeper: Organizes the facilities such as office, technical facilities	Organizing the maintenance of the office and other facilities for conducting the optimal team effort	Needing
Informer: Monitors a correct registration of the hours spent by the team according to the contracts and arrangements with Buurtzorg	Creating and monitoring the overview of the team regarding hours spent and its productivity level and doing the needful through communication	Needing
Developer: Collaborating with initiatives that contribute to the vision and approach of Buurtzorg	Developing and disseminating to employees at Buurtzorg, team members and external stakeholders: knowledge and experiences on the vision, beliefs, methodology, protocol, working designs, syndromes, and techniques and practices for nursing and care	Rethinking
Planner: Organizes the time commitment of the team according to the client's arrangements and employees' contracts and their availability	Scheduling the care commitment according to the arrangements between clients and team members	Rethinking
Team player: Putting effort with colleagues to deliver excellent, efficient and effective nursing and care	Realizing team and organizational goals, subjugating personal interest, serving other team members and encouraging pleasant relationships within the team	Common Sensing
Mentor: Introduces new employees and students for internships and serves as contact person for content related and organizing queries within the team	Supporting and guiding new employees and interns when starting and implementing their work and in developing additional competences	Common Sensing

Goal Orientation in Teams

At Buurtzorg goal orientation is being empowered to avoid extensive discussions and meetings. Very often there is no pre-determined agenda set. For meetings at team level the issues to be discussed are agreed at the start of the meeting. The goal orientation requires each team member to bring forward their queries at the start, these are usually discussed before closure of a meeting. The queries are formulated in such a way that it becomes clear to everyone what the person needs to discuss and with what objective. Given the Buurtzorg context, in practice, teams will apply such a tool according to their own belief of its practicality if they experience the suggested way does not work.

Team Consensus

At team level a main tool for decision making is consensus which implies that a solution will work only if it is acceptable to everyone in the team. This implies that several solutions are sought within the team and when everyone confirms not to have any objections then it is approved at team level. This does not mean that everyone agrees fully with every solution but everyone accepts while at the same time agreeing, that solutions are temporary. People abide to something that has been agreed until someone else has a better alternative. Such a tool acknowledges everyone's input regardless of a person's tenure or team role. It gives the possibility to focus upon the rational arguments rather than personal preferences when justifying a certain solution.

Change is a Constant

At Buurtzorg a decision taken has a temporary character: this means until it works. It is believed that change is a constant. Therefore, there is the experience that nothing is fixed or everything is possible at Buurtzorg. Professionals who are used to predetermined structures do not suit such a context immediately. They need time to adjust to the Buurtzorg way of working.

Team Role Rotation

Team members may express their interest for a specific role. From the organizational point of view it is important to cover all the roles so that all important tasks are carried out. There are no fixed arrangements except the team profiles and teams can implement the way it best suits them. However it is recommended by the training institute, who guides and facilitates the processes in teams, to rotate the team roles. In daily practice teams rotate the roles, some teams twice a year, others less often, some only if a person expresses a new interest for a role or if existing teams are split up, the new team dynamics need to build. Those who apply the rotation frequently experience the team role rotation as a job enrichment tool.

> *Here at Buurtzorg we do not have the possibility for career enrichment because our organizational system is very flat. The enrichment therefore comes from the variety in the work, the client contacts and the different team roles. At the start-up process many former community nurses joined Buurtzorg. Many of them had served as managers in healthcare organizations but they chose to shift to Buurtzorg and not pursue another management position. They were interested in the content of the professional work. Here at Buurtzorg the expertise and experience with clients counts most, not the management expertise or experience (Respondent 4).*

Even with a high education, such as HBO-V, at Buurtzorg we will stay at the level of community nurse. But we should not focus on the position and compare it with other organizations. In the Self-Managed Teams concept the intrinsic motivation for your job counts. Actually I think Self-Managed Teams work well with high educated professionals who do not need supervision. At Buurtzorg we have plenty of opportunities to discover our talents and improve ourselves in our profession but also by occupying several team roles we learn new tasks, things that in my previous job were done by others, such as making the schedules. Here everyone can learn how to make a planning; you can challenge yourself continuously by occupying several roles (Respondent 6).

5.3.2 Mindful Communication

Being mindful towards colleagues and choosing your words carefully creates a good team spirit which is a necessary condition to work successfully.

A client said: Self-Managed Teams do not work automatically. It is not a matter of just agreeing amongst each other; let us start with a Self-Managed Teams approach. One of the basic requirements is the attitude of non-judgment or non-prejudice toward your colleagues. Not trying to develop and express an opinion about everything you see around you. A second requirement is maintaining good relationships amongst team members. Without investing time or showing interest in concerns of colleagues, a team will not be able to sustain with a good team climate. Another requirement is the attitude of being in the present moment and looking ahead instead of looking back and finding fault with colleagues (Respondent 2).

On an ongoing basis we discuss the topic of how to critique your colleague. Expressing your concern about a colleague's behavior and actions can be done in more ways than one. As you deal with small teams with a lack of managers, who manage the culture or solve conflicts, each one of us feel the urge to maintain a positive climate in the team. From a professional point of view you will find faults with colleagues but then you choose the right approach to give your input or to address the issue (Respondent 1).

A coach expressed: As a professional they know their field very well. They may tend to stick to their own beliefs about what is a good approach. If a colleague does not operate in the same way others may induce certain opinions about her and expressing this may disturb the team climate. Usually this person will try to address her concern in such a way that she gets support from the other team members. Here the risk involved is that team members do not support the nurse who brought the issue to their attention. If this happens too often such a person will not feel good in the team and it may cause conflicts, often resulting in a resignation from the team. Therefore each team member needs to be very mindful in how and when they express concerns (Respondent 12).

An employee at the Headquarters said: Every query will be answered, there is respect for everyone's expertise and everyone's strengths will be acknowledged (Respondent 10).

You need to keep the self-managed attitude alive. Like a gardener is watering the plants, so does each team member give attention to the process of Self-Managed Teams (Respondent 2).

5.3.3 Integrating Simplification and Team Synergy

We could relate the roles in the teams to the three organizing principles of Buurtzorg on Craftsmanship. The nurses and nurse assistants apply all three principles of Integrating Simplification. They systematically identify and assess what is needed by asking the questions: why are we doing this; how does it help the client and what are the alternative approaches if they do not meet expected results. During their team meetings they continuously reflect on the client's situation, the rules and regulations, expectations from relevant stakeholders, such as family doctors, and families of the clients. They are open to apply new insights they gain or if someone brings a better alternative to the table. The additional roles represent a specific aspect of Integrating Simplification.

The so called Needing Principle can be identified in the housekeeper and the informer. They have the task to systematically identify and assess what is needed to realize the team and organizational goals. In their roles they justify the hours spent, the facilities that are introduced and they constantly try to see if there are other ways or alternative plans, devices, to help realize the goals.

The developer and planner need to constantly rethink the circumstances they are exposed to externally and internally. Their contribution lies in thinking about cognitive and creative solutions to gain the knowledge and insights that are required to work as a professional team. They create capacity for the flexible space to adjust to new circumstances and to meet arrangements agreed between clients and teammates.

The team player and mentor help according to the Common Sensing Principle which is about designing and implementing tasks sometimes based on current situations and sometimes based on new constructed realities by using the commons sense. They need to have an overall view of the circumstances to adjust to the practices. If they notice things do not work they encourage practical solutions.

5.4   Subtle Expertise for Community Care

Buurtzorg was founded with the focus on the client as a whole person rather than considering the process of care delivery as an economic process with products, targets and customers. The healthcare system has been influenced by economic thinking and approaches. In the past few decades the time spent per client and per illness has been a guiding principle in organizing the work. At Buurtzorg, Craftsmanship has been considered as a main focus rather than following these guiding principles with rules and regulations. Buurtzorg holds the belief that professional dedication and job pride are important drivers for integrated community care. They assume that community nurses and community nurse assistants were trained and have further developed the expertise to consider the client as a whole person. Assessing their social surrounding as well as building networks with other professionals in the healthcare industry such as the family doctors and hospitals is routine. The way the Craftsmanship is being put into practice requires more than only professional expertise. In the previous chapter the attunement to the client has been described and explained as a main factor for Buurtzorg's successful approach in community care. Nurses and nurse assistants need to be aware of in-depth perception of situations and clients in the whole process of their Craftsmanship and they need to develop a subtle expertise. This refers to the ability to acquire subtle cues for processing and retrieving information and applying them when working with the clients. The subtle expertise has emerged in the data as the following three lower level concepts: in-depth expertise; first getting acquainted then caring; "*fingersplitszengefuhl*" (feeing at your fingertips—intuition). Several respondents used this German word to express a kind of intuition or feeling at your fingertips. The following quote clarifies this concept and the lower level concepts will be described in the next sections.

> *As a community nurse I was trained to work as an all-round nurse. I took care of infants and children in a specific village community doing all kinds of tasks. The tasks of a community nurse increased and there was the belief that she was trained too much as a generalist and was lacking specialization. As a community nurse everyone knew you and it was normal if someone stops by, has a chat and expresses her concern regarding her neighbor. As a community nurse we had short communication lines to the family doctors. We worked then with colleagues, sometimes from other villages as well. Together we were responsible for our district. Sometimes we only had a one-person office, everyone could approach you and you could also visit a person without appointments. It was no problem to enter a person's home. They always trusted you because they saw us as nurses working for enhancing the community welfare with an orientation of compassion (Respondent 24).*

5.4.1 In-Depth Expertise of the Professional

Read and Sarasvathy (2005) use the term expertise to refer to a set of skills, models and processes that can be acquired with time and deliberate practice. They formulate a theory of entrepreneurial expertise based on the efficacy of the concept of effectuation for understanding how new markets are created along with how to become more entrepreneurial. In the view of Sarasvathy (2001a, b), entrepreneurs are not different from anyone else. They simply adopt a different approach of problem solving, a different way of thinking. Similarly at Buurtzorg, Craftsmanship is about adopting a different approach to community based care and a different way of thinking. The nurse first makes an assessment of what possibilities, resources and networks are available to them. Second, they ask the simple question: "What can I do with it?" Then the nurse starts designing a solution for the client, in interaction with the client and his social ties. The next question the nurse asks is, "what can I do next with it". The nurse, following Sarasvathy's effectuation principle is a broad base free thinker who goes beyond the existing constraints. In a way the process is simplified. In this perspective, Craftsmanship is an art possible to develop for everyone; people are not naturally born with it. Nor do you need to be a risk taker or have a personality predisposed to taking high level risks. You simply take incremental steps towards your goals.

From the data the concept of in-depth expertise emerged in reference to the deeper insights that are required to work as a professional. The following quotes clarify this concept:

- *At Buurtzorg the professionals know very well what is needed to serve the client well: they are experienced and have got a lot of expertise* (Respondent 23, client)
- *It is their professional attitude, expertise and experience that help in serving the client in the best possible way. But it does not suit every nurse. They need to manage responsibility themselves, dare to be entrepreneurial in their thinking, rely on trusting their capabilities, and able to solve problems when they occur* (Respondent 2, client).
- *An employee in the Headquarter expressed: 'you need to know what is required for the tasks to be done. Sometimes this implies being flexible, sometimes it is about meeting a deadline. You need to assess yourself, what it takes for you to deliver the work well. You do not need to ask for permission. There is a lot of trust in us and a lot of responsibility. You need to be able to act upon these frameworks* (Respondent 7).
- *The more professional the expertise of the nurse, the higher their autonomy, the more they can work as generalists* (Respondent 2, client).
- *Not everyone is being trained as a community nurse. Buurtzorg's way of working pretty much requires such a training to be able to serve the client as a whole person. As this training has disappeared maybe Buurtzorg should develop and offer it to make sure that there are enough qualified nurses available for the near future. Every year we are growing in number of clients and therefore we also need to grow in the number of nurses to be able to deliver the best possible care* (Respondent 3).
- *If you work at Buurtzorg being an expert is not enough. You need to be good at acquiring new clients, seeking education to deepen your understanding, know how to deal with Human Resource issues, understand team dynamics and other business related issues such as planning, financial rules and regulations.*

Normally these are not included in the nursing educational framework (Respondent 12).
- *There are no standard approaches for how to solve a problem or how to implement an idea based on pilot projects to experiment what works, we need to discover things ourselves by trying ideas ourselves, using our professional expertise and our common sense. We integrate these in a natural way. Some colleagues coming from other disciplines such as hospital nursing find this difficult. They have been trained to look at a specific diagnosis while at Buurtzorg that is not enough* (Respondent 6).

5.4.2 First Getting Acquainted Before Caring

From the research it emerged that nurses at Buurtzorg need to have a meta-competence to perceive the whole context first and to understand what is really going on before they proceed. They first acquaint themselves before they go to the detailed procedures of the professional tasks. They need to remove the curtains, the veil, and the hidden agenda in their interpersonal relationship. Otherwise this 'veil' may act as a disturbance. They 'clear the air' to have a positive start when they enter a client's home.

Pool et al. (2011) describe a few approaches that fit this method. Using what is being told and what has been written in the client's reports is a first step. This is opposed to the evidence based working method. This familiarization is required first, to build a good relationship with the client. Removing the veil is a second step. According to Wouters, there is a veil of assumptions hidden between our spontaneous experiences and the reality. If we want to get to know the reality we need to become aware of this veil and then also try to remove it (Pool et al. 2011, p. 70). A third step is completing the picture that is gained through these steps with the professional diagnostic profile of the client.

Some of the following quotes explain this concept further.

It is not enough to be a good nurse assistant or nurse, you need to be able to read the context and to adjust to that context. If you enter a person's house you need to sense that specific context and ask how the person feels, find out what your colleagues have observed and written. Who is the person I am serving, what is his background, what type of family does he have etc. Because you cannot just do your thing and shift to another client, you need to adjust to what is required. Sometimes you need to be a servant of a client, sometimes you listen to him like you are a close friend, sometimes you are the professional and sometime you help navigating them in the context of healthcare institutions. So you have different roles and if you want to stick to just one role you will not make it. And above all you need to be humble to switch to the roles that a specific context requires. We call it in Dutch: 'eerst buurten dan zorgen', which can be translated like: first getting to know the situation and client then providing care (Respondent 24, interview 2).

For professional tasks of course we are all trained and we know exactly what to do but working as a community nurse or nurse assistant at Buurtzorg requires something extra, an extra competence of being aware of the reality and allowing yourself to give it a clear reflection instead of just trying to fit in the situation to a predetermined approach. You try to avoid prejudices on the one hand and on the other hand, you try to avoid fixating upon the professional diagnosis only because you want to get good insight of the client and his situation (Respondent 3).

5.4.3 *"Fingerspitzengefühl"* (Feeling at Your Fingertip)

Fingerspitzengefühl is a German expression, which is also being used in the Netherlands. It refers to great situational awareness and being able to respond according to what is most appropriate and tactful in that given context (intuition). Creating such an awareness requires a perception of the subtle cues in a given situation next to the cues regarding the medical state of the client and finding the coherent 'picture' of that situation and then deciding how to deal with it. Nurses and nurse assistants explained how such cues or instincts help them to recognize changes in the client's condition. Then they act upon the changes. Sometimes it helps them to proactively create solutions for new occurring situations or even help to prevent a decline in conditions of a client.

You develop a kind of special ability to sense extra cues to better understand a specific situation. If you take care of a client for a while you get used to what he or she is able to do and you also notice the changes over time. Sometimes there is a kind of gut feeling that tells you that something is wrong. You may think the client is getting worst or may even die. The first thing that you need to do is to check the condition of the client to make sure that, based on rational information you still have a good overview of his or her condition. If things have changed in his medical condition you will notice it in the blood pressure, temperature or other indicators that you have traced. In some cases you will still have a strange feeling from inside telling you that even if the indicators tell you that things are well, it does not feel well. Then you need to share this with your colleagues because they will be able to understand what you are going through, they may know about similar other cases and can share their views or they may know the client as well and will be assessing what you have shared based on what they know about the client. So there are several ways to validate if the extra cues that you get are right or could be ignored. Often you can assess such cues also because in other situations in the past you may have experience a similar situation. But one thing is for sure, you need to take every extra cue that you perceive seriously. Sometimes it is a certain smell, then you know it is an infection. Sometimes it is the way the client behaves or how relatives or others in his social ties respond or even

if they express certain worries or feelings, you need to take them all seriously.
You should not ignore them or hide them from your colleagues, you should be
transparent towards it. It is an extra antenna for getting information. Those
who do not develop this ability do not survive at Buurtzorg. Usually everyone
has the potential to develop it but some are more open to it than others
(Respondent 37).

It is not strange at all if I call a colleague to share my extra observations
about a specific situation at a client's place or about a change in a client. We
just say to each other that according to my Fingerspitzengefühl I would like
your second opinion or I would like you to go there instead of me or I just ask
for an advice from a colleague. I always do something with it and treat it as
an extra signal to include in my judgments (Respondent 24, interview 2).

5.5   Integrating Simplification and Subtle Craftsmanship

From the data and the concepts that have emerged it has become obvious that nurses
and nurse assistants simplify situations while at the same time remain attuned and
aware of extra information and signals to be included in their evaluations of their
client's situation. They integrate all the different sources of information to get a
good overview for facilitating well thought out and simplified outcomes for the
client.

Intrapreneurial Team Freedom

6

Abstract

An important concept found in the research data is Intrapreneurial Team Freedom. This chapter will explain this concept, its properties and lower-level concepts. Intrapreneurial Team Freedom is about providing the freedom and responsibility for running the Self-Managed Teams by allowing entrepreneurial behavior; creating conditions and maintaining the freedom so that they act with entrepreneurial spirit to innovate and create new solutions for problems and needs with decisive power within an existing organization. Intrapreneurship is often associated with creating a venture within an existing venture. Recent developments have shown that the term has been used in more situations with its main focus on the entrepreneurial behavior that it requires from the intrapreneurs, rather than experimenting with a venture with the help of an existing firm. In this respect entrepreneurial behavior is about having ideas and using initiative, resourcefulness and determination. This generates something of value for the clients, the nurses and nurse assistants, and the organization. Next to specific behavior it requires certain conditions such as structure and actions. While in pure intrapreneurship the aim is to create a venture within a venture, here we suggest introducing Intrapreneurial Team Freedom to focus on the process rather than the results in terms of creating something of economic value.

6.1 Intrapreneurship Within the Field of Entrepreneurship

Both in the data that we collected and employee surveys, two phrases occurred very often: working for Buurtzorg gives freedom and the feeling that you are running your own office or company. Combining both aspects results in Intrapreneurial Team Freedom. The value that has to be created in this context is acquiring and helping the client in the best possible way to enhance her quality and meaning of life. Also for such value creation, teams need to establish their office space, finalize working arrangements and agreements between themselves and with the Buurtzorg

© Springer International Publishing Switzerland 2015   83
S.S. Nandram, *Organizational Innovation by Integrating Simplification*,
Management for Professionals, DOI 10.1007/978-3-319-11725-6_6

organization. It is not as in intrapreneurship, where people are made 'free' to work on a specific venture idea with the aim to innovate and experiment often turning the idea into a spinoff or a new venture. At Buurtzorg the process starts from scratch. Teams create themselves. If a group of nurses think it is a good idea to set up a team under the umbrella of Buurtzorg because they feel aligned with their strategy and are fully equipped with the required competences, they start the process of exploring, discovering whether they can build a team, what it takes from them and what they need from Buurtzorg. In this process they must already consider entrepreneurial related questions. For example, they need to anticipate the future regarding the inflow of clients; changes in the market; rules and regulations in the industry; specific expertise and quality enhancement to stay ahead and an assessment of the expected needs of the client based on his current capacities and resources. Basically these are activities that both entrepreneurs and intrapreneurs continuously perform almost as a habitual pattern. In the following section we will position intrapreneurship and similar concepts within the field of entrepreneurship to get more understanding of its potential application for the context of Buurtzorg. Then we will conceptualize the theory that we introduce: Intrapreneurial Team Freedom where we focus on the behavioral features it takes, the conditions that need to be met and the maintaining elements to have a sustainable result.

The term freedom movement pops up frequently in discussions. In the employee survey of 2013 one of the open ended questions was: what is your motivation to join Buurtzorg? A random sample of 946 employees was approached with a response rate of 51 %. To this open question the majority refers to the experienced freedom, the freedom to help the client in a way that she gets the nursing and care she deserves, the room for autonomy, the feeling of being independent from an organization with supervisors such as managers, running my own business, and the feeling of being part of the organization because of the responsibility for productivity and realizing good quality of services to the clients. At the same time in the answers of the survey we find how employees value the connection they have with the teammates and Buurtzorg as the 'protecting' organization they work for. It seems to them a wonderful combination: being your own boss and still feeling protected by a team and an organization. The following statements have been recorded by a majority of the respondents.

- If you do not know how to deal with a certain issue, you know that you don't have to solve it yourself, there is always a team.
- If you need an answer for something new there is a lot of support at the Headquarters as well. But there is no manager who controls and co-ordinates. This gives recognition and pride that you can do things yourself, it is as if I am running my own business.
- The freedom to do your work and to think of ways to improve yourself is very inspiring.

To find the best fitting concepts relating to this freedom for explaining the case of Buurtzorg, a literature review was done which produced the following terms:

corporate entrepreneurship and *intrapreneurship* (Pinchot 1985; Hisrich and Peters 1998; Antoncic and Hisrich 2001); *intra-corporate entrepreneurship* (Cooper 1981); *corporate venturing* (MacMillan 1986; Vesper 1990); *internal corporate entrepreneurship* (Schollhammer 1981, 1982; Jones and Butler 1992); *firm-level entrepreneurial posture* (Covin and Slevin 1986, 1991); *a knowledge-creation process* (Zahra et al. 1999); *resource configuration process in small firms* (Borch et al. 1999); *entrepreneurial orientation* (Lumpkin and Dess 1996; Knight 1997); and *enterprising behavior* (Kearney 1999).

Although all of these in one way or another can be linked to Buurtzorg the most relative are the scholarly concepts of corporate venturing/entrepreneurship, intrapreneurship or enterprising behavior.

Corporate entrepreneurship or venturing has been referred to as; "a process of organizational renewal that has two distinct but related dimensions: innovation and venturing, and strategic renewal" (Zahra 1993). One specific topic within the field of corporate entrepreneurship is innovation, generally referring to the firm's commitment to introducing new products, production processes, and organizational systems (Covin and Slevin 1991; Lumpkin and Dess 1996). The literature on corporate entrepreneurship however, mainly focuses on its effect on a company's financial performance as well as on the development and acquisition of important organizational capabilities and skills (Kuratko et al. 1990; Lim et al. 2008; Lumpkin and Dess 1996; Soriano 2005; Zahra 1993; Zahra et al. 1999), or on antecedents of corporate entrepreneurial activities (Altinay 2005; Burgelman 1983; Covin and Slevin 1989; Hornsby et al. 2002; Kathuria and Joshi 2007; Kearney et al. 2008; Miller 1983; Zahra 1991).

Intrapreneurship can be described as, "the practice of developing a new venture within an existing organization to exploit new opportunity and create economic value" (Pinchot 1985). Menzel et al. (2007) states that; "anyone who behaves with entrepreneurial spirit within an existing organization... at any level and in any function... can be an intrapreneur". According to this definition Buurtzorg's Self-Managed Teams comprise intrapreneurs. The broader view of Menzel et al. is aligned with enterprising or entrepreneurial behavior as well which has so far been defined as "...a set of activities and practices by which individuals at multiple levels, autonomously generate and use innovative resource combinations to identify and pursue opportunities... (Mair 2002, p. 1)". It has been defined as a more generic behavior that involves recognizing, taking advantage and acting upon these opportunities (Van Dam et al. 2010). Kearney adds to the idea of generic behavior by expanding it to almost a full range of domains of our functioning. He says; "enterprising is about having ideas and using initiative, resourcefulness and determination to generate something of value even when things may be difficult and uncertain. It is taking advantage of what might be, rather than accepting what will be. In a business setting it is called entrepreneurialism but you also need enterprise to run a club, a household, a good classroom or to help yourself and others" (Kearney 1999). Entrepreneurial behavior or enterprising can be considered as a way of living both at the workplace (commercial or not for profit) or at the non-workplace areas.

While all of these concepts have interesting features to describe the case of this book, we faced a challenge. Just applying this literature is not enough because it does not concur with the assumptions at Buurtzorg. Buurtzorg has shown that an organization does not necessarily consist of various organizational layers and supervisors where a few are chosen to experiment with innovative ideas while being freed from existing daily obligations and organizational routines, sometimes in a research lab. Furthermore, while in the Buurtzorg context entrepreneurial behaviors were found, the organization holds a broader view on value creation. In intrapreneurship or corporate entrepreneurship context these behaviors aim to enhance efficiency, innovation and strategic renewal. In the studies on corporate entrepreneurship for example the assumption holds that managers' policy consists of fostering the entrepreneurial orientation, renewal capabilities and activities to realize innovation and strategic renewal as main outcomes. At Buurtzorg the freedom given to teams, directs the outcome of productivity and good business results combined with realizing a client focus in solving their problems in a holistic way considering all important domains in their lives (for example; health condition and family support, preferences and belief systems). It is believed that such a focus will uplift the client's quality of life and foster a speedy recovery.

From the perspective of the employees it is believed that a client focus enhances their creativity, team spirit, the job pride and satisfaction of the nurses and nurse assistants because this is what they have been trained for. It is also believed that it aligns with improving healthcare and community prosperity. Value is thus created with several expressions. Such a freedom concurs to some extent to the concepts of Spaces of Intrapreneurial Freedom (Mourmant et al. 2013) which will be discussed in the next sections.

6.2   Conceptualizing Intrapreneurial Team Freedom

From the Buurtzorg data Intrapreneurial Team Freedom emerged in three sub-concepts: entrepreneurial behavior, conditions for freedom and approaches to maintain the freedom. Intrapreneurial Team Freedom refers to the freedom that Self-Managed Teams have to act as an entrepreneur within an organization. This occurs when it comes to discovering, evaluating and implementing opportunities to create value for the client, their team, organization and themselves while benefitting from being protected financially and enjoying the support given by the organization, in this case Buurtzorg Nederland (Fig. 6.1).

6.2.1   Entrepreneurial Behavior in the Context of Intrapreneurial Team Freedom

From the data it emerged that at Buurtzorg entrepreneurial behavior at the team level is important to be able to serve the client with quality and flexibility. It does not appear under this label but teams conduct several tasks that resemble

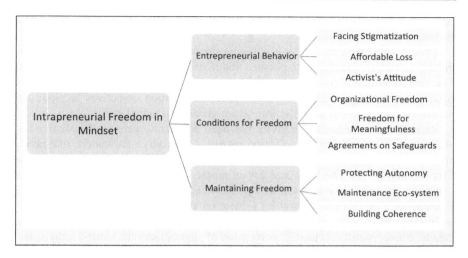

Fig. 6.1 Intrapreneurial team freedom

entrepreneurial tasks. What is entrepreneurial behavior? Stevenson (2000) defines more entrepreneurial behavior, as opposed to less entrepreneurial style, in terms of six dynamic dimensions:

(1) strategic orientation: an entrepreneurial attitude is focused on opportunity,
(2) commitment to opportunity: knowledge of market, willingness to act,
(3) commitment to resources: doing more with less,
(4) control of resources: access to as opposed to owning resources,
(5) flexible management structure,
(6) co-ordination oriented, flat reward philosophy: creation and harvesting of value.

Stevenson offers a dynamic description of entrepreneurship, thereby including corporate venturing and intrapreneurship. "In developing a management theory of entrepreneurship it becomes clear that entrepreneurship is defined more by a set of individual traits and is different from an economic function. It is a cohesive pattern of managerial behavior" (p. 13). Nandram and Samsom (2006) suggest including the use of established entrepreneurial management techniques in larger firms, not-for-profit organizations and even within the public sector to understand entrepreneurial behavior. Timmons and Spinelli (2004) elegantly illustrate the entrepreneurial process as a continuous interplay between opportunity, resources and the entrepreneurial team in an uncertain environment. Adizes (1979) developed a model for explaining life-cycle developments of firms. He suggests that in every stage an organization needs four task orientations that are required in any stage of the company life-cycle in the PAIE model of task orientations: **P**roductive: producing results, production, marketing, sales, distribution, etc.; **A**dministrative: timing, tracking and controlling productive activities; **I**ntegration: team continuously updated on the values, mission and specific goals; Entrepreneurial: creative, innovative, risk taking activities.

This model demands that at each subsequent stage of the venture life-cycle, these four task orientations are pursued and maintained in the appropriate balance. The task orientation common to all life-stages is Integration. In the absence of continuous attention to the integration process, common objectives are likely to breakdown and conflict in the venture team arises as a major threat.

Recently entrepreneurial behavior has been defined as a sense of initiative and ability to turn-taking, ideas into action by using creativity, innovation, risk-taking and the ability to plan and manage projects in order to achieve objectives (European Commission 2006). The EU considers entrepreneurship as a life-long competence that is necessary to live in a knowledge based economy (European Qualifications Framework, Directorate-General for Education and Culture 2006).

In this specific context of Buurtzorg the following concepts emerged from our data as entrepreneurial behavior: perception of stigmatization as introducing something new will not be immediately accepted; pioneering/entrepreneurial behavior that comprises certain risk-taking and a judgment towards losses; an activist's attitude to spark the fire. Entrepreneurial behavior is the ability to identify and exploit opportunities (Currie et al. 2008) while showing evidence of innovativeness, risk-taking and proactivity. Innovativeness is the orientation to be creative, seek for unusual or novel solutions to problems and needs including new services, new organizational forms or new processes (Miller 1983; Currie et al. 2008). Risk-taking refers to the willingness to take moderate risk in committing resources to address opportunities (Miller 1983; Currie et al. 2008). Proactivity is anticipating and preventing problems before they occur by exhibiting perseverance, adaptability and assuming responsibility for failure (Miller 1983; Currie et al. 2008).

In the context of Buurtzorg these behavioral attributes get the following antecedents: an activist's attitude to be able to strive for an innovative orientation, affordable loss principle as a risk-taking behavior and perception of stigmatization to proactively behave in different circumstances. The following sections will explain these concepts further.

6.2.1.1 Perception of Being Stigmatized

It is common that if a person's behavioral patterns are different he will not easily be accepted by others. In entrepreneurship behaving differently is a common pattern as entrepreneurs often create new grounds for their ideas and opportunities especially if they are pioneering. There is a tendency even that he could be expelled from the existing community. From the literature in the social sciences we know that individuals experience stigmatization because of an interpersonal, intergroup, or intragroup belief that stigmatization of others serves to achieve a specific goal (Archer 1985). Giacalone and Promislo (2013) describe how people are stigmatized for their goodness. The goal according to them is to control a person whose generosity poses an instrumental or symbolic threat. Symbolic refers to beliefs, values or ideology, while instrument threat refers to power, safety, health or wealth.

Serving the client as Buurtzorg could be seen as a threat by other organizations in the healthcare industry. Especially because of Buurtzorg's opposite management architecture which shows the smaller roles of having management layers for leadership control. Managers and employees in similar organizations could feel confusion and even frustration due to the existence of an organization, such as Buurtzorg.

From the interviews it emerged that employees at Buurtzorg perceive this tendency of being stigmatized often when they are operating in the external networks. It resembles being stigmatized because of being different. It seems that this perception does not weaken them but rather fuels the entrepreneurial driving force of team members at Buurtzorg. The following quotes will illustrate this concept.

Sometimes Buurtzorg is being labelled as a network organization. Others try to describe how we work in teams and how we relate to the outside world. In the outside world we have to deal with different parties such as volunteer organizations, family doctors, physiotherapist, community worker, district concierge, community offices and various other networks associated with community healthcare but also political networks. We must be aware of all of them, to navigate in this playground of networks. In many instances I have experienced a lack of understanding of how we work. We are not treated as a mainstream community care organization. Often they confuse us with other voluntary organizations or they express a lack of credibility as we are a young organization (Respondent 3, interview 1).

If we tell our story about how we manage all the administrative tasks with a low overhead budget, people do not believe us. They always try to find a way to fit our story into their own approaches or vision of what is best. I always try to be positive even if I notice a strange attitude. Sometimes I don't know whether it is a lack of understanding or envy. It helps us if Buurtzorg appears in the media with positive news. So far this has always been the case. We are very proud of telling people that we work for Buurtzorg. We support our founder for all the work that he is doing. The good thing is that he keeps us informed of important developments, for example issues on the political front. He has good ambitions to reform the healthcare industry (Respondent 8).

People who have had negative experiences with community care in the past decades need more time to get use to us. Clients who approach us are referred to us either by their family doctors or word of mouth. We need to build trust with them then they understand our way of working. At some clients I notice a lack of trust and sometimes it takes them a while to get used to our approach (Respondent 6).

We need to keep telling them the story, our vision and how we work because otherwise they find a way to fit our message into their existing views and stigmatize our work as commercially driven. Especially insurance companies and healthcare bodies, who work from other frameworks, they have lost the humane foundation in their way of thinking. They have followed the trend of using economic terms such as targets, products and revenues. Oftentimes, there is no link at all to the human being behind the system. You may say that the healthcare sector has been economized or rationalized in such a way that it is being approached as a commercial entrepreneurial sector (Founder).

6.2.1.2 Affordable Loss Principle

At Buurtzorg the Affordable Loss Principle is being practiced. This principle has been defined by Sarasvathy (2001a, b) and it refers to committing what you're willing to lose rather than investing based on expected returns. Entrepreneurs are willing to work hard but they tend to avoid doing market research. They rather just go and try to sell their products to the closest potential customer, they just do it and encounter the obstacles while doing it. They do not tie themselves to any pre-conceived theory, market or strategy for their idea. They would rather open themselves to surprises, including which market or markets they will eventually end up building their business in.

An example of Affordable Loss Principle at Buurtzorg could be found in the '*regelarm experiment*', an experiment according to the Buurtzorg principles to deregulate in order to lower administration and reporting burden by creating the freedom to assess the client's needs at team level instead of approaching the external assessment agency, during the period of the experiment. The expected revenues were not the starting point but the ambition to conduct the experiment to show the benefits of their approach. A loss of 9 million Euros in year 2013 was recorded. The effectiveness of the experiment was shown. The Buurtzorg approach requires less number of hours to serve clients in several diagnostic categories. However, insurance agencies refused to pay afterwards for the services that were delivered as they are used to pre-arrangements and only post arrangements for small differences in respect to what was initially agreed upon. They were not able to deal with a huge difference realized by the Buurtzorg approach. Their accounting system was based on the agreements on reimbursement and client's hours as agreed upfront.

6.2.1.3 Activist's Attitude

The activist's attitude could be identified in the interview quotes. Also observations have led to the conclusion that being an activist is rather a rule than an exception at Buurtzorg. It becomes obvious if the employees and founders try to explain what they do. There is always a need to say what they do differently, compared to the current mainstream practices. It seems as if they cannot explain their approach without referring to the dominant approach in healthcare. Such explanations are helpful because they immediately show what the pioneering characteristics are but by always using them they take the activist's attitude. Successes are always celebrated by cakes or other sweets and are announced in terms of 'how a battle has been won or how the 'enemy's mindset has been influenced.' It is remarkable to see how this does not only occur at the level of the founder and his communication style in his blogs but also amongst nurses, nurse assistants, coaches and back office employees. 'Fighting' an external 'enemy' creates coherences in thoughts in the organization which encourages cohesive behaviors and drives the willingness to put extra effort and dedication for unexpected tasks and testing the boundaries and walk beyond them as entrepreneurs do. Currie et al. (2008) refers to the status of being a political agent and describes this as the alertness to policy windows. What they try to explain with this concept is the ability to imagine and discover opportunities to push through or obtain support for a particular proposal within the context of government policies. Having an activist's attitude is probably an antecedent of being such a policy agent.

A few quotes illustrating the activist's attitude:

Our founder is allergic to all of these networks as they also bring institutionalized frameworks and agreements where we as Buurtzorg often do not fit. We have our own approach and our own culture, sometimes it is easier to stay away from them. But in practice we know that our voices need to be heard, if we want to be acknowledged as a serious partner in the healthcare landscape (Respondent 3, interview 1).

Once I have noticed that some hospitals do not refer clients to Buurtzorg. Then, our team proactively approached them and explained our work. We need to be constantly aware of the external context we operate in. We need to remove doubts amongst these stakeholders. Sometimes it feels as if I am continuously 'fighting' or trying to convey our message (Respondent 6).

Just doing your work as a professional nurse is not the main challenge. The challenge lies in a kind of activist attitude that you need to take. We have entered the market as a new organization. Many nurses from existing organizations have left their jobs to join us. The managers of other organizations are not always happy with us as an organization that is constantly growing. We need to be aware of developments to make sure that our work is recognized as the best approach to help the client (Respondent 3, interview 2).

Common negative experiences with the previous employer can motivate team members, but make them insecure at the same time. According to regional coach Yvonne Koopman, home care employees in her area that transferred to Buurtzorg have been threatened by mail from the beginning. Buurtzorg has never made this an issue, until the V&VN professional organization's chairman wrote an indignant column about it in the summer of 2009 (source: De Blok and Pool 2010, p. 33).

6.3 Creating Conditions for Intrapreneurial Freedom

6.3.1 Organizational Freedom

Organizational Freedom resembles the description found in the work of Mourmant et al. (2013). With small adjustments to their definition we refer to the following descriptions:

- Decentralization, agility of the structure, organization in autonomous and flexible Self-Managed Teams organized in regions.
- Flat structure to improve fast and wise decision making by nurses and nurse assistants and reinforcing that their decisions are related to the outcome of the teams and thus letting them become aware of their power of controlling their outcomes.
- Reducing or deleting bureaucracy, power, political games and rules or make them reasonable, flexible and eliminate or reduce formal procedures.

Organizational freedom at Buurtzorg enables the nurses and nurse assistants to spend more time in their client relationship and therefore, creates the possibility to enhance their client focus.

6.3.2 Freedom to Experience Meaningfulness

Freedom to experience meaningfulness resembles the sub-concept Freedom and Lifestyle as described by Mourmant et al. (2013). With adjustments in their definition we describe this as follows: the freedom to have fun, have pleasure, work in an exciting environment, work for an organization to be proud of, work for an organization that brings meaning to the job, to empower job motivation and commitment which in turn will enhance their client focus as that is a main part of their work. Having fun at work within the Buurtzorg organization is being experienced as very important. Many employees have joined Buurtzorg because of their wish to have more fun at work, the feeling to be understood, and getting recognition for their jobs. As an organization with a flat structure the career is not upward but inward. People experience meaning due to these types of intrinsic rewards they experience.

6.3.3 Agreeing on Safeguards

Intrapreneurial Team Freedom contributes to the bottom line of the business which is realizing productivity. Team members value the freedom they get and the responsibilities they have. To ensure the bottom line is not lost, the organization builds in 'safeguards'. The main safeguard at Buurtzorg is the productivity of the teams. The founder gets access to all teams' productivity through the web. The coaches get access to the productivity of their team. During the start-up of a new team or a second, third or fourth team in a region, usually the team will not be productive immediately and this is being taken into account when assessing the productivity. However, it is not the responsibility of the coaches but the teams to realize the productivity level, agreed amongst themselves, their coaches and the founder according to the annual plan. In this plan a team can anticipate on lower productivity if it needs to invest in setting up a new team or if they foresee other investments. At Buurtzorg they strive for a productivity of 60 %. This is the only safeguard which also simplifies co-ordination and communication processes with teams, coaches and the founder. There are no other strict safeguards such as monthly or quarterly reports to coaches or the founder. This leaves teams a lot of freedom, comparable to a real entrepreneur. The teams face similar challenges as actual entrepreneurs do such as finding clients by entering a market where other more established healthcare organizations operate.

6.4   Maintaining Intrapreneurial Freedom

6.4.1   Protecting and Encouraging the Freedom

Protecting and encouraging the freedom refers to ensuring that the freedom is being protected by systematically being reminded. Interestingly, everyone in the organization is protecting the intrapreneurial space they have created. It is considered to be a core element of their existence. The Self-Managed Teams will remind themselves in meetings of their decisive power and their freedom to create their own approach. Even approaches that are offered as the Buurtzorg way of working are not always being followed. Given the guidelines of Buurtzorg they will tend to create their own identity as a team, along with their way of operationalizing the guidelines in practice. Only if the team members themselves are convinced of its impact they will follow an approach that has been offered as solution by others on the website. They will stress that only if they are not sure about something they will contact the Headquarters, the coach or any other supportive staff. Those who are in charge of all ICT facilities continuously remind themselves or are reminded by staff members that new ideas should not be pushed from top-down. They try to let the teams discover for themselves, how some new ways of working or application of some tools will help them to realize the client focus and their productivity goals, while establishing and maintaining a positive team climate.

The founder plays maybe the most important role as protector of the Intrapreneurial Freedom. He reminds the teams who contact him with a problem to refer to their own ability first to solve the issue. If he notices that coaches are acting like managers he will remind them of the intrapreneurial space which makes Buurtzorg unique. Scholar like Pinchot (1985) and Mourmant et al. (2013), refer to the need to protect the intrapreneurial space as well. According to Pinchot intrapreneurship "involves as a role for the in-house sponsor, one who will finesse the corporate politics while the intrapreneur intends single-mindedly to turn the idea into reality". Mourmant et al. (2013) suggest that a company can have more than one protector getting involved in the 'mental battle' with the rest of the organization. Interestingly at Buurtzorg there is also such a thing as protecting the intrapreneurial freedom of teams and the organization as a whole by getting involved in the mental battle with the rest of the healthcare industry. Especially as the Buurtzorg approach is totally opposite to the mainstream approaches, the founder acts as a protector in the industry as well. More about this phenomenon will be discussed in the chapter on leading a higher purpose (Chap. 8).

6.4.2 Populating and Protecting Its Eco-System

At Buurtzorg there are a lot of social ties between employees in teams but also at the Headquarters. When discussing about how personnel is being recruited it seems that the word of mouth approach is a very important antecedent. Incidentally, there are formal job recruitment procedures. Usually teams consist of colleagues whom they have met at a social gathering, a networking event, or through former colleagues by introduction. The Eco-System could be protected. The start-up process of Buurtzorg as an organization itself was formed by former colleagues who were working for an existing organization. They felt that due to bureaucratic rules and regulations they did not have enough freedom to bring forward their ideas and work ethics to serve the client according to their standards. In their IT Intrapreneurship study Mourmant et al. (2013) suggest that populating and protecting the Eco-System is important for intrapreneurship. They refer to the selection process to find the right kind of employee for the organization and defined the characteristics of such people as having entrepreneurial qualities such as: openness, risk taking, passion, entrepreneurial intuition, curious and hard working. They also refer to the attitude of not being hesitant to fire people if they do not fit the Eco-System of the 'ideal' employee in order to protect the environment for getting polluted. In one of the interviews it was said that, "if you do not fit the organization, you will have to leave, there is no middle path".

In a meeting it was announced that a coach was leaving the organization because she found another job that suited her ambitions more. It became obvious that the decision was taken after a process of discussions with the founder and colleagues. Interestingly to note that one of the members at the meeting suggested hosting a special farewell event for this coach, reminding that 'leaving Buurtzorg is not the same as leaving another organization; you have become a close team, almost a family. Emotionally it takes a lot of a person to heal after departing'. It almost sounded like a divorce because of the intense relationships that people have built within the organization. At team level employees enter with a 6-month contract and after this period, only if no member in the team objects will the contract be extended to an undetermined period. This is another way to protect their eco-system in the team.

The following citations are examples of the type of person who fits Buurtzorg:

- *We are not impressed by bio data of people but by their abilities* (Respondent 11).
- *We need people who are down to earth and aim to find solutions for problems of our clients* (Respondent 7).
- *People, who know their professional tasks, can work autonomous and feel responsible for the clients* (Respondent 11).
- *We need creative, pragmatic, open people with a sense of humor and who use their common sense.* (Respondent 2).
- *They need to take initiative themselves, and be proactive in seeking connections with others to improve their work.* (Respondent 6).
- *We like to work with people who are flexible* (Respondent 3).
- *If you like to explore, renew and experiment, there is a lot of freedom at Buurtzorg* (Respondent 37).
- *Those who have the ambition to co-ordinate and excel power over others do not have a space here. We try to work as equal colleagues, be transparent, while respecting everyone's strengths and weaknesses* (Respondent 1).

6.4.3 Enhancing Coherence in Intrapreneurial Freedom

Team members visit their clients individually but as a team they serve a number of clients. It is important to build coherence in the team. Teams come together frequently for discussion regarding their clients, new ideas and improvement of tasks. Next to coherence at team level, the coherence within Buurtzorg is important too. For new employees there are meetings where they can meet other new employees and discuss issues with the founder at the so called "Buurtzorg vision meetings". Here they hear about the Buurtzorg vision and the founder shares his background, his motivation, asks questions and encourages others to share their experiences. Furthermore teams can meet other teams anytime but in practice there is not much time for this unless someone posts a specific query or experience on the web. Sometimes, a coach introduces a team to another because she thinks they may learn from each other as they face similar issues. Buurtzorg organizes 'Buurtzorg Congress Days' a few times a year where personnel can meet each other. Through these activities teams can stay attuned to Buurtzorg while exploring new initiatives and practicing their intrapreneurial freedom.

6.5 Integrating Simplification in Intrapreneurial Freedom

Often Buurtzorg is being associated with an organization hosting freedom as its primary motivator. The most important integrating aspect is found in the way the freedom is being acknowledged in the teams. Members often experience the explorative space they get to find out what works the best in their specific situation and circumstance. The role of the founder as protector of the freedom is an interesting place where integration happens. Later in Chap. 8 his role as integrator will be explained as well. Members of the Headquarters support the integration of freedom by doing the needful only when it comes to the needful, for example forms or regulations. They try to serve as service point to all existing and new teams by reminding them of their freedom by letting them know what the regulations are but allowing them to explore how things could be done at the team level. They do not prescribe routines for tasks. Intrapreneurial Team Freedom has become part of the DNA of the organization.

Pragmatic Will with ICT

7

Abstract

In this chapter we focus on the ICT implementation and relevant factors enhancing a Pragmatic Will with ICT at Buurtzorg. ICT starts with supporting the primary process at Buurtzorg aiming to serve the clients' needs from a holistic focus. How the principles of Buurtzorg are integrated and simplified through ICT facilities will be explained. Another aspect of the Pragmatic Will is the process of implementation and the argumentations behind the decisions to implement ICT. The implementation of ICT at Buurtzorg seemed to be a step by step creativity process that comprises of the following three elements: frugal attitude, smart simplification, and its effectual way of designing the ICT solutions.

7.1 The Concept of Pragmatic Will with ICT

The Pragmatic Will refers to the effort put into realizing the goals of the organization in such a way that it facilitates the primary process at Buurtzorg, which is realizing a client focus in a holistic way and enhancing the quality of life of the client. In the research this core concept emerged with the following three properties (See Fig. 7.1):

- Flexible support to the primary process so that nurses and nurse assistants can access the needful data and information and report time spent with clients. The flexibility creates the possibility to report and monitor client information anytime and at any place to serve the client in a holistic way.
- Step by step creative solutions for the ICT-users which is time saving, iteratively developed with users and which helps reducing complexity.
- Systematic assessment of data to be able to build a common foundation amongst the professionals in serving the client to fit the organization's philosophy of building trust through Craftsmanship (Chap. 5) and enhancing Intrapreneurial Freedom (Chap. 6).

© Springer International Publishing Switzerland 2015

S.S. Nandram, *Organizational Innovation by Integrating Simplification*, Management for Professionals, DOI 10.1007/978-3-319-11725-6_7

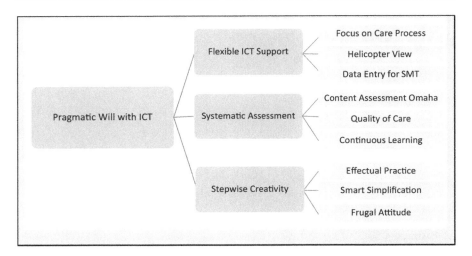

Fig. 7.1 Pragmatic Will with ICT

A systematic assessment seems to be important, especially as the work of serving the client involves several subjective decision making processes. Next to these subjective processes of judging each circumstance and its unique characteristics, it is important to build a common ground for how to treat clients, especially when their circumstances are beyond the status quo. One of the main assets in the organization is trust: amongst the employees, towards the clients and the founders, coaches and others in the chain of care delivery. Relying on trust rather than control requires a facilitating process to improve the quality and continuously learn from experiences and new practices. The ICT targets to facilitate this principle as well.

The following quotes describe the start-up process.

When I think of how I come up with an idea to turn it into an innovation I first ask myself: is my idea sound and do others recognize the message that I am trying to convey? Then, I try it out in a small setting to find out whether it results in the solution that I expect. In these processes I am open to whatever challenges and new opportunities I encounter. I try to bring in the best disciplines to help turn the idea into a sound innovation (Co-founder, creative thinker).

At the start-up of Buurtzorg, the first step was to identify and evaluate the existing and available software. To really make the difference with Buurtzorg it was a main issue to find solutions to facilitate the primary process. The objective was to increase the time that was being spent with clients. With this in mind a system was developed that was accessible from anywhere, at any time, supporting the main process which is delivering care to clients and to serve them as whole human beings. As delivering high quality was also a main issue from the beginning, the ICT system was designed to assess and share the operations in practices. With the ICT facilities Buurtzorg could develop itself further and grow. You can see both processes taking off right from the beginning (Co-founder, creative thinker).

At the start-up research was conducted to assess the products of existing suppliers. Unfortunately nothing could be found that suited the Buurtzorg vision and profile. Therefore Buurtzorg conceived starting its own development track to support the primary process with ICT software. A few established principles were followed. The technical development of the ICT system at Buurtzorg follows the software principles of 'Agile'. The system development focused on interaction with individuals when launching a program. Those working with the programs are continuously being engaged in improvements, feedback and co-designing solutions. Things that do not work are easily changed, simplified and developed to adapt them to the needs of the employees. Therefore at Buurtzorg ICT systems are flexible and they target avoiding wastage in terms of time, effort or money.

All of these concepts are part of the Theory of Integrating Simplification as they are necessary conditions for a successful ICT design and implementation for enabling the primary process at Buurtzorg and facilitating the founders to systematically assess how their policies work in practice. The next sections display the various concepts of Pragmatic Will found at Buurtzorg.

7.2 ICT for Supporting the Primary Process

At Buurtzorg the ICT 'package' consists of:

- Hardware, software, and technical experts to support ICT (helpdesk, BI, maintenance, developers and consultants)
- Visual: Teams, Headquarters
- Hardware support: routers, WIFI, laptops at team locations and tablet computers
- Software support: helpdesk via telephone and e-mail, distant access to the screen of the user

How ICT supports the primary process can be understood through three main aspects that emerged as relevant in the research interviews, company desks reports and other data: the process of care delivery, the role of a back office and the data entry that facilitates the work of a Self-Managed Team. In the next sections we discuss each of them briefly.

7.2.1 Focus on Care Process

The delivery of care is the primary process of Buurtzorg. The ICT has been organized in such a way that it facilitates. It focuses on solutions, establishes and maintains the professional freedom to choose for certain interventions that fit a particular circumstance of a client instead of facilitating the allocations and referral for 'minutes' of care as starting point and focus. As described in previous chapters, a main philosophy at Buurtzorg is 'keep things simple'.

The following quote of an ICT advisor clarifies how the focus on delivery care works in practice.

> *When we get a question from a team we will first evaluate by asking: Does it serve the client? Does it serve the professional? If yes, then we search the appropriate steps to build a solution. It is also important to know where the question comes from. If it comes from a need for control or when it creates additional complexity, then the ICT may not be the appropriate solution. In those circumstances we will advise not to change the current system (Respondent 29, interview 3).*

> *Our approach is to keep the administrative burden for the professionals as low as possible. Usually this concerns the registration of time spent per client and the registration of the overall time worked that day. In our ICT solutions we use limited categories because we believe that less is more. The time spent has to be accounted for but not into pointless detail. We have automated the time spent per client for billing purposes (Respondent 29, interview 3).*

> *We aim to provide the nurses with all client information and consider them the gateway to care and responsible for keeping their client information accurate (Respondent 29, interview 3).*

7.2.2 Helicopter View Back Office

In the ICT facility related things are organized in such a way that there is a big role for the ICT back office in receiving and maintaining a good overview of the processes. There is one back office to support all employees. The back office has ICT access to all areas needed to offer wide support. They provide support by operating with its helicopter view and has decisive responsibility in the whole process. This enables the office to make the right decisions faster and offer quick and effective support.

> *Our task is to keep things that can be done by the ICT back office off the plate of professionals while abiding by rules and regulations for transparency and, accountability (Respondent 29, interview 3).*

7.2.3 Data Entry Attuned to Self-Managed Team

The data entry for the ICT solutions is simple to use and it is attuned to the needs of the Self-Managed Teams. The main principles of the Buurtzorg Self-Management are followed: decentralization of tasks; low number of nurses per client; Intrapreneurial Freedom enabling autonomy in decision making processes and to maintain responsibility for the outcomes. The ICT solutions are designed to foster independency of professional care with the following indicators:

- The duration of the average 'care episode'
- Client satisfaction level
- Employee satisfaction level
- Productivity of team and national benchmark compared to other teams at Buurtzorg (responsibility for production is at team level)
- Client hours and contract hours (because the responsibility for workload and hiring staff is at team level)
- Number of monthly client hours and specification for specific client groups
- Average number of client hours

All this information gives insight in the tangible managerial aspects of each team. The more intangible aspects such as issues and developments around clients, the needs for training and education for nurses and new developments in the market and environment are all discussed at regular meetings at team level (See Chap. 5). Both sources of information; the ICT related and the face to face sessions create awareness in the teams of what is really going on so they are able to monitor and adjust faster whenever required.

The following quotes clarify this concept further:

There is no central planning at the Headquarters, instead there is team planning with individual team members who are responsible for the planning in their team. Every team member has access to the ICT and can view his own workload and performance online (Respondent 29, interview 3).

One of the organization's values is to have as few professionals per client as possible. Therefore the system shows the average number of employees per client (Respondent 29, interview 3).

The software is not built from models of administration, registration and control. It is developed from scratch. We could not find existing software that fit the Buurtzorg profile. The main idea was to see how we could build software to facilitate what Self-Managed Teams really needed to deliver good care (Co-founder, creative thinker).

One part of the Business Information (BI) reveals information at company level for the founders. It provides information about team performance and quality of care. It is not built from a control point of view but to make the relevant information available to manage daily issues and establish goals of the organization.

7.3   Step by Step Process for Finding Creative Solutions

The ICT experts started with a single ICT approach in mind and then related it to a goal that has been agreed with the founder. Subsequently, they generalize how this would be effective in practice by inviting users, asking for their feedback, adding ideas and iteratively adapting it until a large group of employees find it useful. They also monitor the actual usage. If the outcomes are satisfactory, then the experts are available for expanding the facilities with another step and work on new queries from Buurtzorg. They have the attitude of continuously improving the facilities by creative thinking, a step by step introduction and interaction.

The concept of 'Effectuation' emerged from the data when analyzing the process of implementation of the ICT. 'Smart Simplification' emerged as a strategic vision in designing the necessary ICT and deciding what system to build. 'Frugal Attitude' emerged from our data as part of the philosophy of Integrating Simplification to avoid wastage of any kind.

7.3.1   Effectual Practice

The term effectuation was introduced by Sarasvathy in the context of entrepreneurship (2001a, b) to explain how entrepreneurs use another way of problem solving. Their thinking begins with a given set of means and allows goals to emerge contingently over time from the varied imagination and diverse aspirations of the customer and the people they interact with (Sarasvathy 2001a, b). The goals are not pre-determined but the expert imagines possible new ends using a given set of means. The process is diverging into several solutions. Effectuation resembles one of the principles of Jugaad Innovation (Radjou et al. 2012): think and act flexibly. "Jugaad is the antithesis of structured approaches. . ... Jugaad entrepreneurs' flexible mindset, constantly questions the status quo, keeps all options open, and transforms existing products, services, and business models. Unconstrained by structured processes, Jugaad innovators can respond quickly to unexpected changes in their environment" (Radjou et al. 2012, p. 21). Buurtzorg tries as much as possible to keep away structured processes to explore with existing resources new future possibilities.

The following quotes express the effectual practice at Buurtzorg.

When we started with the ICT software, very frequently, usually at least once per month, a new release was published with new tools or extension of existing tools. This gave us the opportunity to interact with the users and then adjust our tool to their needs until it was improved to the level that a majority could work with it easily while retaining the Buurtzorg philosophy (Co-founder, creative thinker).

There are no general predetermined rules for many of the operations. Everything should be generated by individuals themselves. The moment you propose a certain approach it easily gets criticism because people are not used to it. They are used to have enough space for deciding what works in their own context (Respondent 14).

Usually in other organizations there are managers or team leaders to whom you may share complaints about colleagues. They also act as sources for information. At Buurtzorg we have access to the website, our Buurtzorgweb, for getting the relevant information. This requires a proactive attitude. There is no other information available. There is no one who prepares documents for meetings. You generate your own documents if you wish to discuss or present a view (Respondent 20).

An employee in the Headquarters says: We do not need to set up meetings. If there are issues we get them solved at the coffee corner. If you think another approach works better you express your thoughts to your colleagues and they will share their feedback and together you will agree to apply the alternative approach. Sometimes you do not know upfront if this approach will be better, so you just try and find out yourself as far as it does not disturb processes others are involved with (Respondent 7).

We do not develop rules upfront. Usually you solve a problem, learn from the experience and when it occurs often, you try to find out whether a certain strategy would be good to agree upon for preventing such a problem in the future (Respondent 8).

Stage 1
At the start of Buurtzorg a framework consisting of four components was constructed:

- tools for organizing the work at team level
- a dashboard where the team performance could appear
- a knowledge system and a platform for sharing and communication between members of the system and platform
- a digital reporting and filing system

First, the focus was primarily on *organizing the work*. For example, an administration system for clients and employees, a planning system and a simple user friendly HR (Human Resource) department portal for monitoring sick leave and for facilitating official correspondence between back office and the employees such as contracts, letters and pay slips. Buurtzorg also had to submit its accountability report according to the rules and regulations which led to the development of tooling for the registration of the productivity.

At the same time simple tools were developed for *communication purposes*. For example internal 'blog', 'Facebook' and 'WhatsApp' possibilities were launched for discussions, communication and sharing experiences between team members. These facilities for communication were built in the portal of the employees to enable them an easy access because they did not require a separate log in.

While becoming acquainted with the functionality, it appeared that teams started to ask for additional possibilities such as own stats on team perfor-mance: how well did they perform as a team, and were they contributing enough to the organization's performance? A first dashboard was presented with individual productivity compared to the average team productivity (Co-founder, creative thinker).

Stage 2
While all these activities resulted in innovative practices there was still a main challenge. Buurtzorg was still operating in a so called 'backwards accountable care delivery system'. The national government and healthcare financial bodies still preferred accountability on production and several other indicators which were not attuned with the daily practice. The conversation that was going on concerned accountability on products and time spent while this is not the main focus point at Buurtzorg. The *content-based reporting* at Buurtzorg was still a paper and pencil exercise. There were no good electronic health records and no supporting tools to enable the professional thinking and working approach of the nurses. This resulted in the next ICT innovation: *structured electronic health records.*
Brainstorming between the creative thinkers, the ICT experts, Buurtzorg founders and users on this issue resulted in following requirements:

• Connection to the vision on integrated community based care
• Based on or comparable with international standards
• Pragmatic in application
• Suitable for research, reporting and monitoring

The search for such a system resulted in the Omaha System, a USA system of 'unified language'. This system was not well-known or widely used but it seemed most suitable (www.omahasystem.org).
The nurses and nurse assistants used paper and pencil reporting in a way of story-telling. The change that was introduced however required reporting on incidents and exceptions generating more standardized data.

From other disciplines such as family doctors we knew that this was a big challenge. Even if you introduce proper ICT facilities, this does not guaran-tee success. It is the user who decides whether it is a success or not. If they apply it you know it enables their work and that is the Buurtzorg philosophy (Co-founder, creative thinker).

Again it was decided to go for a step by step development of the software according to Buurtzorg's approach of introducing ICT in interaction with employees. This is a constructivist research approach where employees give a lot of input and feedback, then construct together with the ICT developers the founda-tion for the unified language for the classification. Through discussion of cases and E-learning facilities employees get acquainted with the language.

The development and implementation consisted of two stages. The first stage involved a back office module to make healthcare plans according to the Omaha System structure. In the second stage, this was expanded with a module for a mobile application for care. Both modules were developed and integrated with the other modules from the ICT framework.

Due to the chosen strategy, Buurtzorg is able to develop itself in implementing digitally written accounts adequately, without causing a big bang at the organizational front. All old accounts need to be replaced by new digitally written accounts. Whenever a team announces its readiness to implement this new style of accounting, the ICT company facilitates (Co-founder, creative thinker).

7.3.2 Smart Simplification for Users

Interesting to note that implementation of the ICT facilities was accepted as a natural part of the processes at Buurtzorg. Employees all knew from the start that using ICT would be an important aspect of their work. New employees learned from their colleagues how friendly the ICT applications were. Frequently they noted "it is not difficult at all, even I can use it".

There were no courses, no manuals, and no training programs. Employees were introduced to the ICT facilities in a pragmatic way: at their own pace, just by using it, they discovered the possibilities and became attuned to the ICT approach at Buurtzorg. Based on their positive experiences they showed openness to new facilities as well. The development of the ICT facilities accompanied the development of the Buurtzorg organization. Both strengthened each other during the process of discovering what works according to the Buurtzorg vision of a client focus. In perspective they benefited each other: because Buurtzorg grew, the ICT-platform also had to be developed further and because the ICT platform expanded, Buurtzorg could grow more easily.

The different tools, the integration of these tools and its broad implementation have resulted in the Buurtzorg community which works as the backbone for policy development, knowledge development and innovation. At Buurtzorg there are no projects, working groups or policy papers available as the policy is very pragmatically formulated when the need occurs. Everyone can enter a discussion, give input and assist in improving, developing and organizing things. The underlying assumption is that the wisdom of the crowd is the pragmatic reality.

With the implementation of the Omaha System, Buurtzorg has set an important foundation for further development and innovation. The ICT development however is not completed. There is a continuous effort for improvement at present at Buurtzorg and among the ICT experts. Currently the following three topics are on the ICT agenda:

- Health data communications should be made available to the client and his family by integrating the data with Personal Health Records. A pilot with Microsoft HealthVault has taken off.
- Optimizing the collaboration from a multi-disciplinary perspective in the chain which makes it easier to share data with family doctors and hospitals.
- Tooling for supporting E-Health initiatives. The complexity of the care and nursing activities at residences is increasing. It is almost as if 'Hospitals at Home' are being established. The available technology in home care also enables research, monitoring and controlling at a distance. It is important that new ICT is being integrated with Health Records.

The following quotes express the smart simplification at Buurtzorg. An employee explained a situation where teams were purchasing medical products from different suppliers and how smart simplification enables the daily practice. *"At the back office it was noticed that each supplier had its own standards when it came to quality, delivery and price. The overview was lacking. Together with the founders I studied the possibilities and then set up a list of suppliers and conditions to incorporate for deciding where to purchase such products. Teams still had the room for choosing their own supplier from the list that was offered to them. Standardizing too much would be against the principles of Buurtzorg. But at least the process is a bit simplified for them so that they can spend the time for their care activities"* (Respondent 3).

An ICT expert explained how important it is to develop everything from the focus of a service to the Buurtzorg community. *"Only if you meet the Buurtzorg philosophy or if it is pushed by the founders, which is against the philosophy but if they would push it, it would raise effects. When you meet the needs, people use the facilities we offer. It should always be as simple as possible and they should be convinced of the gains"* (Respondent 27).

7.3.3 Frugal Practice

At the start-up a few crucial decisions were made. The distribution of the ICT should take place through Internet Technology. Buurtzorg was about to start working with small Self-Managed Teams. Setting up an infrastructure based on their own connections in a conventional manner would become too expensive. It was decided not to set up a separate business unit for ICT within Buurtzorg but to start partnership with an ICT supplier. They decided to use what was already available. A big saving was the use of web-based or in the cloud solutions. Therefore no expensive, special hardware or software was required, just what was available (source: Pool et al. 2011, p. 164).

Buurtzorg preferred software based on pricing as per usage. The ICT supplier therefore was willing to invest in the development without the guarantee whether or not it would turn out to be beneficial for him. The supplier, Ecare Services, took the main risk.

A frugal practice is about doing more with less, which is one of the principles of Jugaad Innovation. "The practitioners of Jugaad, work with what they have got" (Radjou et al. 2012, p. 21). At Buurtzorg a pragmatic approach of doing more with less is key to Integrating Simplification and it is present not only at ICT practices but in the whole organization. Saving time by organizing the work in order to spend more time for the client is one important principle as has been discussed in the previous sections and chapters. Frugality is not only an expression of money but also of other types of resources such as time and professional expertise. Currently E-learning modules are being developed and one of the aims is to nourish specific knowledge and expertise of nurses. There are often circumstances where they apply a certain expertise only a few times a year because in practice while they have been trained for it, there are not enough clients for whom that particular expertise could be applied. Instead of going to a refreshing course a nurse could gain the knowledge from the E-learning modules where senior nurses and experts explain the details through knowledge sharing, explaining cases and visuals. In the long run, time and money could be saved because the E-learning modules will be studied only when needed.

7.4 Systematic Assessment

The third expression of Pragmatic Will is Systematic Assessment. This is about continuously asking yourself and colleagues: How does my activity serve the mission and could the impact be made transparent? Especially in the professional context it requires a common ground for the content of care for serving the client in the best possible way and enhancing his quality of life. The Omaha System has been acquired for the purpose of systematic assessment in respect to the content of care. Another expression of systematic assessment is enhancing quality assurance and yet another approach for systematic assessment is a continuously learning orientation. In the next sections these three expressions will be explained.

7.4.1 Content Assessment with Omaha

As we deal with professionals, there is a basic foundation for the content of the care that is being delivered. There is also a need for high quality data collection that supports the nurses and reflects the vision on quality of care. As explained earlier there was a need for a classification system to support a unified language, exchangeable data and data that can be used for internal quality improvement purposes. The Omaha System fit these needs. The Omaha System is a classification for documenting client care from the moment of admission to exit. It is seen as a comprehensive way to standardize the documentation of practices. It also gives the possibility to research the impact of certain practices because of its systematic reporting. The system has three main parts: assessment overview where problems of clients are classified; an intervention scheme to decide what intervention would be appropriate and a part where outcomes are rated.

It has the following features that are aligned with the Buurtzorg philosophy:

- It has a holistic view on health and human functioning
- It is multidisciplinary
- Uses understandable terms
- Requires a limited amount of data
- It is easy to automate
- It has been validated

It also gives the possibility to include Integrated Care factors such as:

- It supports an innovative mind with regard to the selection of solutions
- It offers a system that includes the full spectrum of client needs
- It suggests interventions based on best practices and evidence based practice.

The Omaha System supports the employees of Buurtzorg in their work: thinking and reporting about care according to a healthcare nursing language. It offers the possibility of internationally validated standards. The team dashboard develops itself into a more accurate instrument for assessing team performance. Meanwhile according to Omaha Systems about 75 % of the teams are planning and about 40 % of the teams are applying written accounts on Point of Care with tablet computers.

> *Also at a strategic front it seems that the Omaha System is having an impact. Buurtzorg is now much more and better able to prove that its approach results in more effective care. It seems that it is also being received positively by other organizations in the Netherlands. Amongst the professionals the awareness is increasing that standardization is important for reducing the bureaucracy that has been created in the past decades within the healthcare industry. This will enable the professional freedom and it will enhance the ability to innovate. The Omaha System exists in the 'public area' of Buurtzorg's web. The Dutch translations are also hosted there. Currently there is a data warehouse available for scientific research with possibilities for international collaboration (Respondent 19, interview 2).*

7.4.2 Quality Assurance and Improvement Through ICT

ICT could also assist in assessing and improving the level of quality by collecting data on clients' needs, interventions, and outcomes in a structural way. Currently, several existing instruments are being combined and integrated in the ICT framework. Additional information about teams' needs and ideas of coaches are being gathered and discussed by a working group. This will help to decide what type of data should be gathered for reviewing and enhancing the quality of the care at the team level. They are not intended for standardizing the work as each circumstance requires its specific solution to be designed by the professional in interaction with the client. However, signals could be built in the system when reporting about a client's interventions and benchmarks with other teams could be generated to be used as feedback by teams.

7.4.3   Continuous Learning Through ICT

There are several possibilities to improve expertise. One can learn from colleagues, learn by each other's experiences and best practices and by sharing her own experiences. The Intranet is already a community for sharing experiences but it could be improved towards an online nursing community. A team can already access online data and business information reports to reflect on its status. In addition, E-Learning modules are currently being developed to be used in the coming months while constantly having the possibility to improve these modules.

7.5   Integrating Simplification and ICT

The features of the ICT, the process of designing and implementation, and the process of monitoring are all integrated with each other. The Headquarters that supports employees and handles most of the administrative tasks is equally trusted and considered as part of an integrated whole (not as separate to front-line delivery of care). In the Buurtzorg organization and at team level there is significant emphasis on use of ICT and meaningful access to data. The Headquarters plays an important role in providing effective support so front-line teams can make good decisions quickly to serve the client in the best possible way.

Acknowledgement   The author acknowledges the input given by Ard Leferink and Nicole Koster for writing this chapter.

Leading Higher Purpose

8

Abstract

This chapter describes the leadership features at Buurtzorg, how the common purpose resonates in the organization and operates as a higher purpose. Leadership is an area in management studies that has received much attention for decades, leading to several perspectives of leader's motivational approaches and governance. In this chapter a brief overview of the relevant literature will be presented with the aim to explain how at Buurtzorg leading a higher purpose is the central view of leadership in respect to the main concern of this study.

The literature review will be presented after the three concepts that were induced from the research data. These concepts are expressions of the three principles of the Integrating Simplification Theory: needing, rethinking and common sensing. The first one represents expressions of the belief system of humanity over bureaucracy, stressing humane needs of clients and how this relates to the higher purpose of serving the client. The second concept refers to the various roles of the founders and the ability to integrate thinking processes and generate rethinking for realizing innovative approaches. The third concept is the communication style and how using common sense and pragmatic approaches help in reaching out to all employees.

8.1   Introduction

Next to the data from the interviews and by attending meetings the findings in this chapter are based on the content analysis of the web blogs posted by the founder. In total, 113 blogs were posted in the period of 2008-02-17 until 2014-03-02, which is about 1 blog in every 3 weeks.

The properties and lower level concepts of 'Leading a Higher Purpose' are presented in Fig. 8.1.

© Springer International Publishing Switzerland 2015   111
S.S. Nandram, *Organizational Innovation by Integrating Simplification*,
Management for Professionals, DOI 10.1007/978-3-319-11725-6_8

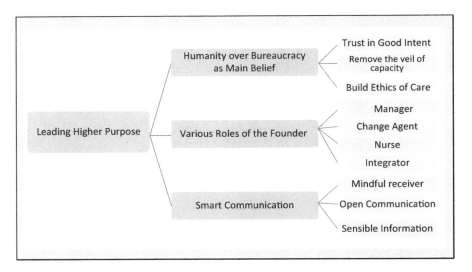

Fig. 8.1 Leading a higher purpose

8.2   Leadership at Buurtzorg

The terms management or leadership do not resonate very well at Buurtzorg. Employees stressed that Buurtzorg is an organization without managers. This is formally the case as there are only coaches facilitating teams; employees working on specific projects; support staff for the teams in the Headquarters; coaches or directors; and nurses and nurse assistants in teams serving clients and managing their day to day issues. There are no other job positions than these next to the two directors. An interviewee noticed: "*In fact, everyone is a leader in a team. So there is informal leadership. Every team member is responsible for the productivity of the team. You could compare this as management by objectives*" (Respondent 1).

Some even think of Buurtzorg as an organization without a leader while others find the role of the leader, many referring to the founder, others referring to both the founder and the co-founder, both operating as directors-, as most important for its survival and growth. Self-management is based on the principle of mutual trust between the teams and the leader. Some employees think that the founder is not a manager nor a leader but a pioneer. Some feel the organization is moving towards a next phase where management will be required and structures will be needed to maintain effectiveness and efficiency. In one of the interviews the founder expresses his views on management and recalls a few courses that he took as an MBA student on Innovation Management. He realized that many topics being taught were not relevant or useful in daily activities at the workplace. Consequently, he did not feel the motivation to complete his MBA. He recalls that in management courses, the topic 'what makes people happy', had never occurred, which he thinks is a big lacking. He expressed this further as follows: "*A lot that you learn is not practical, terms are too much economic oriented and people's communication focuses on language to express and explain competition, negotiation, and maximizing profit. They hardly focus on strategies for enhancing things that really matter such as the perspective of the client or the employees*".

In the job satisfaction survey of 2013 conducted by the market research office Effectory, on the open ended question 'why did you join Buurtzorg' almost 20 % (90 respondents out of 481) spontaneously expressed that their own vision on care delivery resonates with the Buurtzorg vision. The vision then becomes the higher purpose for many employees as it is more than a vision about their workplace but a way of 'professional living based on their professional calling'. Many of them felt that their job had been taken away from them or that they were educated for a practice that did not exist. At several positions in the organization it seems that people are driven by a purpose that transcends their personal interest of earning an income. They want to contribute to Buurtzorg, based on their personal determination, but there is more that drives them. The founder's task then becomes, leading these extra drives, expressed as a higher purpose.

Here follow a few quotes to illustrate how the higher purpose has been expressed during the survey, in interviews or on the website:

Higher purpose is being humane towards client:

The philosophy at Buurtzorg which is about spending time for the human being behind the client is the most attractive part of working at Buurtzorg. It makes me aware of why I have chosen for this occupation (nurse/nurse assistant in Survey 2013 Effectory study).

The Buurtzorg vision resonates very well with the norms and values that I believe are important for the way I want to conduct my work as a nurse in taking care of the client in need. Furthermore, working in a Self-Managed Team is very attractive as I am allowed to have more responsibilities and explore and develop more of my competences (nurse/nurse assistant in Survey 2013 Effectory study).

Higher purpose is a joined effort:

We carry this together. The whole is more than the sum of the parts! That is the strength of Buurtzorg, which also turned out in your message, Jos. I am happy to be part of it and wish all colleagues a lot of good luck and joy at work. (Toos Buijssen—7th of March 2009 19:41 as response to the Web blog on Strong Ladies ('Sterke vrouwen') written by Jos de Blok. 7th March 2009 at 00:21).

Higher purpose is revitalizing community care with the respected role of the professional:

The founder aims to give nurses their job as a community nurse back. They have been trained well and are dedicated to their profession but in the past decades too many protocols and reforms in healthcare have resulted in unacceptable situations for them but also for clients who have become numbers and products instead of human beings with certain needs for which they are dependent on nurses and nurse assistants (Client representative).

When we were preparing the start-up we discussed about what would be the best entity. I preferred a foundation instead of a private limited company. It was not an easy job as we had to be cost-effective but we all thought this would be the best fit as we had a higher goal of making the difference in the community care (Co-founder).

Even while we have grown so fast, the principles of self-management have been maintained. Many of us have had a management position in our previous job, so it was a normal habit to structure and coordinate. So far, the founder has always been opposed to the tendency for structuring and coordinating. For me this has been fine and it was good to discover how much I tend to organize and take the lead. But Jos has put effort in leaving the decision power and self-management at team level. I am also very fond of autonomy and I know how well it works, but I think Jos has a deep faith that self-management is important to realize the higher vision of the organization. He doesn't follow any management training for developing such a belief. It is just who he is. You may say he is much more spiritual in the belief that giving autonomy is a key organizing feature, than I am (Respondent 3, interview 1).

In the healthcare environment, including the insurance companies, it often happens that judgments of professionals are not valued or respected. Buurtzorg responds to this by respecting the professionals (Respondent 19).

Jos has ideals, higher goals and he would like to change the world. He tries to influence change and that shows his guts. Many things he does are not new in the sense that if we logically think about them, we may come up with those ideas as well. But he is the one who does not only think; he brings those ideas into practice (Client representative).

Higher purpose is enhancing quality of client care:

Usually in community care the quality systems aim to monitor the activities of the nurses and caregivers. Buurtzorg consciously avoided implementing such a system. The founders sought for a system that resonates with their vision of a client care delivery and they found that in the Omaha quality system in USA. This already made a lot of difference and nurses and nurse assistants could experience how this was different compared to what they were used to in their previous jobs (Client representative).

At Buurtzorg productivity is not the main goal. Employees should be aware of its relevance but they should know that quality is very important. Delivering good care is the main aim. The primary process is about good care and if this is not done well, there is a problem. You will see the impact immediately. If other parts for example in the secondary process such as ICT do not function well, there is also an impact but we may not feel the consequence immediately. There is time to solve issues but when it comes to serving a client, things should be in place and they should be done very well (Co-founder, Creative thinker).

Higher purpose is realizing shared values:

When Jos started there were 20 people. I listened to his ideas and ambitions but I thought, he would not succeed with those big ideas. But he succeeded with 100, with 1,000, with 2,000 and more employees. He has grown tremendously and it still continues. Therefore who am I to stop him in his ambitious dreams? I would never be able to do the things he does; that is just not my thing. We both share the same vision on community care, have same views on human beings and share values on how things should be organized. This builds the trust that we have in each other. But I am also interested as an expert. I see myself as a servant, a pioneer. I generate an idea, think of ways how to put it into practice and I just try it and find out how meaningful it is for Buurtzorg. I have a certain budget for innovations and I try to be frugal and step by step I introduce a new idea. If the innovations are good enough they will be implemented in larger scale as well but that is not my aim (Co-founder, Creative thinker).

In the interviews the respondents mentioned the following words in respect to the founder, to characterize his leadership while stressing his 'soft' skills mainly:

- Charismatic
- Humane
- He maintains the helicopter view
- Has a simple business strategy
- He knows intuitively whether he could count on you or not
- He gives you space to develop yourself or your idea
- He does not have a sales pitch but is real in his communication
- He has a lot of people knowledge
- He has a naïve curiosity, as a child would to explore how things work
- He mobilizes people who could work for him.
- He is a noble person, the innovator, the leader at Buurtzorg
- He enjoys meeting other people
- He is not sensitive for authority
- He often is opinionated
- He is respectful to everyone
- He enjoys life
- He trusts people

The higher purpose found at Buurtzorg is about the reasons for which Buurtzorg exist beyond simply realizing the bottom line of a business in the sense of serving the needs of clients and striving for continuity of this service. As it became clear there are also non-financial business related strivings such as revitalizing the community care, giving the job back to nurses, thus also realizing social impact.

8.3   Belief System: Humanity over Bureaucracy

From the data of the interviews it emerged how employees believe that they need to *put time and effort in such things that really matter and that this is built around **the assumption of trusting the good intent of those involved**.* If you put time in what does not really matter for a client care approach, they feel it contradicts with the Buurtzorg way of doing things. From the blogs and interviews with the founder, the belief that humanity should prevail over bureaucratic rules and regulations, emerged as basis for creating more autonomy for the employees and for organizing a client care focus. His thoughts regarding humanity have been presented in the book 'Humanity over Bureaucracy' (De Blok and Pool 2010). This belief system could be expressed in several ways, it is an overarching psychological concept where intentions, attitudes, norms, values, expectations all fit in but finally it is more important to notice the way it is being expressed in the behaviors, actions, images and the rituals in the organization. The main conclusion regarding the belief system that one can draw is that there is a lucid belief system in place everywhere in the organization. Organizations define their vision, mission, and strategies. Often these are formulated at the top tier without a clear link to the grass roots level or daily practices. In this situation, they function as superficial or abstract wordings only, instead of inspirational sources for conducting tasks in the primary processes of the organization. At Buurtzorg the vision, mission, and strategies resonate in the whole organization. So far by explaining the main concern of the study, several elements of the belief system have been implicitly described. A belief system of an organization is its culture, which is an integral phenomenon that needs to be experienced. Schneider et al. (2013) review the various perspectives and inconsistencies in views of what organizational culture is. They suggest the most widely used perspective which indicates an integrationist idea about culture. The integrationist view is that organizations are or have one culture shared by all: conflict, ambiguity and differences are ignored and, if mentioned, are seen as something to fix or an aberration (Schneider et al. 2013, p. 370). This view has been expressed in the previous section as well by illustrating the way the higher purpose works as the integrating factor. Here the underlying assumptions are being considered. Assumptions are not easily articulated and they require in-depth interviewing to illuminate them (Schneider et al. 2013, p. 371). Therefore here I only intend to illustrate the belief system as could be found in the assumptions with a few quotes from interviews and a selection of a few conversations that took place on the blog posts of the founder. They are so deeply embedded or ingrained. Hence, by illustrating some of the conversations it tells it all.

   Many employees stress that they are being trusted by both founders. In respect to the trust they receive, they mentioned how important it is to be open in your communication. "*If things do not turn out the way you have planned you just go to them and tell them or you go to any other colleague, it depends how important you think it is to share it with the founders. As we are so committed to the work, from their side there is no doubt that you would have put enough effort in getting the best out of it and that gives such a good feeling. You then automatically come up with solutions yourself. I always try to inform them and especially as the co-founder is so accessible I just drop by to her office and check with her my alternative path or use her as a sounding board*" (Respondent 39).

In observations during meetings where the founder participated, it emerged that he acknowledges that *people are in general capable of more than they have been trained for* so far and that they should be given the space to develop their talents and **remove the veil** to see what a person really is able to deliver. The assumption behind the belief system in this example is that 'people are smart by themselves'. In many interviews employees expressed how well the founder has been in tracing their talents. "*It is as if he is extra ordinary in tracing what your capabilities are. Often you are not even aware of them yourself. But it is also the case that nobody cared about your extra capabilities in the past. Here it is not important what you have on your CV, how smart you are based on your formal degrees, simply because in practice those things are not enough. It is more important who you are as a person and whether you are willing to explore yourself and your hidden talents to discover how you can contribute and then you notice how smart you are. Actually I created my job myself; because there was so much work and I saw opportunities that I discussed with the founders*" (Respondent 40).

One other assumption is that *people care for each other and there is a culture to* **build an ethics of care for each other**. One such illustration can be found in the following quote:

> *You could also compare it with a family business. In other organizations, if the founder or director is ill, things will just go on. In a family business or at Buurtzorg it makes a difference if the founder is ill. Everyone feels involved and acknowledges how important the leadership of the founder is. Even while in practice he is not physically present all day, in such circumstances everyone is empathically involved. This could potentially put the organization in a vulnerable situation. To prevent this it would be wise to think of a small management layer who is representing the leader (Respondent 1).*

> *In teams there are conflicts just as in every team. The only difference is that they are solved in the sphere of a family; just like brothers and sisters. With such an atmosphere you express things directly but somehow it also creates a bond. If there is an issue with the directors as well, you can express it. Your vulnerability will not be misused; there is a safe environment also for conflicts (Respondent 12).*

The following blog illustrates how people care for each other.

Box 8.1 Blog founder and some reactions: with tears in your eyes
With tears in your eyes
   Written by: Jos de Blok, November 14, 2008 at 17:15
   Have you ever experienced when you are reading something and suddenly you have tears in your eyes, you can't just stop it, you are so moved that you just start crying? It happens to me quite often, lately.
   I was reading the very nice letter of the client from Meppel and saw how the people in that team in front of me; apparently did just the right things to help this client on his way again. Beautiful how the client puts this into words. Also, the reaction from Marjo on the Cuijk/Boxmeer team, again almost brought me to tears. Wonderful that such a prize-winning Buurtzorgweb can cause these kinds of emotions. (Thanks guys from Ecare!!!) This because I am such a sensitive human being. Maybe a little overstressed? Not at all, it just moves me because it is exactly the core of what we are doing: helping people on their way to a next destination. If you experience a crisis, your body is not functioning properly anymore, you get to hear that you have a disease beyond cure, sometimes your world just collapses, you don't know how to go further, you don't want to give up. At a moment like that and the period following it, you can only hope that you come across people that understand what this means for you and go to work on it together with you. Everybody will eventually have to deal with a crisis like this but the life you will have after it depends for a great deal on your environment and how your caregiver deals with it. Do not give up on it, darn it, just look what is still possible and at the same time realise that there is a mourning process necessary to process setbacks. Make sure that a new perspective is created and after a stopover, the journey to the next destination can be picked up.
   Last week I was asked again by Ernst & Young: Which products do you supply? How do you clarify with them what we are doing exactly? Somehow we will manage to answer this, but in the mean time we will just enjoy what our clients experience as very valuable and our sometimes very stubborn nurses!!
   Selection of a few responses:
   "Wow, these are different web blogs than from our previous manager! These 'Buurtzorgers' are quite lucky!" Ilona Berkhof—November 15, 2008 at 09:08
   "Hi Jos, just a small reaction from a pigheaded nurse. It is really great to show your emotion. And you also set a good example, yes men can also cry. Because, the work at Buurtzorg is intensive and definitely exhausting you can't do this without emotion. If you want to work in an experimental way, emotion is just a part of it!!" Miriam Wasser—November 14, 2008 at 22:52

(continued)

> **Box 8.1** (continued)
>
> "Maybe you can let Ernst & Young know that we deliver a product called 'humans with feelings'. And the tears in your eyes are recognizable and so kind, the feelings that come with our work are not yet killed by society, what else do we want????" Petra Bothof—November 15, 2008 at 16:56
>
> "With my former employer we worked based on a vision called, "Experiential Based Care". Caregivers were supposed to approach clients with that vision. From the managers it was expected that they, provide the example and also approached their associates that way. Little of that actually happened. What you show with your input is that leading by example really works and action speaks louder than words. Nice, finally a human being as a manager!! I did not know that it was still possible!" Theo Broekhof—November 17, 2008 at 08:51

Another assumption is "*we can make the difference*" in community care. Due to attention and recognition for what Buurtzorg has achieved the belief that it is worth it to strive for the higher purpose has been strengthened. The following blogs are about the higher purpose at Buurtzorg and the attention and recognition received from the government and society.

> **Box 8.2 Blog founder: Minister Schippers visits Almelo today!**
> Minister Schippers visits Almelo today!
> Written by: Jos de Blok, August 20, 2013 at 13:12
> This morning I received a message from Edith Schippers with the question if I would like take an hour to update her about senior care/AWBZ. Of course I wanted this and because she happened to be in the east, she was able to stop by our office in Almelo. I will let you know tonight how this meeting went.
> What are we going to talk about?
> Of course I do not know about what our minister would like to talk, but I would like to tell her that we should occupy ourselves with what is necessary and useful for people with disabilities, handicaps, and injuries. What is necessary for this, are good agreements with care-offices/insurance companies/municipalities. Which expertise is needed in order to do this properly and how you can organize this in the best way. How we should co-operate together instead of competing: with other first line professionnals, with informal care and other organizations. How we can learn from experiences. How we can make younger people enthusiastic for this profession and much more. . ..
> Kind regards,
> Jos

Two blogs about receiving the award for the best employer of the year.

Box 8.3 Blog founder: Buurtzorg best employer of The Netherlands
Buurtzorg is the Best Employer in The Netherlands!!

Written by: Jos de Blok, September 29, 2011 16:39

Dear colleagues,

WE HAVE WON!! This afternoon at 15:30 we received the prize for the Best Employer of The Netherlands with the highest score ever! We got an 8.7 for general satisfaction and for some areas even higher. For example a 9.5 for involvement and a 9.1 for low employee turnover: so you seem to keep working for Buurtzorg for a while still. It is special that despite (or maybe thanks to) the huge dynamics within Buurtzorg we win this prize. There is in fact no real distinction between employee and employers and I would like to congratulate you all on the result. I propose that each team orders a cake, at the expense of Buurtzorg of course. Winning this prize does not mean that there are not things that we can improve. The coming years we will invest a lot of energy in the balance between work and personal life. Buurtzorg thanks her growth to the effort of all colleagues. We will keep searching for a good balance in all that we do. But now it is time to party! Also on behalf of Kety and Gonnie: THANK YOU VERY MUCH!! We have the sweetest, nicest, best, most beautiful, most creative and intelligent colleagues of the entire Netherlands!!

WE WON AGAIN: FOR THE SECOND TIME THE BEST EMPLOYER OF THE NETHERLANDS!!! CAKE!!!

Written by: Jos de Blok, October 10, 2012 07:09

Dear colleagues, as you might have heard or read already: yesterday we received the prize for the Best Employer of The Netherlands for the second time at a special meeting in the La Mar Theater. I propose that each team orders something nice to go with the coffee and celebrate this. I would like to thank you all very much for the trust you have in us and Buurtzorg (and yourself).

We already knew that we scored well with a 9, but it was still great to receive the prize yesterday. This puts us in the spotlights in a positive way again. From various presentations it was clear that it becomes more and more important for the organisation that social values are pursued. This is what we have been trying since the start of Buurtzorg. This has resulted in a lot of nice things already. I hope we keep doing the right things and that despite the occasional huge pressure, the enjoyment in the work remains and that we keep inspiring each other with good ideas. Again, thank you very much: it is an honour to be the employer of so many great people!!!

Kind regards,

Jos

The blogs address every type of management topic that would be addressed by a CEO in regular meetings with employees. These are for example:

- nursing specific issues and enhancing quality of care
- about incidents such as a death, of a colleague or a colleague with a severe accident
- when a colleague receives a knighthood
- strategic issues and the position of Buurtzorg in the industry
- new developments and international scope
- experiences and worries in respect to new governmental policies and developments at local district level
- experiences with insurance companies and other healthcare agencies
- self-management issues
- views on management and control
- views on institutions and bureaucratic climates in the healthcare
- views on training and education, the bottom line such as productivity
- illness rate
- expenses on training and education and balancing work and home.

Especially the blogs related to the higher purpose of reforming community care get very affectionate and engaged reactions from the employees. This shows how employees are committed to help the founder in achieving this higher purpose because it almost becomes a universal value to strive for. A majority of the employees are professionally experienced and therefore could resonate to the urgency of this striving.

The next section will show that it is not only the content that is being discussed but also the way it is being discussed which increases the engagement of employees in the discussions. First, we explain the various roles and how it helps a client care focus.

8.4 Founder's Various Roles

The founder has four roles: change agent; community nurse; manager and integrator. With these roles he stays connected to the market, the employees and the Healthcare Industry for community care. Next to these roles, employees recognize in the founder a person just like everyone else, a human being with preferences, insights, courage, strengths and some weaknesses. Being simple in this role is one of the greatest compliments he receives. Employees regard his behavior as being authentic and courageous to think independently.

The founder is not strict in dividing his time between these roles. During some periods in the year he is more engaged as change agent presenting his views to the local and national government, political parties, other colleagues in community care, other organizations in the healthcare such as general practitioners (family doctors) or other healthcare professionals who show interest in the Buurtzorg way of working. At other times he is the leader expressing the Buurtzorg vision at meetings to employees, to the board of directors, or to people outside the organization. Here he is also taking on a manager's role in discussions with stakeholders such as insurance companies, as at the end of the day the organization should be financially healthy as well. As the organization has grown and is still growing his role as nurse is decreasing. According to many interviewees he is now spending much more time as a change agent compared to the early years.

Many employees are proud of being a part of Buurtzorg. They appreciate it if the founder visits their teams at important occasions. The roles as discussed in this section do not seem to conclude as conflicting in practice and take a natural flow.

While these separate roles are important in leading the higher purpose, integration is also just as important. The integration happens at the level of the founder who due to operating in different roles could bring together and synthesize the knowledge and insights. Integrating these roles has some positive side effects at organizational level.

One of the interviewees noticed the following in respect to roles between the founders. *"The founder is charismatic in his nature. He is real, he is authentic. As a gardener he should 'water' continuously because leadership is not a mechanism that functions itself. Gonnie the other director is brilliant, and she organizes everything. She is very friendly and has a natural authority. In other organizations you have managers who try to manage decision making processes. But here there is no manager and no need to formalize management processes. Gonnie does all the needful internally. Both Jos and Gonnie do not realize that the success of Buurtzorg lies in the power of the coincidence in the fit of their personalities. Without this fit, we would not have the same Buurtzorg"* (client representative).

Both founders seem to fit to the tasks that need to be done very well.

The role of both founders has not changed. Their personalities have not changed neither has the approach changed. The only change we notice is that Jos is more active outside Buurtzorg (Respondent 1).

As the organization grows there is much more information accessible. In the early years every type of information was available in the minds. We did not need to make notes. Jos took along employees to meetings but now he asks even more people to join him. The strength of the founder is that he recalls all important issues (Respondent 1).

8.5   Smart Communication

The way the founder reaches out to the employees who are based all over the country with a smart way of communication is another expression, of leading the higher purpose. It is labeled as smart because it is a combination of affectionate and business like communication. If necessary the founder is bold and direct, but usually he is respectful and kind. Based on the findings at Buurtzorg we induce the following characteristics as ingredients that make such communication successful.

- The way it is being expressed should give the receiver a feeling that the communication is sincere, respectful, and warm. The receiver should be mindful (without judgments and attentive) to understand what is being said. As the job satisfaction is high at Buurtzorg, usually employees are dedicated to give the best of themselves to the organization. They are committed to get involved and they will be aware of the relevance of the information that is being communicated on the virtual platform. As not everything is fixed in rules and regulations at Buurtzorg it requires to *'read between the lines'* which means that employees believe you should always try to see what is being said and how this relates to the client care focus. In other words, it is about being mindful to what is being communicated. *"Just listening to words is not enough; you should try to make sense out of what is being said, why and how it relates to the Buurtzorg vision"* (Respondent 38). This holds for communication with the founders but also for working with colleagues.
- Furthermore, the sender of the information should be able to express himself openly when it comes to his emotions, thinking processes and doubts. People almost feel the communicator is around while he is not. This is realized as a person is being perceived as a human being with strengths and some imperfections. The communicator should not try to hide the imperfections if they occur to be relevant in the communication. Such is the case for example, if the founder says he does not know what is the best solution for an issue and that he is struggling himself with things, thus showing his vulnerable side of being human. In the blogs it turned out that the founder actively asks for input from the employees.
- The information that is being sent should connect to what makes sense to the reader by addressing things and experiences that he recognizes in his daily life. Avoiding information overload is another way to increase the willingness of the reader to read the blogs.

Here follows a blog that is expressing the more business like messages and a selection of a few responses.

Box 8.4 Blog Founder and reactions: Alarming message about high phone bills
Jos de Blok, May 4th 2012 22:19
  Alarming message about high phone bills
  The last few months, there has been an alarming increase of the number of high telephone bills, sometimes between 200 and 400 euro per month. Some even exceed 400 euro. We suspect that some SIM cards are being used in smart phones. For the Buurtzorg phones there is no data plan subscription,

(continued)

Box 8.4 (continued)

which means that downloading images or movies and the use of the internet results in high costs. Besides this, it is of course not intended that the phones are being used for personal use. Please give your attention for this issue.

Everybody with a high phone bill will be contacted personally about this. The extremely high bills form a financial risk for Buurtzorg. We will keep a close eye on the developments and see what we can do to reduce the costs. Also it came to our attention that quite some people spend a lot of time on their phones, sometimes more than 15 hours per month. A good conversation might be necessary, but there are limits to this.

I count on your cooperation,

Kind regards,

Jos

Selection of a few responses:

"The bigger we grow as Buurtzorg, the greater the chance is that we experience becoming just a reflection of society with all sorts of people in it. Small is clear and transparent and big is more difficult to stay transparent. Please let us all keep the ideals and ideas of Buurtzorg high and we will all prosper. And in the meantime stay alert in a healthy way because unfortunately this is simply necessary and is also a part of self-steering".

Annette Souverijn—May 7, 2012 at 12:51

"Hello Jos, I have a different kind of reaction on your message. I see that everybody immediately thinks about themselves as ideal and sound employees. Really, I don't mean this in a cynical way. I would like to use your message to discuss the use of smartphones for our work in the 21st century. I only use my Buurtzorg phone for calling and sending text messages about work, which is what it was intended for, I thought, as others also indicate. Besides this I have a smartphone, an I-phone, with which I do a lot of things 'for work purposes' for example: looking up medication or other questions on the internet, finding directions, or making movies of a colleague showing how to perform a specific task. Taking pictures of a wound and sending it to a colleague for judgement, making and send notes, scheduling appointments, you name it. I pay this all myself. I find it indispensable in order to work as a professional in the area. I think it would be great if we would think about making a smartphone and data plan part of our standard equipment".

Juul van Ogtrop—May 7, 2012 at 09:51

"Very good to inform people personally, all the liberties that we have at Buurtzorg have to be guarded, unfortunately. Success, Greetings from Jenny".

Jenny Cornelisse—May 6, 2012 at 02:30

But also in such messages it seems that employees are very engaged to seek a solution which is aligned to the organizational aims and that they are open and respectful in their communication.

Here are more explanations and some citations from the research data for illustrations. Practically speaking the founder will not be able to solve issues that occur at a geographical distance and he does not have the time to do so. When employees want to share a new idea and need permission because its impact and costs are higher compared to what has been agreed, they will ask the founder's opinion. Usually he will encourage new ideas if they are well thought out and the risks are reasonable. If the founder himself thinks of something new he will usually not push it but post it on the web to share his rational as well as his doubts. By engaging the whole organization he gets input and sometimes even without spelling out what he may have in mind, others will themselves come up with similar ideas and feel themselves as owners of these ideas and therefore will be committed to implement them.

The times when he decides something himself and announces this through the web everyone tends to take his 'commands' seriously. Several interviewees mention that team members make sure they take care to read messages from "Almelo" (the location of the Headquarters). If they do not have much time, which is usually the case as they prefer their professional role rather than attending the website for doing office work, they will skip other news. Often in each team there is one person in charge of following the communication. Formally this fits the team role of the developer as was expressed in Chap. 5 of this book. While the founder tries to be mindful of what he communicates, based on his role, at times he needs to push some ideas as well to realize some of the organizational goals. When he does this too often, he will be reminded by the coaches, the co-founder or others he works with as it may have negative side effects. This all requires an open communication. There is this belief at Buurtzorg: *"if you need to get something done then you ask the founder to communicate because if he says something, people perceive it as important and everyone listens to him (Respondent 29, interview 2)"*.

Overall it is being experienced that communicating through the internal virtual network is an effective way to reach out to the whole organization. At the Headquarters it turned out that both founders are direct in their communication style. If they do not find something good enough they will express it. If they think someone has done a good job they will express it as well. In the web communications the founders try to avoid expressing too much information. It seems that they think carefully about the information they send out in their blogs. It should not be complex or elicit side effects but it should be helpful to solving issues, serving the client care focus and it should be short and clear. Questions that are used in communication: Do you need it? Does it make sense to you? Do you understand how it serves the client? Another interesting feature emerged when reading and analyzing the blogs of the founder. The communication is very personal and it expresses emotions. The founder puts himself in a vulnerable position by asking advice for some issues, by sharing some doubts or just a few ideas. In the personal way of expression he engages employees in the communication as if they are very near while they are far away at several locations in the country.

Overall it seems that communication is both personal and professional at the level of the founders, a feature that was found amongst the nurses and nurse assistants as well (Chap. 4). They are able to balance between the affectionate and the business-like communication especially when it is face-to-face. For the virtual communication, the affectionate approach in conveying messages and starting discussions is the dominant pattern.

8.6   Leadership Views in the Literature

8.6.1   Leadership Views on Motivation and Control

At Buurtzorg leading the higher purpose in respect to the main concern which is: 'What does an organization (Buurtzorg) do, to deliver services that are fulfilling the client's needs and how does it design and organize its activities for realizing a client's focused service'? The questions of what needs to be organized and how to realize client care focus, has been more important than a certain leadership style or characteristic of the founder. The founder's style of leading is intertwined with his higher purpose which resonates with the higher purpose of the employees. This becomes then a shared higher purpose. By turning to the literature we may draw a term which resonates better to the Buurtzorg concept of leadership, next to the concept of the higher purpose. Here I review existing main theories on the model of man, which is being reviewed by focusing on the views on motivation and coordination, the basic concepts of management. The rational model of man and the organizational self-actualizing model have been dominating the perspectives in management. Here we refer to the dialogue on these models by Lovrich (1989). In this context the Agency Theory and the Theory of Self-Actualization are often described as opposed views. Many leadership models have been influenced by them. Recently the Stewardship Theory and wisdom based views have been proposed as alternatives which also will be mentioned briefly.

When we talk about the 'model of man' in Organizational Theory the main attention goes to the question of what motivates employees and what needs to be done to achieve organizational goals such as clients' satisfaction, high efficiency and effectiveness. Along with this there is the assumption that someone other than the employee is the actor in organizing the work to achieve the goals. More often we see employees taking responsibility themselves, in organizing things such as is the case at Buurtzorg but this is rather an exception than the rule. Therefore, it is more common to believe that individuals who are taking part in any organization each has their own interests, in addition to the organizational interests. In daily practices of many organizations, it turns out that often the personal interests are not fully aligned with the organizational interest. A main personal interest could be receiving an income for the job being done in the organization, the so called Transaction Costs Approach aiming an economic exchange of talents for earnings.

Many managers and employees in organizations hold this economic model of man, each seeking for maximizing their self-interests sometimes at the expense of common goals or higher purposes that could be served. On the side of managers and entrepreneurs control mechanisms are built. Those employees who feel attracted to these contexts choose to work for such places and remain in the organization, according to the ASA (Attraction-Selection-Attrition) theory of Schein (2004). They may have several reasons for this. They restrict their full motivation capacities from these workplaces to find other contexts for those motivational strivings for example in their leisure. If we look at Organizational Theory there are different models with a changing intensity of control mechanisms.

For example, Taylor, in his scientific management and efficiency ideas, states that jobs should be specified in detail so that the leader can get an overview and apply control to realize organizational efficiency. Inspired by these ideas, Skinner's Reinforcement Model was developed with the assumption that human behavior could be modified through punishments and rewards. Furthermore, the Path-Goal Theory based on reward systems became very well-known in the organizational context (House and Mitchell 1974). Controlling can also be linked to the hierarchy of needs (Maslow 1954); or McClelland's (1953) four types of human motives: power over others, goal achievement, attachment to others and avoidance of pain or suffering. McGregor's theory X stated that man is evil in nature. This led to theory Y which finds that human beings are self-actualizing in nature and fundamentally good (McGregor 1960). Ouchi's theory Z, hailing from Japan, talks about being more employee-centered by acknowledging that each employee has his own drives, an open attitude to learn and change and can be motivated in certain types of situations. His theory involves collective decision-making and holistic ideas on motivation that include involvement of the employees' families (Ouchi 1981). Ouchi's theory however did not get much attention in the West. Nor did the Indian's holistic and integrated view of governance and organization hailing for example from Kautilya (Nandram 2011a, b, 2013; Jain and Mukherji 2009).

Observation of individuals' tendency to focus on loyalty towards their profession rather than the company or employers led to the development of new models for control by moving to psychological control. Steers & Porter and Vroom stressed the cognitive ability of subordinates whose focus on results is driven by their expectations and values (Steers and Porter 1987; Vroom 1964). Vroom introduced the Expectancy Value Theory which stressed that motivation is directly related to one's expectations and to the value he places on an activity. Adams (1965) says that people perceive outcomes of their efforts and compare them with the efforts and outcomes of others. The Tasks Characteristic Model of Hackman and Oldham (1975) is another example of a cognitive motivational model. It finds that employees become motivated by the perception and experience of autonomy while performing their tasks. The higher the level of independence and autonomy, the more fulfilling it is. Highly fulfilling tasks generate more motivation. At Buurtzorg, employees experience high levels of autonomy and they value this aspect very highly as well (See Chap. 6). In line with this perspective, Deci (1971) developed the concepts of intrinsic and extrinsic motivation. Intrinsic motivation relates to the experience of pleasure while executing the tasks. Extrinsic motivation relates to the inspiration that comes from rewards that one get from executing the tasks.

Other models focus on the effectiveness of the leader's behavior. Bass and Avolio quantified the components of leadership behavior by creating the Full Range Leadership Development (FRLD) model (Bass and Avolio 1994). The FRLD is commonly used for identifying leadership styles. The model describes specific leadership styles in terms of effectiveness, degree of activity and frequency of utilization.

The notion that employees are good and have work ethics that drive them to fulfill their potential and their self-actualization aspirations becomes the mainstream in some models. An example is Bass and Burns' Transformational Leadership (Bass 1985, 1990; Burns 1978). Another one is the Servant-Leadership Model. Here Greenleaf introduced the notion that to lead, one also has to serve (Greenleaf 1977). Servant Leaders facilitate the growth and development of their followers, promote community, share power and resources, and provide the support they need to achieve the goals that lead to the common good of individuals and the community as a whole (Greenleaf 1977; Spears and Lawrence 2002). They believe that organizational goals will be achieved on a long-term basis only by first facilitating the growth, development, and general wellbeing of the individuals who comprise the organization. While employees at Buurtzorg have a service oriented attitude, this duality is not necessary as they are often aligned to the organization's philosophy. The primary distinction between Servant Leadership and other leadership styles is that a servant leader is genuinely concerned with serving and he trusts the self-actualizing drive of followers (Greenleaf 1977). All these approaches so far position the employee and the organization as opposite parties, each with its own motivation where accidentally some ambitions may meet and some giving more space to the employee strivings to cultivate. Another key feature is that they either focus on motivation or on control. Recently scholars have turned to more focus on the motivational side and less on the control side in the model of man by introducing the concept of stewardship as a way to reconcile motivation and control in leadership theories.

8.6.2 Stewardship Views on Governance

Next to the motivational models, as an extension to organizational theory building, scholars have introduced the concept of stewardship. Some associate the term stewardship in the biblical sense of taking care and feeling responsible for what has given to mankind by God. In management context it refers to one who manages another's property or financial affairs. This resembles the concept of an agent. The concept has also been adopted in the environmental and sustainability domain of corporate governance. Lawrence and Weber (2008) use stewards or trustees for referring to corporate executives who act in the general public's interest. Hart (1997) define it as commitment to do no harm to the natural environment. In the context of leadership it is used in more general sense as managing the affairs of other's. If we recall how nurses at Buurtzorg take care of the clients and arranges things for the clients in the community context by incorporating the whole chain of professional caregivers (Chaps. 4 and 5) the term steward seems appropriate. Also the reciprocity element between team members can be defined in terms of steward-ship. Furthermore, coaches act as stewards on behalf of the founder. Nurses and nurse assistants act as stewards for the Buurtzorg organization as well. However the term management is less strictly applied but taking care of what needs to be done is more appropriate.

Stewardship fosters the idea that organizations can be built in such a way that followers put aside their personal interest for the group interest and they focus on the long-term interest rather than the short-term (Hernandez 2008). Thus instead of focusing on mainly the motivational views of human beings, they have thought of an organizational architecture to foster cooperation by employees for achieving organizational goals. Davis et al. (1997) explain stewardship as an alternative for the Principle Agent Theory (Eisenhardt 1985), often labeled as the economic model of man, as mentioned earlier. Within this economic theory it is believed that agents (e.g. employees) do not care for the benefit of the principal (the leader). The principal builds in control mechanisms like performance compensation schemes and governance structures with the hope that these mechanisms will align the goals of both, the agents and leaders/organization. The main message of Davis et al. (1997) is that if we follow psychological assumptions of individuals such as have been developed in the motivational theories, then we may structure organizations in a different way.

Stewardship assumes a benevolent view of human nature (Davis et al. 1997). While Davis et al. (1997) focused mainly upon the psychological idea of the self-actualizing man based on the work of Maslow. Hernandez (2008, 2012) builds further on the psychological dimensions of support as mechanism to motivate followers to consider the broader implications or organizational decisions and for accepting the personal consequences of their actions. These are: interpersonal, contextual and motivational support for fostering self-efficacy, self-determination and feelings of purpose. The assumption behind such thinking is that this subse-quently leads to high productivity and high commitment, thus an experience of a meaningful workplace.

Based on the findings of the research of this book, we could conclude that Buurtzorg fosters all three conditions. People are encouraged to put into practice what they are capable of, thus their efficacy. By empowering them, their perception of what they are capable of grows (self-efficacy). Furthermore, there is space for self-determination and for deciding how to put one's talents into practice next to his professionalism which is based on knowledge and expertise. At Buurtzorg employees generate the feeling of purpose, as could be concluded from the previous sections. One important factor behind these support mechanism is trust. In Chap. 6 of this book we have presented the Intrapreneurial Freedom and the experienced trust of employees at Buurtzorg. A main contribution lies in how Buurtzorg succeeds in building trust which is one of the main topics in management practices of community care but also in other industries. Building trust is also an important concept in discussions regarding revitalizing societies and the role of financial systems and governance. It is also becoming a phenomenon to be studied in the domain of organization behavior and theory development on stewardship. Kulkarni and Ramamoorthy (2011) introduce the aspect of *subordinate stewardship* as determinant of governance mechanisms of control and coordination. They suggest trust and loyalty as important critical characteristics in the exchange relationship between employee and leader. In their view, trust represents a risk orientation of an individual to be vulnerable to the actions of another person or party regardless of monitoring (Kulkarni and Ramamoorthy 2011, p. 2777). The risk orientation is the willingness to incur any loss while fulfilling the organizational obligations. In their view, trust reduces the costs for controlling self-interest-seeking behavior by the organization and it builds the belief that a trustee will act beneficially because he cares about the wellbeing of the trustor. They define loyalty as a situation where an individual's primary interests are to serve the organizational goals rather than to serve themselves. This can be built in contracts between the leader and the employees. It can be viewed as relational or psychological and include beliefs about reciprocity and acceptable norms (Kulkarni and Ramamoorthy 2011, p. 2778).

Next to subordinate stewardship some scholars explicitly focus on leader's stewardship. Caldwell et al. (2008) suggest that great leaders are ethical stewards who generate high levels of commitment from followers. They introduce *ethical stewardship* as the honoring of duties owed to employees, stakeholders, and society in the pursuit of long-term wealth creation (Caldwell et al. 2008, p. 153). The assumption behind this concept is that leaders can work on creating long term wealth and build organizational trust by operating as ethical stewards. Caldwell et al. (2008) stress how important it is to earn trust and followership by creating integrated organizational systems for enabling these conditions. Ethical stewards earn trust if they themselves are perceived as trustworthy.

In stewardship theory the steward will not replace his personal interests for cooperative interest but will seek to maximize utility for the organization based on rational principles (Davis et al. 1997). Block (1996) thinks of stewardship containing two features: service over self-interest and employees as owners and partners.

In previous chapters of this book it has become obvious how important service is compared to personal interest. Chapter 4 has shown how attuned nurses and nurse assistants are towards the client's needs and capabilities. In previous sections of this chapter it is clear how engaged employees feel at Buurtzorg and how informally they consider themselves as leaders, owners and partners. Buurtzorg is theirs. Furthermore the aspects of trust, long-term orientation, relationship and loyalty have been demonstrated as important in stewardship theory. These aspects are all lively at Buurtzorg in the process of leading the higher purpose. The analysis of the leadership theories by incorporating the concept of stewardship has resulted in two conclusions: Buurtzorg has demonstrated that employees perceive trustworthiness and are able to focus on the higher purpose of the organization which is serving the client in the best possible way. A long-term orientation is present as well as the higher purpose, which is about revitalizing the community care which also requires a long-term perspective. Building relationships between essential parties is a key component in all possible settings at Buurtzorg: nurse and client; team members; team and coaches; teams and other nurse assistants or community stakeholders; the founder and the coaches; the founder and the team members; the founder and the staff at the Headquarters; and finally between the founder and other care related agencies and institutes. As a leadership-follower relationship does not resonate well at Buurtzorg, the concept of stewardship seems to fit much better.

While focusing on stewardship and the role of followers as stewards (at Buurtzorg the nurses, nurse assistants and coaches are the stewards), it is also important to focus on the role the leaders have to play in such stewardship context. Caldwell et al. (2008) suggest ethical stewardship as a response. Are there alternatives that fit the Buurtzorg way better as leadership is still part of the organization's design? However, also alternatives such as stewardship are reflected in an untraditional sense of the concept of leadership in terms of motivation theories or control mechanisms. Hence, we reflect on the wisdom based literature to find more suitable input for understanding the concept of leadership at Buurtzorg.

8.6.3 Wisdom Based Leadership and Purpose

While stewardship moved from a control to a motivation focus and many leadership views are dealing with both motivation and coordination, they all still depart from a dualistic perspective of self and organization, self-interest and organization-interest. Wisdom based models however, often take away the dualistic perspective. They assume that people are altruistic in nature and they are seeking a sense of meaning, purpose, interconnectedness and harmony with the environment and maybe even belief in a higher power. They provide assumptions for a higher power for which human beings would like to act in the interest of all.

They also give means to enhance the wellbeing for coping with stressful events. They give tools for awakening higher consciousness levels so that our perception increases in lucidity and enhances creativity. They provide the ontology that all existence is united to one force, a state of oneness and therefore we all need to contribute to that solidarity of oneness. With this they often combine the idea of all beings having spiritual needs for developing and maintaining relationships; inner harmony and a belief in transcendence of our desires and situations.

The altruistic need doesn't require control or coordination as it is a natural process that only needs to be awakened. The main condition is the acceptance and acknowledgement of such needs in the organizational context. So while stewardship focuses on building trust, loyalty, and a long term perspective, its epistemology about reality can be fully rational. Spiritual models however, acknowledge non-rational aspect such as affection and various other non-rational belief systems.

The interest for spirituality in the management practice is new. Only in the past two decades management scholars have started seeking for alternative approaches to enhance the quality of life of employees and fostering sustainability in businesses by incorporating views on spirituality. One of the main assumptions for introducing spirituality in management is that employees want to be recognized for who they are. This means as a whole person with spirit, heart, soul, passions, hopes, talents, aspirations, families, private lives, emotions, ups and downs, and diverse perspectives on several matters in the organizations they work for. Leadership is then a way to give an answer to this holistic need with the impact that the employees subsequently will aligned fully with the Buurtzorg goals.

The scholarly debate on spiritual models for management concerns the character of spirituality, its features and its impact on businesses. In a review of Karakas (2009) based on 140 articles, three different perspectives were mentioned as approaches to contribute with spirituality in management: it is recognized as a way to enhance the employee wellbeing and the quality of life; it provides employees a sense of purpose and meaning at work and it provides employees a sense of interconnectedness and community. Academicians see spirituality as something that comes from within the person (Krishnakumar and Neck 2002; Schwartz 2006). Some stress the interpersonal dimension; connectedness to others. Marques (2006) defines spirituality in the workplace as an experience of interconnectedness and trust. Bandsuch and Cavanagh (2002) see spirituality as enabling a person to develop good moral habits. In some views the focus towards connectedness is central. Kelemen and Peltonen (2005) for example describe spirituality as a positive emotion that serves to bring together the rational and the embodied aspects of human life. At the same time it is about reaching out to make a connection with a larger universe (Kelemen and Peltonen 2005, p. 60). They use the term 'technology of the self' and state that spirituality is rooted in the here and now and that it opens the way to the inner side of the individual and connection with the larger cosmos. Another such view stems from Pandey and Gupta (2008, p. 6): "Spirituality is defined as harmony with oneself and with the social and natural environment and it is a potential every human being is born with".

Nandram and Borden 2010; Nandram 2011a) define spirituality as a process of evolution of a business climate bringing it to a higher level of meaning for its entrepreneurs, employees and stakeholders. It starts where individuals feel the wholeness of their being. This makes it possible for them to work from their inner senses and to invent new forces and talents to improve. The new strengths and talents that emerge from the empowered and inspired entrepreneurs will increase business performance on both tangible and intangible levels with economic and social gains for the internal and external stakeholders of the business.

Few researchers have developed means to measure spirituality thereby creating the possibility of testing their conceptual models (Miller 2004; Piedmont and Leach 2002; Ashmos and Duchon 2000; Bhal and Debnath 2006; Miller and Ewest 2011). The key aspects are harmony by experiencing meaning and purpose, connectedness to others and living beings and the belief in transcendence.

While spirituality is being introduced as a broad concept for management practices (individual techniques; way of building relations; approaches to foster commitment and connectedness) there are scholars who explicitly focus on leadership. Margaret Benefiel (2005) describes stages in the transformation of the goals of individual leaders giving them increasing relevance at the organizational level. Fry's spiritual leadership model (Fry 2003, 2005; Fry and Slocum 2008) is based on spiritual values such as altruistic love leading to hope and faith, and inducing a shared mission and vision. This leads to spiritual well-being enhanced by listening to their inner calling and creating a sense of belongingness. Ultimately, this leads to greater productivity and commitment to the organization.

Inspired by the Yogic philosophy, Nandram (2010a, b) introduced the Yogic Leadership model operationalized in five levels of being and as a synthesis of inner and outer harmony. The belief system of oneness encompasses the assumption that there is an inner life and an outer life that needs to be integrated for which we tap from our potential of self-transcendence to strive for oneness. In this model spirituality is operationalized as attitudes, behaviors or a practice stemming from the inner self and it makes it possible to examine it as a part of management science. The current trend in management is to address spirituality from an extrinsic perspective. Here it is assumed that spirituality has both an inner and outer quest. Just as there is outer and inner consciousness, spirituality can also be experienced and expressed both outwardly and inwardly (Nandram 2011b). The outer aspect of spirituality refers to mentally learning about spiritual concepts; our relationship to others and the world as expressed in trust, respect and our commitments. Inner spirituality, rather than being conceptual is an experience, a transformative process which involves transcending our habitual state of being, expanding the consciousness, becoming more subtle and ultimately connected and fully aligned to the indwelling force. The existing research on spirituality in the context of business deals mostly with the outer side of it. This is because the non-tangible nature of spirituality makes it difficult to access from a dominant traditional scientific perspective. For example, in the literature one can find the opinion that spirituality is not measurable, and thus not a topic for research (Dent et al. 2005). Those who are convinced that spirituality is measurable try to respond to this view by saying that we need alternative models to allow the study of spirituality due to its non-tangible, individual and subtle nature. They seek to replace the more positivistic methodologies that work with predetermined frames of research with a constructive view by proposing, natural inquiry methods, action research methods, a first person approach or reflective and experience-based models for learning.

The biggest challenge is to develop a model integrating both the external and internal sides of spirituality as relevant to leadership. Integrating both aspects will give more synergy between private life and professional life creating a workplace to which entrepreneurs, leaders, employees can bring their whole self. The result of this creates an environment in which they can be free to simply be human beings aligned with their authentic, inner self. Those who develop their authenticity feel more centered in all situations, and thus they will be fully motivated to perform according to their hidden talents (Kernis and Goldman 2006).

There are several techniques to fasten this process. It requires, such as the word yoga implies: discipline and letting go as two sides of the same coin of oneness the whole system of life. Such a belief system requires freedom to let go but also a clear governance framework for building discipline. If reforming the community care by attunement to the client's needs is the higher purpose of an organization then a Yogic Leadership approach requires transcending self-interest to the higher interest of the client as is the current case at Buurtzorg. Buurtzorg's concept of the higher purpose can be labeled as a yogic spiritual value. It is a fundamental part of life, an ongoing and thus dynamic process that is not fixed but that requires discipline to work on for changing the community care. It requires an attitude of never give up, and yet let go when things do not work: a yogic attitude. Because it is acknowledged that change is the constant, there is not a fixed reality. This has been expressed in the way clients are served, in the way complexity is being avoided and by going back to the basics of human relationships of trust, respect, loyalty and harmony.

This elaboration of the literature on leadership leads to the conclusion that stewardship and Yogic Leadership are appropriate concepts to enable the process of leading a higher purpose in the Integrating Simplification Theory. This enabler will be discussed in Chap. 9 in more detail and within the theoretical principles and its scientific contribution.

Scientific Contribution of IST in the Domain of Organizational Innovation

Abstract

In this chapter the added value of the Integrating Simplification Theory (IST) for the management field of organizational innovation will be argued. We have seen that Integrating Simplification comprises of principles that refer to aspects of perception of available information, seeking additional information and synthesizing the information in such a way that practices are simplified. This can be reviewed at the individual level of the nurse and nurse assistant, for example and at the organizational level of information processing and implementation by focusing on the process of knowledge creation in organizations and how this works in the five dimension of Integrating Simplification. These five dimensions; Attunement to the Client, Craftsmanship, Intrapreneurial Team Freedom, Pragmatic ICT solutions and Leading a Higher Purpose, refer to building trustful customer relationship, entrepreneurial aspects of creating and innovating and the managerial aspects of motivation and organization. These are topics that almost all types of organizations experience. The IST will be discussed in the light of the Knowledge Theory, Vedic Theory on Knowledge Creation and Subtle Knowledge, and Effectuation Theory.

9.1 Introduction

The main concern in the study was: 'What do entrepreneurs and professionals do in an organization, to deliver services that are fulfilling the client's needs and how do they design and organize its activities for realizing a client focused service'. The underlying assumption at Buurtzorg is that a client focus is the best approach to serve the client's needs. The main concern includes both the individual professional/entrepreneurial level and the organizational level of a client focused service. So far the chapters have given an understanding of how Buurtzorg is designed to operate from a client's perspective. Serving their clients in the best possible way is one of their core values. The best possible way refers to the quality of the care and the empowerment of the client to be self-reliant again as soon as possible and guiding him in preventing situations that make him dependent of care. Such a question of delivering what a client or customer needs, lies at the heart of every organization as every organization needs its clients and customers to survive. Moreover, a high client satisfaction level will contribute to the bottom line of business. Serving the client also requires a continuous innovative perspective to meet the client's needs. The practice at Buurtzorg could be put in the contexts of organizational behavior and organizational innovation. The way professionalism is being organized with nurses and nurse assistants in the front-line with various entrepreneurial tasks and responsibilities and how the main process of delivering care is being facilitated with pragmatic ICT solutions and a small Headquarters form the main building blocks of its organizational design. This means that both processes, the primary which is delivering care, and the secondary process, which is the organizational architecture, are simplified but still integrated to acquire the organizational outcomes of efficiency, effectiveness and experienced meaningfulness by the clients and employees.

The primary process is in practice the main process which sounds more than logic. While this seems so logical in the community care industry it has been the other way around. An explanation could be found in unraveling the question of who is the client, a question that is so familiar to the public sector. Is it the national or local government who has constructed the insurance law and policy? Is the insurance agency that brings this policy into practice, the client of Buurtzorg? Is it the citizen who actually requires the care? From a business perspective the client is the one who pays for the service. Buurtzorg is being paid by several insurance agencies from two types of expenditures that have been reserved at governmental level, the so called ABWZ and the WMO for the services they provide to the citizens. The citizens themselves pay a certain percentage based on their own income level to a governmental administration office. The remaining costs are covered with these two types of expenditures. In practice Buurtzorg does not receive payment directly from the citizens, who are the actual clients of the services they provide.

The innovativeness of Buurtzorg lies in the fact that it sees the citizens who receive the services as its client irrespective of the parties from which they get their earnings. In community care, organizations are usually trying to serve all the types of clients, often losing the overview of what was really required for a smooth primary process. This was going on for a few decades. In the public sector of community care, the effort and time spent for the process of administration has become dominant. It aimed a transparent practice of the rules and regulations that were defined by law. As reforms were introduced, assuming economies of scales, these practices have become very complex, more time consuming and often hardly manageable. By introducing several management layers to control due to the accountability goal in respect to the expenditures, the costs as well as the complexity increased. Organizations became too busy in managing the complexity and began losing the perspective of the clients. Clients became of secondary importance while managing the complexity became of primary importance.

By choosing for the citizen, who actually experience the care, as the main client, and not the parties from whom the payment is being received, Buurtzorg has placed the client central in the process. It has positioned the process of delivering care to the client as primary importance in its strategic operation and policy. It has identified two processes, the primary and the secondary. It has reflected on these and disentangled them in the operations to keep them both transparent but at the same time at the level of the whole organization. The processes are integrated in such a way that operations in both support each other. Furthermore it has defined and implemented the delivery of care to the client and the relationship with the client as the main operation while the administrative part explicitly has the role of facilitating. In designing this philosophy of 'the client in the center', Buurtzorg has introduced a new way of organizing based on Self-Managed Teams, thus by putting the professional in the front-line, as could be read in the previous chapters. While this new organizational design was developed for the community care industry, several of its features are applicable to organizations in general as each organization deals with similar questions in respect to how to serve the client in the best possible way and how to maintain a committed employee in the organization. A special feature of the employee is his professionalism referring to the space he has to operate according to his profession. In daily practice this means that he has autonomy to take certain decisions based on his occupational expertise and insights. He does not need to be managed for each activity; he is the expert on a certain field and has the relevant competences to operate in a certain way that is being expected by its occupational framework.

Actually here we are talking about knowledge hailing from the expertise of nurses and nurse assistants as main asset to be organized and implemented to gain renewed practices for enhancing the effectiveness of the care delivery process. Hence, is it a worthwhile exercise to reflect on how the insights that we have gained in the study, could be relevant for the management field of organizational innovation. More specifically, how organizations create innovation by nourishing their main asset which is expertise.

In this chapter we will focus on the *dynamics of knowledge creation*. Based on the implementation of the Classic Grounded Theory we have found that Integrating Simplification lies at the heart of the Buurtzorg way of organizing. The main contribution of this theory could be placed within the knowledge creation framework discussing different types of knowledge concepts where Nonaka's Theory fits best. Furthermore to deepen the discussion on knowledge we will borrow insights from Vedantic views. The Effectuation Theory will be addressed for understanding the thinking process and building expertise as part of the IST. Finally the Yogic Leadership concept (See Chap. 8) is being presented as the integrating factor of the knowledge types, cognitive process and the operations at the several dimensions of IST.

9.2   IST in the Context of Knowledge Creation

9.2.1   Nonaka's Model of Knowledge Creation

In his interview for reflections, Ikujiro Nonaka explains his ideas on innovative organizations and according to what principles organizations create knowledge that fosters innovation (Scharmer 2000). His theory has been applied in several studies to explain and test how knowledge creation helps organizations in their endeavors to continuously innovate (Nonaka et al. 2000; Von Krogh et al. 2012; Gueldenberg and Helting 2007; Nonaka and von Krogh 2009). Scholars also focus on what could be possible critiques to his theory (Gourlay 2006) and address challenges regarding its inter-cultural dynamic (Hong 2012). The main critique of Gourlay is that not all modes of knowledge converting are plausible; there is lack of evidence and the language used by Nonaka is subjective and does not explain how collaboration works. This paragraph is not meant to give an extensive review of the applications, debate and challenges of his theory but will only focus on those points that are relevant in the context of Integrating Simplification Theory.

Nonaka's Knowledge Creation Theory contributes to the understanding of innovations in companies by distinguishing between tacit and explicit knowledge and by stressing how knowledge comes to exist in organizations. As well as what mechanism could be helpful in managing this process so that it serves the discovery of opportunities for continuous innovation. A basic assumption in his orientation on innovation is that; *an innovation comes from a subjective belief or an image of the world* (Scharmer 2000, p. 1). This is an important assumption as it certainly corresponds with the findings at Buurtzorg Nederland, where it was the founder and co-founders concerning subjective belief that the community care industry could be revitalized in such a way that the client was getting what he needs. Such statements like the best possible care and the care that serves the clients' needs, are all subjective indeed and they had been developed based on experiences in the healthcare by those who founded Buurtzorg Nederland. Due to their experiences, they have created certain mental models or images of how community care could be organized differently. This does not mean that they all started with exactly the same mental model in detail or the same subjective beliefs but in terms of humane values they were all on the same wave length. Through brainstorming they have developed a shared mental model with the belief that clients' needs should be put first, thus the primary process should be main and supported by the secondary process and not the other way around. They have succeeded to share this mental model with others and get them aligned to it so it has now become a higher purpose of the existence of Buurtzorg Nederland. The founders have been able to convert their mental model into an objective language as well; they have justified it in the organization and are able to realize the concept of setting up an alternative way of organizing. This gives them confidence and strengthens similar beliefs or awakens new beliefs regarding innovations which they have proven as well by starting other concepts such as "Buurtzorg Diensten" specifically for providing domestic services such as house cleaning; a "Buurtzorg Hospice", "Buurtzorg Jong" for youth who are requiring guidance and "Buurtzorg T" which offers therapeutic services to people with psychiatric diseases and disabilities.

The notion that subjectivity is important in generating ideas is one of the first steps of innovation that has been acknowledged in the entrepreneurship scholarly works such as in the works of Saras Sarasvathy. She explains that, the entrepreneurial opportunities need to be imagined, therefore claiming it is a matter of the mindset and thus a subjective process (Sarasvathy 2000). Her theory on Effectuation, one of the most accepted entrepreneurial theories, has also demonstrated how the entrepreneur effectuates the process from idea or concept to the start-up in creating a market for a product or service. Some authors demonstrate how even more subjective beliefs hailing from intuition has an impact on inventions and discoveries in our history (Vaughan 1997). There are scholars however, who only focus on information processing which excludes beliefs and images of reality but which stresses the objectivity of phenomena such as in the works of Herbert Simon (1967). At Buurtzorg we have witnessed how beliefs and images of reality are important in the process of Craftsmanship.

Let us start describing the main principles of the Knowledge Creation Theory followed by a reflection on how these could be linked to the Integrating Simplification Theory.

1. In Nonaka's Theory *there is a difference between knowledge and information* (Scharmer 2000, p. 1). He explains that information is passive while knowledge is proactive. Knowledge comes from beliefs and is created by the accumulation of information. Therefore, information is a necessary medium or material for eliciting and constructing knowledge but information is not enough. He compares information with the flow of a message which can be send out to a person regardless of his commitment of receiving it while knowledge requires a commitment to understand it by applying a dynamic human process of justifying personal beliefs towards the truth.

   At Buurtzorg the web provides a lot of information and employees can choose whether to use it or not. The discussion always pops up whether people read the information or not and how to ensure that people get the information that may really make a difference in their practice. In the study it appeared that when information was regarded as relevant for everyone then it is the founder who conveyed the message through blogs and messages. This resembles the so called 'commander's intent' (Johansen and Euchner 2013). When it comes to knowledge it is ensured that this appears in the E-learning environment. Here employees who are interested in a particular topic will actively search for the knowledge and apply it to a current practice or share it with other team members to improve the quality of the services. In the team the so called developer is supposed to be the person who proactively searches for relevant knowledge from the web and from other professional networks. Additional knowledge is gained through other externally offered professional training and education. To conclude, the distinction between information and knowledge is an important one in the Buurtzorg practice, while leaving the freedom to use the information provided to the individual professional.

2. Nonaka distinguishes between *two types of knowledge—tacit and explicit* (Scharmer 2000, p. 2; Nonaka 1991). Tacit knowledge is personal and specific to a context and often hard to formalize or to communicate. "Tacit knowledge consists of mental models, beliefs, and perspectives so ingrained that we take them for granted, and therefore cannot easily articulate them (Nonaka 1991, p. 98)". Explicit knowledge however, can be put in words in a systematic and formal way to be used in communication. "Knowledge that is uttered, formulated in sentences, and captured in drawings and writing is explicit (Nonaka and von Krogh 2009, p. 636)".

It is interesting to note that at Buurtzorg both types of knowledge are present and have room to be expressed. On the website people can express what they have experienced and by doing so they share their insights. Although not every experience can or should necessarily be put into words, a positive side effect of the ICT facilities is that internet posts are short and contain the main message and therefore has a clear goal. If it does not serve a purpose, people will not spend time communicating on the website which leads to the conclusion that the person who shares the tacit knowledge expect to nourish a certain need. In team meetings individuals can have more lengthy expressions and reflections if needed. Therefore, here there is also capacity for tacit knowledge. But as having lengthy meetings is something that is being avoided at Buurtzorg in practice, also at team level, the tacit knowledge serves a goal in all communication. Web communications have impact on others as well as there is the possibility for interaction on the web and it can always be traced back.

The founder also expresses tacit knowledge. He posts blogs to share his feelings, thoughts and experiences on particular topics in the healthcare system or to convey a message related to a special event or celebration such as Easter or Christmas. In some of the messages he takes a vulnerable attitude by just expressing his concerns and asking for input on how to solve an issue or to get insights for possible solutions. In face to face session there is a very open atmosphere of communication and there is space for reflecting.

There is also space for explicit knowledge and this is presented in a formal way. This concerns for example: professional related knowledge, forms to be filled in, about rules and regulations or on developments in the healthcare system. From the Headquarters explicit knowledge is being posted on the web and team members share their experiences regularly within the team. The E-learning website conveys knowledge related to a specific professional activity.

3. These two types are *both mutually complementary entities in innovations* (Scharmer 2000, p. 2). Nonaka says that tacit and explicit knowledge do not act as totally separate entities suggesting that without experience one cannot truly understand a phenomenon and without converting experiences into explicit knowledge we cannot reflect upon what it means and how it relates to things that are going on in the organization. Thus we cannot share it further in the organization. He makes the distinction between technical tacit knowledge (knowhow

and skills) and cognitive tacit knowledge (mental belief systems of the world). He suggests *a dynamic interaction between both types of knowledge* which is the key to organizational knowledge creation where personal knowledge becomes organizational knowledge (Nonaka 1994, p. 16). And knowledge that is available in the organizational infrastructure as explicit knowledge fosters individuals to develop new knowledge through new experiences.

While both types of knowledge are present at Buurtzorg we should note that there is a thin line between them, they are closely intertwined. Except for some basic principles that need to be followed as legally prescribed in the healthcare system, in the explicit knowledge there is enough room for a contextual interpretation because that is the way it works at Buurtzorg, nothing is engraved in stone. In the study it occurred that there is a lot going on in practice and making this knowledge explicit may be helpful to others but there is always a trade-off to be made whether to formalize it or keep it tacit.

4. The dynamic interaction is a key to organizational knowledge creation and brings forward four processes which Nonaka labels as *four modes of knowledge converting* (Scharmer 2000, p. 2; Nonaka 1994; Nonaka and Toyama 2003). These four modes are: socialization, externalization, combination and internalization (SECI). He used the analogy of the spiral to explain the process of knowledge creation leading to knowledge accumulation (Nonaka 1994; Nonaka and Takeuchi 1995; Nonaka and Toyama 2003). The process of *socialization* requires sharing experiences and space to create common unarticulated beliefs or embodied skills. At Buurtzorg this happens on the web and in teams. An unarticulated belief could be, for example: being frugal in expenses or avoiding waste of time in bureaucratic procedures, minimalizing overhead costs or very practically such a belief that you schedule your vacation plans in agreement with the plans of the client or you show more attention in the client who is going through a tough time.

The process of *externalization* is about articulating the tacit knowledge into explicit knowledge which can have several forms such as concepts, metaphors, sketches, diagrams. An example at Buurtzorg is the concept, in Dutch, '*eerst buurten, dan zorgen*' which started as an expression but now it is having a certain common ground of getting acquainted with a client before you start providing the care. It is as if you remove a veil that is between you and the client before you really get to understand what the client needs for designing a plan of action.

Combination is the third mode of knowledge converting which is about assembling new and existing explicit knowledge into systematic knowledge to make it tangible. During team sessions experiences are shared by team members representing their roles; new and existing knowledge is being created and combined to make the activities more effective.

Internalization is an important mode in knowledge converting. Nonaka sees this as a process of learning. It is about embodying explicit knowledge into tacit, operational knowledge such as know-how. The best way to get into this mode is by learning by doing or by applying knowledge in a specific context. At

Buurtzorg this mode is found when team members teach new employees on how things work at Buurtzorg or if they apply knowledge which they have gained from a specific training into their daily activities or if someone with 'seniority' on a specific topic teaches other colleagues on the job what to do to have the best results for the client. We can conclude that all the four modes are present at Buurtzorg in their client care focus.

5. Knowledge base layer: Nonaka suggest a hypertext organization where there is a dynamic synthesis of a bureaucratic structure with the task-force structure. The bureaucratic structure uses combination and internalization aiming for efficiency and stability, while the task-force uses socialization and externalization aiming for effectiveness and dynamism. Next to these structures there is a knowledge base that serves as a clearing house for new knowledge that is being created within these structures.

At Buurtzorg the Headquarters operates as the stable structure aiming efficiency in the support towards the Self-Managed Teams. The idea of a task force is not structurally built. There are possibilities to start an expert group catering specific knowledge on specific diseases but these are not formalized. There is not a formalized knowledge base however the Ecare organization for providing ICT services and the Buurtzorg Academy for providing E-learning modules, serve a bit as clearinghouses.

6. Enabling conditions: Nonaka explains five enabling conditions for knowledge creation; intention, autonomy, fluctuation, redundancy and requisite variety (Scharmer 2000, p. 4). In respect to fluctuation he asserts that this either leads to creative or destructive chaos. By requisite variety he means a minimum internal variety for the purpose of organizational integration and a maximum internal variety for an effective adaptation to the environment. He explains that knowledge creation, knowledge application and knowledge dissemination all interact with each other. He further addresses the importance of socialization by referring to strong organizational cultures enhancing a team oriented spirit with strong individuals. If individuals can function autonomously they could be perceived as a part of the holographic structure. In this structure the whole and each part has access to and share the same information and knowledge (Scharmer 2000, p. 6).

9.2.2 Added Value of Integration Simplification Theory

How is Integrating Simplification different from knowledge converting or where does it add to the knowledge creation process? Integrating Simplification actually departs from a very pragmatic context where nurses and nurse assistants are continuously trying to deliver the best care that is possible in the given context. They will use all types of knowledge such as concrete data on health status of the client, professional frameworks for designing a plan of action, the perception of subtle cues and insights drawn from experiences. They will share the tacit knowledge through the socialization process; they will externalize the tacit knowledge to make it explicit; they will combine experiences with the formal knowledge from their training and formal education, formal knowledge of the organizational and of the community care policy. They will try to present it in a systematic way; they will internalize it and apply it in practice and embrace it as their own Buurtzorg way of doing things. This means that Buurtzorg can be described by the elements of the Knowledge Creation Theory of Nonaka. However, the idea of this book was not describing the Buurtzorg practice with existing theoretical frameworks, but explaining what processes and factors contribute to the Buurtzorg's approach towards the client without preconceived theories. It turned out, that Integrating Simplification process is the key explanation and it gets expressed in the five dimensions which are enabled by Yogic Leadership. The Yogic Leadership concept occurs as a moderator in the conceptual framework. Here follows a description of the added value of the IST.

a. The four processes of knowledge converting first require the orientation of re-setting or converting the mindset or thinking process. This is the core process for starting integrating simplification. Converting knowledge as can be found in the SECI model could be part of integrating simplification but Integrating Simplification Theory embraces a cognitive step of perceiving; an evaluative step of constructing reality and a pragmatic or behavioral step of putting it into practice. *Converting the thinking* is about a proactive mode of perception, evaluation and construction of reality. From a scientific point of view this is suggesting a constructivist epistemology, according to the interpretation of the work of the developmental psychologist Piaget and philosopher Baldwin (Sánchez and Loredo 2009). In essence it refers to the claim that we have the ability to create the reality ourselves using our perception interactively with what is out there. This will be further discussed in the context of the Theory of Entrepreneurial Effectuation.

b. Another feature of Integrating Simplification Theory is that it uses more sources. While tacit knowledge refers to experiences, at Buurtzorg nurses and nurse assistants talk about a '*fingerspitzengefül*', which comes close to the concept of intuition. Furthermore they interact in a team where new knowledge is being created. The context of being a member of a team itself provides new knowledge when interacting with each other. Interaction with clients is another context where new knowledge is being created. We could think of the knowledge based on intuitive stimuli and the knowledge that is created in interaction as a third type of knowledge to be used in the process of knowledge converting. Further on in this chapter, the concept of intuition and other types of knowledge from the literature will be explained to see if these can add to deepen the conclusion here that there is a third source, a third type of knowledge. For now it is labeled as *subtle knowledge*.

c. While the Knowledge Creation Theory distinguishes a knowledge base layer for establishing and maintaining the intellectual capital, at Buurtzorg there is not such a specific layer. The intellectual capacity is integrated in several levels. Hence *integrating intellectual capacity* is more appropriate for Integrating

Simplification. The Ecare organization fosters new ideas but does not operate predominantly as a separate knowledge based unit. They largely work demand-driven which means that the queries to develop a new tool or approach hails from the nurses, nurse assistants, coaches and founders mainly. At times they introduce new ideas themselves. Each idea gets implemented in co-creation with the users. Coaches also serve in creating and maintaining intellectual capacity. Some of the knowledge is shared in the Buurtzorg Academy. At each team level new knowledge and innovative approaches are being developed and utilized mainly by applying in their own settings and by sharing with colleagues on the web. In co-creation with coaches and the IVS office new approaches are developed to serve the primary process of delivering a client care focus. Some of the interviewees expressed their need to have the overview of what is going on in respect to innovative ideas and approaches. Actually no one, including the founders, has a comprehensive or systematic overview. It is the whole that makes it work the way it works.

d. In Nonaka's theory the link with the organizational context has been introduced through acknowledging the enabling conditions. In Nonaka's work ideas are born with beliefs. Beliefs first host individual's knowledge systems. According to him original ideas that come from autonomous individuals, subsequently diffuses within the team they are part of and then become organizational ideas. In his perspective there seems to be a natural flow of interaction between individuals, teams, departments, divisions, organization and back to individuals.

Integrating Simplification Theory survives through *a balancing act or twin principle* which will be explained further in this chapter under the label of *Yogic Leadership*. This functions as a metaenabler to hold together the dimensions of IST and to link the individual level to the organizational level. It requires nurses, nurse assistants and coaches who operate as stewards. The *phenomenon of entrainment* helps in explaining the working of the leader as an enabler in Integrating Simplification. In Chap. 4 of this book this phenomenon has been introduced in respect to attunement to the client.

Nonaka refers to hypertext organizations where the foundations of his theory will work more effectively. In such an organization, for example, there are members of an urgent project team, given the freedom to work on a specific issue where everyone is empowered to use their best potential to complete the project on time. Roles and functions may rotate here to get the particular job done, depending on the stage or process of the project. Interesting to note is that at Buurtzorg teams have the possibility to divide amongst each other different roles to get tasks done. These roles are not fixed and could be applied flexibly for a certain period of time and then roles can be rotated within the team. When teams grow, which often happens given the facts at Buurtzorg, and reach a maximum of 12 they need to split and form two teams. So next to the changing roles this process as well creates the dynamics in the teams.

Another interesting aspect in Nonaka's perspective is that he sees the knowledge creation process as the heart of organization design. While neo-classical economics conceptualize the market as a place for competition usually in terms of price, he introduces the notion that the market could be seen as a reservoir of knowledge. The critical knowledge there, is the tacit knowledge and the main idea is to build a system where this knowledge can be converted in the market to explicit knowledge finding its way out in a product or service to be delivered as a fundamental function of an organization.

Following this reasoning the IST acknowledges that knowledge creation is an important factor for organizational design and for discovering potential opportunities. There are three types of knowledge to be considered in this process and the process of converting the mindset. This will be discussed in the next section.

9.2.3   Vedantic Ontology and Epistemology on Knowledge

Inspired by the critique of Nonaka that Western learning perspectives are trapped in their Skinnerian behavioral thinking, and his encouragement of incorporating the view on fundamentals of epistemology and my own previous work on spirituality based on Indian yogic epistemology and ontology mainly in the settings of leadership (Nandram and Borden 2010; Nandram 2010a, b, 2011a). I will search for alternative insights to position IST in the management science. First, the ontological and epistemological views from a Vedantic perspective will be presented to further position the concept of knowledge in this paragraph.

Vedanta here refers to the Indian School of Philosophy. While there are many Indian schools of thought, here we use Vedanta in the general sense referring to the underlying foundation of all these schools which is inherent in all scientific discussion: what is reality or truth (ontology) and how do we know what we know about that reality (epistemology). There are three main assumptions (Chakraborty and Chakraborty 2008):

- Vedantic Ontology speculates that eternal reality or truth is a foundation for the changing reality. This implies that accepting and studying the changing reality gives us input for knowing the truth reality.
- It also suggests that there is a 'whole' which comprises both eternal and changing reality.
- The third assumption is that we have an outer self and an inner self. This outer self is expressed by our actions and the inner self is who we essentially are. We could say there is this duality between doing (outer self) and being (inner self).

These assumptions add to the discussion of the IST, the concept of holism and the potentiality of transcending the duality. While Piaget talks about assimilation and accommodation in respect to reality, it seems that he considers this as a process of human development and maturity, something that is beyond the scope of big influence. Whereas Vedantic ontology provides the notion of transcendence as an active process to work on to find the equilibrium towards the wholeness. Integrating Simplification is a holistic process but in our daily lives we are not experientially holistic; first we need to be aware of it and then strive for joining both, the inner and the outer self. It is something we can train ourselves for. The inner self refers to how we use sources of cues that we perceive from within ourselves for making interpretations. The outer self refers to how we use the external cues for interpretations. If we see both as part of the whole they merge and synthesize towards new knowledge.

The Vedantic epistemology assumes that the functioning of mental reasoning is not sufficient for knowing this 'whole'. Our sense of reason and intellect works by analyzing which requires dividing and fragmenting. For perceiving this 'whole' and thus experiencing the inner self, Vedanta assumes the path of mental silence. We could translate this into the path of building reflective moments in our 'mode of doing'. In the next section the cues that derive from the inner self are discussed further as forms of knowledge.

9.3   Subtle Knowledge and IST

9.3.1   Subtle Knowledge from Vedantic View

The Indian Philosopher Sri Aurobindo (1872–1950), has described the types of knowledge from a Vedantic perspective in his philosophical magnum opus, the *Life Divine* (Sri Aurobindo 7th edition 2006) and in his work on Integral Yoga (1993). Western conception of knowledge is that it stems from the mind, whereas Sri Aurobindo says the mind gives us thought, observation, reasoning and cognition through separation and analysis of information. What the mind actually does is to process information about our lives and our environment. Psychological research has shown us that this process is prone to errors that occur due to our mind's tendency toward preferences, desires and preconceived notions. These biases ultimately stem from our senses. Sri Aurobindo says, "The thinking mind does not lead men, does not influence them the most—it is the vital propensities and the vital mind that predominate. The thinking mind for most men, in matters of life is only an instrument of the vital (Sri Aurobindo 1993, p. 243)". It is the vital part that embodies the interaction between the inner and the outer self. In practical terms it is this vital part that nourishes relationships between people. Without its involvement the mind has a limited function. It is the vital aspect that creates possibilities for change. It continuously asks what to do next with the change. The mind sees things in parts and uses the process of reasoning and synthesis to put things in appropriate relation to each other. So, the mind gives us partial knowledge. Sri Aurobindo suggests that this process results in incomplete and inaccurate knowledge which he terms "*knowledge ignorance*". Because the mind cannot see the true wholeness or essence of that which it seeks to know, man developed an ego to help organize and develop effective capacities. This resulted in identifying with the ego and separating from the deeper subtle knowledge that is the source for our potential competences. Based on this perspective, Sri Aurobindo distinguished four different types of knowledge (See Table 9.1) present in our outer and inner mind (Sri

Table 9.1 Types of knowledge from a Vedantic perspective of Sri Aurobindo and compared with Nonaka's knowledge types

Nonaka	Sri Aurobindo's terms	IST terms
Information	Information (indirect and separate)	Objective knowledge
Explicit knowledge		
Tacit knowledge (technical and cognitive)	Experience (direct and separate)	Reflective knowledge
–	Realization (direct and intimate)	Subtle knowledge
		Inner knowledge
–	Transformation (knowledge by identity)	Self-knowledge

Aurobindo, book 2, Chap. 10, pp. 543–544, 1939). While he explains them in reverse sequence, here it makes more sense for the purpose of this book to explain it in the sequence below.

1. Objective, scientific knowledge: Sri Aurobindo calls this indirect knowledge as it is mediated by our senses. He points out that this form of knowledge is inherently separate from our inner self because here we experience a difference between our self as knower and the world as known. In this mode of knowing we partly identify with the world but we dissociate with it as well when we say there is a world out there. Ordinary science only recognizes this first type of knowledge. To get an understanding of this knowledge we gather information by listening to others, by reading or by conducting objective experiments. Usually the emotional aspect of the person is not involved unless the topic of study is related to emotions.

2. The knowledge of our inner processes: this covers emotions, moods, desires and thoughts. According to Sri Aurobindo this knowledge is direct but still separate. In this mode of knowing we partly identify with the mind and use it to view another part of the mind. The cognitive process separates the knower from the known. This type of knowledge is thus based on one's experience and it becomes the knowledge of the person. It is private and subjective but one can talk about it and share his experiences. This second type resembles what Nonaka labels as tacit knowledge.

3. The third form is knowledge that we do both; experience our inner processes and identify with them. This occurs, for example when we are completely consumed by a feeling such as happiness or anger and this feeling drives our action. This mode of knowing is more or less pre-conscious and pre-reflective. In this type of knowledge the person is directly involved in the experience. It refers to a state of realization. The thoughts, basic attitudes, perspective on reality are changed but one's nature remains largely the same. It is knowledge of deeper sources, not just a description of what someone experiences. There may be parts of that which cannot be described fully, meanwhile they influence someone's belief system and then his behavior. For example if someone says "today I am really happy", the person is the thought. There is no distinction between both. This type of

knowledge is rarely being studied in research while we know that people use it also in their professional context, some more than others. It is often labelled under the heading of experiential knowledge without further distinction. In the spiritual and philosophical focused literature it is acknowledged that there are deeper aspects of knowledge. The third type is called by Sri Aurobindo, the realization. For making it applicable and based on what has emerged in our study a further distinction seems appropriate between the knowledge that is being constructed by being open and using all kinds of subtle cues and knowledge of the inner dimension of consciousness. This last one, according to spiritual focused literature, could not be approached directly. Spiritual techniques such as disciplined practices of meditation in various forms can open up the way to get into contact with this inner knowledge. The subtle knowledge could be labeled as wisdom or intuition, representing the subtle dimension of what someone experiences, perceives and applies in his interpretations for giving meaning to what happens around him. In the next section this knowledge type will be explored under the heading of intuition from a Western Ancient perspective.

4. Then according to Sri Aurobindo, there is a fourth type of knowledge where there is no separation between self and knowledge, not even a cognitive process. Our comprehensive picture of this type of knowledge has no foundation in the senses. We can train our inner instruments of knowledge to become as reliable and unambiguous as our outer senses. This stage is totally beyond the mind. In the fourth type of knowledge the whole nature of a person has undergone transformation.

In the philosophical and spiritual literature there are many further elaborations on such deeper knowledge. Especially in the Vedantic philosophy, the idea of wholeness is being described and explained where it is assumed that we can only become aware of the deeper power if we use instruments that extend beyond the sensual ways of knowing. Only then can we know what we know about this fourth type.

The third and fourth types of knowledge are the sources of deeper intuition in the teachings of Sri Aurobindo (2006) as he saw intuition hailing from a higher consciousness. We often ignore these intuitive sources. Our impulses, desires and habits obstruct the stream of this perception from the intuition. Based on his teachings I define intuition as follows: On the material level of consciousness, we all appear to be separate, we are in touch with the body's instinctual needs. On the vital level of consciousness, we are in touch with our affective drives, cravings, desires and emotions. On the mental level of consciousness, we can grasp and put order into both the lower and higher drives and learn to navigate through them with clarity. Intuition can sometimes be of the mind, a flash of awareness whereby various fragments or ideas in the mind all of a sudden come together and take on a cohesive form. There are also higher forms of intuition coming from higher or transcendent parts of the mind. This stems from the soul or directly from the universal consciousness. All these sources form the subtle knowledge that people use in their professional context, in finding opportunities and constructing reality to design solutions for issues that occur.

According to Sri Aurobindo there are four ways to develop the power of intuition which he labeled as the intuitive mind (2006): silence the mind; visualizing the descending of light from above: listening to the voice within the heart and developing the intellect.

Overall we can say that the fourth type and the process it involves is transformation, however is a gradual process that comes as a result of gaining the other types of knowledge. It is not something that can be achieved by putting direct effort. The fourth stage is not approachable in modern 'scientific' approaches. As this type of knowledge is beyond the mind it is out of the scope of this book or further discussion.

In the second and third type of knowledge the first person approach of research is relevant as they go beyond objective facts but they can still be traced through experiences and talked about in interviews and surveys. The second type can be approached by objectively explaining experiences. It requires reflection on what is really going on. The third type, the way it is explained based on the IST (See Table 9.1) has two dimensions. The first dimension can be approached by objective introspection of various kinds of subtle cues such as intuition, by looking objectively at what is happening inside oneself; and what has been experienced before. One can say e.g. "My hands feel cold". Someone else can test whether the hand is cold or not. This could end up with an observation of the person testing and an observation of the person who is experiencing, then both can be compared. The outcome may turn out to be fully aligned or different. The second dimension could be based on contemplation and what the insights reveal rather than proactively elicit. The observer perceives holistically without active discipline on the application of a specific type of cue. It can be a combined outcome of what one gets as objective information, experiences, subtle cues and deeper feelings that are not easily put into words. It is the person himself who is observing without being able to fully express this process in words but it has implications for his behavior. In the process of Integrating Simplification the professional taps from several types of knowledge. It is the first type, second type and first dimension of the third type of knowledge that are considered in the IST, while acknowledging that other more deeper sources may be present. But since they cannot be studied, I do not consider them. They also did not emerge themselves in the research. Especially this dimension is perhaps something that occurs in a service oriented setting where a nurse works with clients in caring and where she has built a relationship with them such as is the case in the community healthcare context. For those who use this type of knowledge it becomes a natural aspect of getting knowledge by listening to the 'fingerspitzengefül' (as was mentioned previously). Perhaps it may be the case that in other healthcare contexts or in context outside the healthcare industry where relationship building is less important with customers, that this type of knowledge is not being used consciously or perhaps with less intensity.

From our explanation so far we can say that intuition is a function of consciousness, which goes beyond the ordinary senses and mental mind, which does not have a logic sequence, which has multiple sources, and which is connected to our intellect and emotions. In scientific research we can grasp some parts of intuition. The more we use reflective approaches, the more we come to know about intuition and thus the subtle knowledge. While in this section a Vedantic perspective has been followed to explain subtle knowledge as part of the source for integrating simplification in Western Ancient view subtle knowledge, mainly under the concept of intuition was present as well. A few main ideas will be discussed in the following section.

9.3.2   Western Ancient Views on Subtle Knowledge

In prehistoric and ancient literate societies there was no clear-cut division in the minds of ancient people between the external stimulus and the internal impression (Noddings and Shore 1984, p. 3). There was a validation of internal impression with outward stimulus and the other way around and the intuitive insights or intuitive experiences that were generated were regarded as messages from the Gods. The seers who were sharing these insights and their interpretations were considered as someone with great knowledge but this knowledge was claimed inaccessible by rational means. Several Eastern notions of intuition have influenced Western philosophical and educational investigations of intuition (Noddings and Shore 1984, p. 5). In these views rituals, meditation and disciplined control of the mind were important practices. For classical Greeks and Romans, both rational and intuitive knowledge were valid but irrational sources were valued not only for solving real life problems but also for the contact with the immaterial world. Several philosophers referred to insights or inductive known truths. Aristotle claimed that intuition was more accurate than scientific knowledge and it was given to all which means that everyone has access to it. Intuition was related to sense perception and memory. Noddings and Shore (1984) explain that a claim on intuition as truth rarely exists anymore. Intuition is now more a way of knowing, a way of seeing the objects of knowledge. They argue that when intuition is viewed as a source of knowledge or guidance, the restrictions that are placed by exaggerated claims are removed and intuition can be treated as a human experience and it can be processed as a tool for education (Noddings and Shore 1984, p. 7). In Appendix 4 of this book an overview has been given of the various views on intuition, based on the historical analysis of Noddings and Shore.

Noddings and Shore (1984) explain the diminishing role of the seer in the West due to the establishment of Christianity. The Medieval theologians continued to be interested in intuition and they were the first to use the word intuition to describe an ineffable mystical experience of identification with God. In their view intuition reveals to some people but not to all. In the medieval period the concept did not develop much in a scientific context. With the work of Ockham the tendency to attribute any intuitive experience to an agency outside of the individual continued in philosophy for many centuries and is still alive. While in the period from Renaissance no new theory was developed (Noddings and Shore 1984, p. 12) on the notion of intuition, in the seventeenth century thinkers began to return to non-rational sources of knowledge by stating that talking about knowledge, proofs and linear reasoning were not enough. In the eighteenth century, however a more rationalistic view became dominant not leaving space for the non-rational or more affective views on human psychology. In the nineteenth century there were a few relevant attempts to build theory on intuition by using previous views. It is interesting to note that Schleiermacher made a distinction between several types of intuition: self-intuition, intuition of the work, aesthetic intuition and philosophical speculations of intuition. Another attempt was that of Schopenhauer who acknowledged an intuitive capacity through the concept of will as an important aspect of the knowledge of reality. He believed that the human mind can be brought to a higher intuition. Such a higher intuition could be beneficial to realize collective goods such as a higher purpose. A third attempt was Bergson's claim that a person, object, or situation may be intuitively perceived, but never completely known, analyzed, or described in intellectual terms. By making this claim he actually acknowledged subtle aspects of perceptions while warning us for the incomplete capacity of our intellectual mind, as we could see in the teachings of Sri Aurobindo in the previous section.

It is remarkable to notice a lack of the terms consciousness and unconsciousness in explaining intuition up until the twentieth century. There was no link made to the unconscious aspect of intuition that has been referred to in most of the definitions that are being used currently in the field of management and entrepreneurship (Dane and Pratt 2007). The interest for unconscious processes to understand intuition as a source of knowledge may have started with the work of Jung who referred to intuition as an unconscious perception. Noddings and Shore (1984) argue that Jung deserves the recognition as the first modern psychologist to investigate the importance of intuition.

This brief description has given us an idea that there is openness towards subtle aspects of knowing in Western Ancient scholarly perspectives as well. It seems that the Vedantic has more tradition in dealing with such concepts for generating discussions on how to make such insights a part of scientific views of human functioning in creating knowledge. This may have to do with the Vedantic ontology: the wholesome notion of reality and the room it provides for constructing reality based on a holistic perception and experience of things that happen. In Chap. 5 of this book it has been explained how subtle aspects of cues are used as knowledge in Craftsmanship at Buurtzorg. It is not the only source of knowledge but certainly it is a source that should not be ignored. IST has contributed by providing some insights on the black box of the mind.

9.4   IST in the context of Entrepreneurial Effectuation

9.4.1   Entrepreneurial Effectuation Theory

Next to the Knowledge Creation Theory the Theory of Effectuation could be considered when reflecting the added value of the IST. This theory has been developed based on studies amongst entrepreneurs and its main focus is the process of discovering opportunities. The Theory of Effectuation explains the cognitive processes of decision making amongst start-ups who need to create new markets for their products and services, and how they engage relevant stakeholders. The clients in the IST can be considered as relevant stakeholders or customers in a way as well and the nurses and nurse assistants are then considered as the entrepreneur who is making decisions in respect to their Craftsmanship. First an explanation of the theory will be provided followed by an explanation of how the IST, especially the converting thinking process, fits in the Theory of Effectuation.

Sarasvathy proposes the concept of effectuation as the dominant model for entrepreneurial decision-making (2001a, b). She examined the cognitive processes of 27 expert entrepreneurs and 37 MBA students who were asked to identify the market for a given new product. Her findings indicate that over 63 % of the experts used effectuation more than 75 % of the time. 78 % of the MBA students did not use effectuation at all. The experts start with a single customer; generalize the profile of that customer into a larger segment; add segments in an iterative fashion and end up literally creating a market for their product. She also found that the experts were more successful in starting companies compared to the MBA students: 18 versus 9.

Based on another study of 30 founders of companies (Sarasvathy 2001a, b, 2004) explains effectual as inverse to causal by describing three modes of thinking: (two causal, one effectual):

- Managerial thinking—causal reasoning: This reasoning begins with a pre-determined goal and a given set of means. Students are then encouraged to seek to identify the fastest and most efficient or optimal way to achieve the goal. The process is converging towards the goal.
- Strategic thinking—creative causal reasoning. Sometimes they are encouraged towards strategic thinking and a form of creative causal reasoning where they show interest for the creation of additional alternatives and means to achieve the given goal. New goals can be created during the process of creating new means. In this mode of thinking there are also pre-determined goals. The process is converging towards the goals.
- Entrepreneurial thinking—effectual reasoning: Effectual thinking however begins with a given set of means and allows goals to emerge contingently over time from the varied imagination and diverse aspirations of the founders and the people they interact with (Sarasvathy 2001a, b). The goals are not pre-determined but the entrepreneur imagines possible new ends using a given set of means. The process is diverging into several ends.

The same person though can use effectual reasoning and causal reasoning at different times dependent on the circumstances. The Effectuation Theory states that the best entrepreneurs are capable of both and do use both models well. However, they prefer effectual reasoning over causal reasoning in the early stages of a new venture. In later stages they need to transition to more causal reasoning which is rarely a smooth process. This means that effectual reasoning is mainly helpful in the initial stages of an entrepreneurial process.

Another difference between both types of reasoning is that causal thinking may or may not involve creative thinking while effectual reasoning is inherently creative. Sarasvathy explains both types by the example of the task of cooking a dinner. In a causal reasoning process the chef is given a specific menu and he has only to pick out his favorite recipes for the items on the menu, shop for the ingredients and cook the meal in a well equipped kitchen. When effectual reasoning is involved, the chef is not given a menu in advance and he has to cook in a strange kitchen by exploring the unspecified ingredients available.

Sarasvathy (2001a, b) has defined the following principles of the Entrepreneurial Expertise in effectuation:

Start with your means:

In the Effectuation Theory entrepreneurs start with three types of means:

- Who they are: traits, tastes, abilities
- What they know: education, training, expertise, experience
- Whom they know: social and professional networks.

Based on these means the entrepreneurs begin to imagine and implement possible effects that can be created by them. They start without a careful planning. They often start very small with the means that are closest at hand, and move almost directly into action without elaborate planning. Effectual reasoning lives and breathes execution. Sarasvathy (2001a, b) mentions that, plans are made and then unmade, revised and recast through action and interaction with others on a daily basis. At any given moment, there is always a meaningful picture that keeps the team together, a compelling story that brings in more stakeholders and a continuing journey that map out uncharted territories (Sarasvathy 2001a, b, p. 3). Means and effects change and get reconfigured and eventually landmarks begin to emerge.

Control Instead of Predict

Effectuation advises an entrepreneur to operate from what he is able to control so that he assures a desired outcome rather than by trying to predict the future. An effectual worldview is rooted in the belief that the future is neither found nor predicted, but rather made or discovered. "In the effectuation process, the unexpected is the stuff of entrepreneurial experience and transforming the unpredictable into the utterly mundane is the special domain of the expert entrepreneur" (Sarasvathy 2001a, b, p. 4). Effectual reasoning is based on a different logic from causal reasoning. Causal reasoning is based on the logic: 'to the extent that we can predict the future, we can control it'. Effectual reasoning is based on the logic: 'to the extent that we can control the future, we do not need to predict it'. The main thing then is to control the future by identifying the uncertainties. According to Sarasvathy, entrepreneurs act as if they believe the future is not out there to be discovered, but that it gets created through the very strategies of the players. In this sense the entrepreneur uses effectual reasoning.

The Affordable Loss Principle (Focus on Downside Risk)
Committing what you're willing to lose rather than investing based on expected returns. Entrepreneurs are willing to work hard but they tend to avoid doing market research. They rather just go and try to sell their products to the closest potential customer, they just do it and discover the obstacles while doing it. They do not tie themselves to any pre-conceived theory, market or strategy for their idea. They rather open themselves to surprises as to which market or markets they will eventually end up building their business in. In that process they think of what they could afford as risks and losses.

The Strategic Partnership Principle
The focus is on building partnerships rather than on doing a systematic competitive analysis. In the start-up phase it doesn't make sense to do a detailed competitive analysis since the entrepreneurs tend to start the process without assuming the existence of a pre-determined market for his idea. They start building partnerships from the start, to get pre-commitments from key stakeholders so that they avoid extending a lot of capital out.

The Leveraging Contingencies Principle
The ability to turn the unexpected into the profitable. According to Sarasvathy, "great entrepreneurial firms are products of contingencies. Their structure, culture, core competence and endurance are all residual of particular human beings striving to forge and fulfil specific aspirations through interactions with the space, time and technologies which they live in (Sarasvathy 2001a, b, p. 6)". It is not the contingencies themselves that shape the company but how the entrepreneurs leveraged the contingencies that came upon them has formed the core models of effectual reasoning. In effectuation reasoning surprises are not avoided but used as resources into the new venture creation process.

9.4.2   IST and Effectuation

IST is not based on a causal thinking process but rather on an effectual thinking process. It resembles strategic thinking because there is a fundamental goal which is serving the client in the best possible way while considering the effectiveness and efficiency of the team and the Buurtzorg organization. But how to realize that goal is determined by the individual professionals. During that process new goals will emerge as per the effectual thinking. The professional has the freedom to decide on site, what is best for the client, as well as the possibility to get advice from the other team members. He can also engage the coaches and the Headquarters as well for issues he cannot solve himself. As was discussed in Chap. 6, the professional experiences freedom, labeled as intrapreneurial freedom. In this process of providing and delivering the care, new goals emerge.

The thinking processes in the IST include several kinds of input, as explained in the previous section on knowledge creation. The Effectuation Theory suggests imagination of opportunities without explaining how this process cognitively occurs but rather explains it according to design thinking and operational behaviors referring to effectual expertise and principles.

Three out of the five principles of effectual expertise are applicable in the Buurtzorg context. The first two functions, the means and the logic, differ in the context of Buurtzorg. Effectuation starts with the means by putting the psychological foundation first, where the entrepreneur asks himself a few questions regarding his talents, networks and resources. The IST however does not depart from what the individual knows but from the context he has to operate in, which in the case of Buurtzorg is the client's physical situation and psychological status. The IST is a very pragmatic approach of solving a problem or preventing a problem in an interactive manner where constructing the reality plays an important role. Furthermore while the logic is based on controlling the context in effectual reasoning, in the case of IST neither control nor predictions are important. Trust is the logic behind the processes in the organization and in the approach with the clients and other stakeholders. It requires a balancing act between being empathic and being professional towards them.

Effectual thinking gives room to creativity as does IST but in the IST the professionalism and relationship with the client and how he experiences this relationship is another important source that influences the thinking process of the nurse and nurse assistants. An entrepreneur can start a business without a certain professional background while a nurse or nurse assistant has the professional background as an important base for input for his decision making process.

In recent discussion on effectuation Venkataraman et al. (2013) suggest that opportunities may be of several varieties and they are drawing further on suggesting that knowledge is an irreducible tripod consisting of the objective, subjective and intersubjective. With such views scholars create capacity for further debates on knowledge and topics such as converting thinking within the field of management. A main contribution of the IST in the context of effectuation is the process of converting reality as this provides a pragmatic approach for application and understanding the process of designing opportunities in a specific context and the role of trust over controlling in certainties.

9.5   Construction of Reality as Converting Thinking

When we talk about perception, evaluation and construction of reality as key processes in the Integrating Simplification Theory, then we need to reflect on the work of Kurt Lewin. Lewin's work takes on the influence of social context in the construction of reality and on the teachings of Jean Piaget, the Swiss psychologist as he has built an influential theory on cognitive development for constructing reality. Below this mechanism of constructing reality will be explained. In learning theories we could distinguish three main paradigms (Mueller 2012). The behaviorist paradigm sees learning as a change in behavior (Skinner 1950). The cognitivist paradigm considers individual cognitive processes as important for learning (Bandura 1977; Piaget 1950). And the constructivist paradigm sees knowledge as constructed by the individual (Gergen 1999; Von Glaserfeld 1996). While Piaget's work belongs to the cognitive paradigm, all constructivist theories base their ideas on constructing reality on the work of Piaget concerning assimilation and accommodation (Mueller 2012, p. 30; Von Glasersfeld 1982).

For understanding how people construct reality in the social context, psychologists use two main processes which are labeled as *differentiation and integration* (Wegner and Vallacher 1977, p. 29). The first one refers to the separation of thoughts or structures of thought; the second refers to their combination. These terms were originally borrowed from biology by Kurt Lewin (Wegner and Vallacher 1977, p. 30). In biology when the human being grows, his cells differentiate and then certain groups of cells combine to form organs, bones etc. This process of formation of systems is called integration. This analogy of the development of the body is being applied in describing the development of the mind where also the process of differentiation and integration helps us to understand how people construct reality. As Wegner and Vallacher (1977) nicely say; "no two people live in the same skin, so no two people have exactly the same set of experiences" (p. 32). We construct reality or in other words, we organize our observations of reality in a particular way which is unique. This construction of reality is done in a social context where interaction with other people takes place making the construction of reality a unique process.

If we look at the process of Integrating Simplification then we notice that differentiation and integration are main aspects in the two first principles of IST. The first one, the process of systematically identifying and assessing what is needed consists of two questions: 'what are the needs of the client' and 'why do we do things as we always do'. These two refer to the process of differentiation while the question of 'how does it help the client' refers to integration. The same happens in the second process of IST which is about continuously connecting to different types and sources of information and cues, then reconstructing the perception of reality. The first two questions refer to differentiation: 'what is really going on' and 'are we doing the right things'. When nurses and nurse assistants ask themselves, 'is there a simpler way of doing things' then they start to integrate the stimuli around them to construct reality.

While Piaget's initial ideas for his theory were based and built on observations of children's behavior during experimental settings, the principles that he has suggested for understanding the process of constructing reality are also largely applicable to human behavior in general. A study of his teachings revealed similarities between IST and his two processes of *assimilation and accommodation* of cognitive development. Assimilation in the work of Piaget is the integration of

Table 9.2 Conversion of mindset

		Low IS	High IS
		Assimilation	Accommodation
Low IS	Differentiation	LL	LH
High IS	Integration	HL	HH

external elements into evolving or completed mental or knowledge structures. Accommodation is any modification of an assimilatory scheme or structure by the elements it assimilates (Block 1982). In *assimilation* new information is fitted in existing knowledge structures. In *accommodation* it is the existing knowledge structure that is being restructured to fit in the new information (Renking et al. 2000). Assimilation is a necessary activity; otherwise the person will constantly feel a dissonance, a difference between what he gets as new knowledge and what he already knows. From the theory of Festinger we know that human beings tend to solve any dissonance (1957). In the theory of Piaget this is an ongoing process and in concrete activities often they are not separated. It is two sides of the same coin of the process of adaptation and finding an equilibrium which is important in the further development. The more matured a person's experience, the more he seeks for accommodation as assimilation does not satisfy his curiosity. Interesting to note that in the theory of Piaget, both processes are subordinate to the external reality. Assimilation is subordinate to accommodation and accommodation itself is subordinate to the already existing structures to which the situation must be assimilated (Piaget 1950, p. 709). In the case of Buurtzorg the client serves as the external reality towards which the nurses assimilate and accommodate.

We can explain *how the process of converting the thinking works* in the IST by using these four concepts, which contain two dimensions: social construction of reality and cognitive construction of reality. They are the antecedents of IST. It is proactively preparing the perception of reality by differentiating and integrating cues from the social context and cognitively fitting these cues into our existing knowledge framework (assimilating) and restructuring existing frames to the perceived cues. These dimensions go from low intensity to high intensity when it comes to the question, 'how they influence the behavior of the individual' (See Table 9.2). A person, who mainly proactively differentiates what he perceives, is converting his mindset in another intensity compared to the situation if he cognitively accommodates his knowledge structures. In a situation where the person is able to accommodate and integrate, the intensity of the converting in terms of Integrating Simplification (IS) is the highest (HH). We may see it as a transformation in the mindset. IST has an additional step to this transformation through the common sensing principle. This is about designing and implementing tasks according to the current circumstances or new perceived reality until this doesn't work because the context has changed again or someone has a better alternative. This process requires a reflection on resources and acting in a pragmatic way. It may result in *reallocating resources* (mobilizing several types of resources) *and creating renewal*. The person asks himself: 'what do I require for this novel approach', 'how do I bring this simpler way into practice' and 'how does the new practice improve my service'?

9.6   Yogic Leadership Enables Integrating Simplification

What is reality and how do we know what we know about reality, were the basic ontological and epistemological questions in the previous sections. In this scientific philosophical context the building blocks of Integrating Simplification have been discussed in the light of construction of reality based on psychological concepts of differentiation, integration, assimilation and accommodation. Furthermore a Vedantic perspective and Western Ancient views have been introduced to incorporate the third type of knowledge which is the subtle knowledge. It is also important to discuss the follow up question: how do we nourish the way of knowing and reality construction?

This invites a discussion on the enabling factor and for addressing the process that links the individual with the organizational context at a meta-level. This process is labeled as integrating and the enabling factor is Yogic Leadership. With presenting the five dimensions in Chaps. 4–8 the process of integrating simplification has been explained in detail. The multiple properties of these dimensions and their lower-level concepts have illustrated in detail what is required for establishing IST in the organization. In this chapter so far, the principles of integrating simplification were discussed at an individual level. Nonaka's knowledge creation departs from mental beliefs and connects to the organization through the enabling conditions. By addressing psychological and philosophical views on the construction of reality and subtle knowledge potential, the added value of the IST has been positioned in the scholarly discussion. IST is linked to the organizational level and construction of reality also occurs in a context. The aim here is not explaining the contextual framework but to focus on the enabling condition for Integrating Simplification. As previous chapters have shown, the higher purpose is the starting point for the whole process of delivering client care. An interesting question then is: 'what is the mechanism behind this higher purpose?' In Chap. 8 it was explained that people need to be able to transcend personal interest for the higher purpose and how the founder does that as a role model.

As I am reaching the last part of the book now, I can give a meta-reflection from a meta-lens to the several components of the IST. This meta-reflection has resulted in the meta-conclusion that behind the IST there is a Yogic leader—in the case of Buurtzorg it is Jos de Blok—and Yogic stewards— the nurses, nurse assistants, coaches, co-founders—for enabling the process of Integrating Simplification. Through this enabler, Integrating Simplification serves as a successful process for governing Organizational Innovation in facilitating a client care focus. Integrating Simplification is a way of knowing and a way of constructing reality in the organizational context. It comprises of three phenomena that could be applied in any organization for explaining human behavior: converting the mindset; a holistic perception and application of various types of knowledge and Yogic Leadership. Let us now further address, the enabler.

To explain Integrating Simplification we can reflect on a more analytical level where we can find an analogy with the Yogic philosophy. The term yogic here is about balancing with the aim to integrate. An entrepreneur who starts up an organization with Self-Managed Teams resembles a franchise business model. However the Self-Managed Teams are not franchise entities but all part of the organization, in this case, of Buurtzorg. This organizing principle was consciously chosen by the founder to avoid high costs for overhead and focus on the main cause which is organizing the primary process of delivering the best possible care to the client. In the interviews it emerged as could be read in Chap. 8, that the leader avoids excess coordination, management and control. Such a flat organization structure could be seen as a way to centralize the status of the leader. Such a leader could feel he is in charge of everything or he could experience it as having freedom himself to do the needful. Employees could either perceive him as a 'commander' and be sensitive to the commander's will or see him as a servant leader. Both can happen and it depends on the culture that is present in the organization and the aim of the leader himself. As shown in the previous chapters the leader has a higher goal and employees perceive a high level of trust for their talents and a high level of freedom for decision making. Such a way of organizing requires an attitude of letting go, the ability to delegate, the ability to improvise, a positive attitude towards the unexpected, being able to cope with uncertainty, and the main attitude he requires being in the position of the leader or entrepreneur, is the ability to balance between control and trust. The concept of Yogic Leadership seems to fit such a description. From a meta-lens such a conceptualization is interesting as it also explains the integrating feature of the theory in more detail.

We can think of the two Yogic Concepts of *"Abhyasa"* (effort, will, practice, discipline, control to win) and *"Vairagya"* (acceptance and insights of what distracts and let go to renew), both necessary wings to join or integrate and simplify. The art of "Abhyasa" leads to sincere devotion toward realizing the goal. This is an attitude that we have seen among the leader, nurses and nurse assistants. The art of "Vairagya" leads to in-depth understanding of different paths and experiences to serve the goal. This is an attitude that we have noticed as well in the organization.

What the Yogic leader does is: balancing between these two actions, as an attitude in general sense in running the organization and in more specific sense, he is integrating several dimensions so that all function in harmony. From a meta-view, the integrative processes where balancing is required occur at four aspects. Each requires a certain dominant ability where the principles of Integrating Simplification are part of (See Table 9.3):

- Balancing between the primary and secondary process where the main tasks occur in the primary process. In the primary process he has the attitude of Vairagya and in the secondary process he applies the attitude of Abhyasa. Here he can use control mechanisms if required and foster a discipline and put effort to win. *The art of creating effectiveness is important.*
- Second is balancing between the higher purpose and the leadership visibility, both at the level of the leadership of the coaches and at the level of the directors. Choosing for client focus is the starting point of the whole organizational process. The more the client focus is being perceived as a higher purpose the more easily the employees and other stakeholders are committed and feel a

Table 9.3 Features of yogic leadership

Activity: Abhyasa–Vajragya	Dimensions in the IST	Integrating abilities
Balancing primary and secondary process	Overall organizational architecture	Art of *creating effectiveness* – Needing – Rethinking – Common sensing
Balancing higher purpose and visibility leader	Higher purpose	Art of *entraining to common goal* – Needing – Rethinking – Common sensing
Balancing between systematic and dynamic process	Pragmatic ICT solution and Entrepreneurship	Art of *opportunity discovery* – Needing – Rethinking – Common sensing
Balancing between professional and empathic relationship	Craftsmanship and attunement to the client	Art of *building trust* – Needing – Rethinking – Common sensing

Input for the integrating role of the leader in organizational innovation:
Offering of professional services by stewards in the form of different kinds of knowledge and their expertise in converting their thinking process to fit the client's needs, capabilities and context

belongingness to put effort in realizing this higher purpose. The coaches do not act as watch dogs but as facilitators, giving the support when needed. They can be made visible when the team needs them. They can make themselves visible when they think the higher purpose is at stake. The same holds for the directors. They can be made visible when the employees need them. They can make themselves visible when they perceive a distraction from the client's focus or when they believe the organization's higher purpose is at stake. *Here the art of entraining serves as a key component representing a higher mental dimension.*

- Pragmatic Will and Intrapreneurial Team Freedom at the mental and physical level: there is another dimension of Integrating Simplification. Pragmatic Will serves as a discipline of putting a continuous effort to realize the aims without being distracted, discouraged or bored. It allows a systematic assessment of its features at several levels in the organization. It serves like a thread that resonates as a common approach to be followed in the organization at whatever position or task a person operates. Entrepreneurial attitude as the twin partner, acts as another discipline to dissociate from routines, to dispassion from habitual thinking and acting. It generates an openness to renew. We could imagine both as two wings that are necessary to act for making Craftsmanship a success. Whether to choose either for Pragmatic Will or Intrapreneurial Freedom is a matter of discernment based on professional maturity. Patterns of Pragmatic Will are always present in the teams, among the coaches, and in the Headquarters of the organization. Based on experiences, spaces are created for the unexpected.

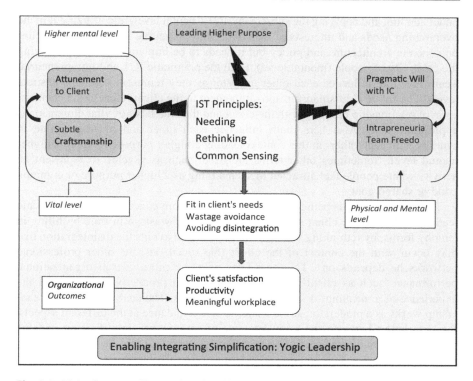

Fig. 9.1 Main elements of integrating simplification theory

Discovering of opportunity becomes the key art in this dimension of Integrating Simplification and represents the physical dimension of the organizational architecture and a mental dimension as the knowledge force.

- Craftsmanship and Attunement as a vital process: Craftsmanship ensured mastering the skills that are required to get the holistic view of the client and attune to him with the expertise to help the client in the best possible way. Here it requires to combining Craftsmanship and clients' capabilities to maintain or enhance their quality of life and independency. *Trust building is the key art of Integrating Simplification at the level of nurse/nurse assistant and client relationship, representing a vital dimension of the knowledge force.*

This leads to the final overview (See Fig. 9.1) with the core category in the middle of the figure and all core concepts of Integrating Simplification around. The concepts in italic represent abstract levels to be used as metaphor of expressions of how reality is being expressed in an organization (Fry and Kriger 2009, p. 4; Nandram 2010a, b) or as psychological needs (Maslow 1943) or consciousness levels in corporations (Barrett 2013). Just building an ICT system, for example, focuses on the physical level—and this is not enough without people really understanding and applying the subsequent ICT (mental level) and utilizing it in the overarching needs and interests of the client. Intrapreneurial Team Freedom relies on concrete architecture and policy but it needs to be implemented with involving the creativity of people (mental level). Both the pragmatic ICT and Intrapreneurial Team Freedom influence each other to foster as they represent the same abstract levels. The subtle Craftsmanship and attunement to the client refers to the phenomenon of relationship building with the client and thus the label of vital dimension is appropriate here. Also here, both influence each other and ideally operate in synergy with each other. In this context leading a higher purpose refers to a higher mental level. Sometimes other terms are used, such as psychic to represent an activity where people feel attracted to such a thing as a higher purpose or common good or shared goal.

The core category is being expressed in the five core concepts (dimensions) and leads to a fit with the client's need, an avoidance of wastage in time by filling in lengthy forms, by rethinking what can be done, and it avoids the disintegration that may occur with the context of the client (his social ties, the other professional networks he depends on). This correlates with the more overall organizational performance such as client's satisfaction, expected productivity levels and the experience of a meaningful workplace by employees. The enabler of Yogic Leadership works as a moderator. If the leader is able to balance at the different aspects, the correlation between the core category of integrating simplification and the organizational outcomes (both in concrete ways such as client fit; wastage avoidance, avoidance of disintegration and in terms of overall outcomes) will be stronger. If the leader is not able to balance well the correlation will be lower. This holds for each of the five core concepts.

Implications and Discussion

10

Abstract

In this chapter the implications of the research findings and a discussion on how the findings could be related to current management issues are presented. The following issues are being addressed: what are the implications of the findings and how do the insights from Buurtzorg Nederland contribute to the understanding of the VUCA problem in management?

10.1   Implications

10.1.1 The VUCA World

The world today needs responsible entrepreneurs and innovators to create solutions for many types of issues in organizations and society that cannot easily be solved by applying the current management practices. Overall we could say that the critical problem at the level of economies is scarcity of resources, at the social level it is ethical decline and at an individual level it is loss of meaning and purpose in life. Every day the global outlet changes a bit more, becoming increasingly complex and therefore less tangible. We can summarize a few developments.

- The scarcity as can be found in the form of financial constraints at consumer, organizational and governmental level. Consumers look for cheaper products and services. New professionals are entering the labor market while the number of job opportunities has decreased, leaving them with frustration and uncertainty.
- Companies and governments are cutting costs often without considering the impact of decisions for the new generation inducing feelings of uncertainty about their future.

© Springer International Publishing Switzerland 2015
S.S. Nandram, *Organizational Innovation by Integrating Simplification*,
Management for Professionals, DOI 10.1007/978-3-319-11725-6_10

- Resources such as oil and water are dwindling while needs of the new generation are increasing due to the availability of greater technologies than in the past. This elicits high levels of uncertainty.
- Velocity is changing at different fronts: technology (e.g. cloud computing, social media, mobile technologies).
- Market competition is high: the need to develop a business attitude to be frugal and doing more with less, staying updated by the needs of our customer, freelance skills offered by several self-employed persons with lower fees.
- Ambiguity in the interpretation of the needs of diverse consumer groups is increasing. Due to globalization entrepreneurs have to deal with religious diversity and political sensitivities of stakeholders in different societies. They need to learn and adapt to the rising ambicultural values of their employees and customers due to influences from different continents.
- Employees wishes are changing (diverse values and expectations of a multi-generational workforce such as, baby boomers, generations x, y, z).
- Organizations have become very big and powerful, yet their flexibility is declining and therefore often lacking efficiency.

Companies face the challenge of how to: keep connected to the workforce; deal with higher costs for raw products; keep consumers and partners involved in innovations within their firm, not strictly by relying upon a R&D unit but the larger group of stakeholders, consumer and partners who are focusing outside the firm for innovations; empower employees to quickly and effectively cope with change; develop a more flexible attitude; foster an improvising attitude to deal with unexpected situations and how to foster an ethical business climate to build trust.

In management these challenges are labeled as VUCA: Volatility, Uncertainty, Complexity and Ambiguity. It is told that the term was first coined at the Army War College, the graduate school for future generals (Johansen and Euchner 2013). In the organizational context VUCA is characterized as follows (Horney et al. 2010): *Volatility*: the nature, speed, volume, magnitude and dynamics of change; *Uncertainty*: the lack of predictability of issues and events; *Complexity*: the confounding issues and the chaos that surround any organization; *Ambiguity*: the haziness of reality and the mixed meanings of conditions.

At the more concrete level, management scholars are exploring new ways of leading as a solution to tackle the VUCA challenges. Primarily, to confront the feeling of alienation among employees from the meaning and purpose of activities they are carrying out in their daily workplaces. There are alternative models of leadership and organizing being developed. Some are suggesting leadership agility as a way to cope with the VUCA world (Horney et al. 2010). Leading the continuous shifts in people, processes, technology and structure requires the capability to sense and respond with actions that are focused, fast and flexible (Horney et al. 2010). Others mention wise leadership practices and internal spiritual journeys under the label of suited monk leadership (Adams and Thompson 2013). Some authors mention the development of the leadership skill, 'design strategic conversations'. This refers to making people who will be executing strategy as part of the conversation. This allows them experiencing that getting all engaged may achieve better results than if a leader tries to solve something alone (Ertel and Solomon 2014).

10.1.2 Navigating VUCA by Organizational Innovation

The VUCA challenges become a critical problem if societies and organizations are not able to cope with them and they may raise confusion and fear. Specific forms of innovations are often seen as the tool to such challenges. Innovation is grouped as follows: as a new product or service; a new production process, a new type of marketing or overall behavior on the market including a different way of engaging the state or societal organizations; and a new organizational or management structure (Sundbo 1998). Innovations can have different characteristics: technological, intellectual, logistics and behavioral. Mainly the last two categories have the attention from management scholars. For example, Chesbrough's concept of open innovation (2003, 2006) to describe how a combination of resources is being used and organized to generate new ideas, services and products in an organization. This view is one of the most influential ones in the academic and business practice on innovation in different sectors. He shows that innovation does not necessarily come from a single source, perspective, organizational context or structure. According to Chesbrough (2012, p. 20); "The open innovation paradigm can be understood as the antithesis of the traditional vertical integration model in which internal innovation activities lead to internally developed products and services that are then distributed by the firm". Chesbrough also claims, open innovation concerns the use of purposive inflows and outflows of knowledge to accelerate internal innovation and expand the markets for external use of innovation. It requires collaboration and involvement of a wide variety of participants or stakeholders and implies that the innovation capabilities of an organization do not stop at the boundaries of the organization.

Looking at the VUCA world it mainly helps to deal with the volatility by co-creating with resources to cope with the rapid change in market needs and it aligns to the complexity that has occurred due to interdependencies and complex connections among communities, including the business. Instead of moving away from these connections in open innovation, entrepreneurs aim to benefit from them.

Another type of innovation that attracts attention is 'Jugaad' Innovation (Radjou et al. 2012). It refers to an innovative fix: an improvised solution born from ingenuity and cleverness (p. 4). It is a unique way of thinking and acting in response to challenges. Radjou et al. (2012) describe it as the gutsy art of spotting opportunities in the most adverse circumstances and resourcefully improvising solutions using simple means. The following characteristics are found in 'Jugaad' Innovation: it is about doing more with less; it is about making the most of what you have; it is about finding simple yet effective solution for vexing problems that fellows face. The innovative entrepreneur needs to think frugal; act flexible and aiming to generate breakthrough growth. If we look at the VUCA world, this form of innovation deals with the volatility by seeing rapid technological advances as a source for innovative practices. It deals with uncertainty by nourishing the attitude of flexibility and the skill of improvisation. It deals with complexity by stressing how entrepreneurs can end up with breakthrough innovations by just using simple means. It does not tackle but accepts ambiguity by leaving it to the entrepreneur, how he translates a context based on his own wisdom and maturity.

Both Open and Jugaad Innovation can incorporate technical, intellectual, market related and behavioral features, thus are not only labeled as organizational innovations though they focus on a new way of organizing resources and a different attitude towards resources. They are more integrated forms of innovations aiming to add value either by a new product, process, market approach or organizational approach. Based on this book, innovation by Integrating Simplification of the organizational structure could be added to this category of innovations. How does it help to navigate the VUCA challenges?

10.1.3 Navigating the VUCA World by IST

Integrating Simplification Theory is a type of organizational innovation consisting of:

(a) Systematically identifying and assessing what is needed;
(b) Continuously connecting to different types of cues and reconstructing the perception of reality;
(c) Designing and implementing tasks according to the current circumstances or new perceived reality until this doesn't work because the context has changed again or someone has a better alternative.

In this process the following questions are asked:

- What are the needs of the client?
- Why do I do things as I always do?
- How does it help the client?
- What is really going on?
- Am I doing the right things?
- Is there a simpler way of doing things?
- What do I require for this novel approach?
- How do I bring this simpler way into practice?
- How does the new practice improve the client focus?

It is being expressed in an integrated way which means that it is present in five main concepts (dimensions): Attunement to the Client; Craftsmanship; Pragmatic Will by ICT; Intrapreneurial Team Freedom and a Leadership of a Higher Purpose. Furthermore the enabler of Yogic Leadership helps to integrate the individual and organizational level. Integrating simplification aims to avoid what could lead to disintegration in the primary organizational process and avoiding any kind of wastage (in time spent, money and material) in terms of unnecessary complexity in realizing organizational goals.

The IST assists in navigating the VUCA world in several ways. It helps to get aligned to the volatility through a self-managed architecture that makes it easier to take decisions fast and to adapt to the changes that occur. Such an organizational structure puts the managerial and decision power close to the activities of the primary process so that in a dynamic and natural way the volatility is being managed. The IST embraces uncertainty by avoiding the tendency to predict future events as main process for decision making and the development of policy. As the name itself already suggests, it tackles complexity as well. Thinking processes, business processes, organizational structures and climate all breathe simplicity as a main ingredient of the organizational innovation. In organizations there is much more ambiguity due to the worldwide web of inter-connections that we are part of and the different interpretations of values, cultures and systems it may lead to. There is not one unique way of dealing with issues, there is not a dominant worldview but several roles we all have to address. The only unified system that integrates activities and efforts could be found in a so called 'universal belief system' which embraces the values on humanity. One that no matter which position or role one fulfills; religion, class or culture; humanity will stay alive. It has become obvious how in the IST a unified system of humanity prevails over rules, regulations, and notions of competition, power and control. Talking the language of a higher purpose and of love for humanity is not ambiguous. It rather integrates.

In Table 10.1 the core concepts (5), their properties (17) and the lower-level concepts (45) that were presented in the Chaps. 4–8, are summarized. The second column presents the results of an analysis on which VUCA concept is being addressed in the several properties of the core concepts.

– Volatility is being executed with the following properties of the concepts: context attunement, entrepreneurial behavior, a flexible ICT support, and various roles of the founder.
– Uncertainty is being solved by: emotional attunement to the client, temporal attunement to get the client empowered as soon as possible to get him back to normal situation, application of subtle expertise to help the client, and smart communication.
– Rhythm attunement: self-managed, teams, setting intrapreneurial conditions for freedom, a step by step introduction of creative ICT solutions, all are related to solving the issue of complexity that surrounds an organization.
– The issue of ambiguity is being solved through the properties of professional attunement, team synergy, maintaining intrapreneurial freedom, systematic assessment, putting humanity over bureaucracy as the basic human belief.

It has become obvious that IST provides a solution for navigating the VUCA world in different ways. IST does not only have implications for the community care but it gives a theoretical framework and a dynamic model with variables to be implemented and translated to sectors where the VUCA problem is present.

Table 10.1 Antecedents of dimensions of integrating simplification

Concepts, *properties*, lower level concepts		Navigating VUCA
Attunement to client		
	Rhythm attunement	Complexity
	Professional attunement	Ambiguity
– Trusting professionalism		
– Holistic perception		
	Emotional attunement	Uncertainty
– Acknowledging humane values		
– Parenting responsibility		
	Context attunement	Volatility
– Engaging social ties		
– Community coherence		
– Awareness conflicting interest		
	Temporal attunement	Uncertainty
– Empathy-based care		
– Empowering independency		
Subtle craftsmanship		
	Self-managed teams	Complexity
– Support for secondary tasks		
– Small teams		
– Close to the client		
	Team synergy	Ambiguity
– Balanced team composition		
– Mindful communication		
	Subtle expertise	Uncertainty
– In-depth expertise		
– Removing the veil		
– Fingerspitzengefül		
Intrapreneurial team freedom		
	Entrepreneurial behavior	Volatility
– Facing stigmatization		
– Affordable loss principle		
– Activist's attitude		
	Conditions for freedom	Complexity
– Organizational freedom		
– Freedom for meaningfulness		
– Agreements on safeguards		
	Maintaining freedom	Ambiguity
– Protecting autonomy		
– Maintenance eco-system		
– Building coherence		
Pragmatic Will with ICT		
	Flexible ICT-support	Volatility
– Focus on care process		
– Helicopter view back office		
– Data entry for self-managed teams		

(continued)

Table 10.1   (continued)

Concepts, *properties*, lower level concepts	Navigating VUCA
Systematic assessment – Content assessment with Omaha systems – Quality of care – Continuous learning	Ambiguity
Step by step approach to creativity – Effectual practice – Smart simplification – Frugal attitude	Complexity
Leading higher purpose	
Humanity of bureaucracy as main belief – Trust in good Will – Remove the veil of capacity – Build ethics of care	Ambiguity
Various roles of founder – Manager – Change agent – Nurse – Integrator	Volatility
Smart communication – Mindful receiver – Open communication – Sensible information	Uncertainty

10.2   Discussion

The case of Buurtzorg has received attention mainly from a descriptive research perspective and less from an explanatory perspective. By using the ethnographic approach Van Dalen (2012) has tried to explain the organizational structure of Buurtzorg. This book has provided an explanatory view for the client care system at Buurtzorg. The descriptions and different angels that have been used so far demonstrate the interest it is gaining and the perspective that could be used for scientific research designs.

The Buurtzorg vision and its approach have been discussed in De Blok and Pool (2010). One of the main messages was that humane values should be the key driving force for all activities in the primary process of serving the client instead of bureaucratic structures. The humane values which have been discussed by them and illustrated in weekly diaries of professionals are: solidarity, freedom, trust, equality, and autonomy. Its community care approach and Craftsmanship have been described by Pool et al. (2011) and Werner and Pool (2013). Werner and Pool focused on the experience based care in different ethnic societies and how cultural values could have an impact on their expectations and communication in the community care practices by the Buurtzorg approach. Vermeer and Wenting

(2012) describe a practical booklet which is being used as a toolkit in self-management at Buurtzorg. They address a set of principles which they have induced based on their experiences with self-management in the healthcare system in general and more specific in the Buurtzorg teams. They have also made a booklet for coaches to assist them in guiding the Self-Managed Teams (2013). Both serve as practical principles for Buurtzorg care teams and coaches and are presented in such a way that they can be made context specific in their application. Because Buurtzorg does not work with predetermined guidelines to be followed by everyone, these are rather a set of guiding principles to be explored in the field. The Buurtzorg case has also been described in English articles. It has been considered in the context of whole systems thinking and social innovation as well (Nandram 2012; Kreitzer et al. 2014); organizational innovation (Nandram and Koster 2014); and in the nursing context (Monsen and De Blok 2013a, b). The case has received attention in Japanese magazines as well (Leferink et al. 2014) from a public management perspective addressing the various steps and arguments for applying ICT and innovation. In several consultancy reports and professional articles Buurtzorg has been described as a best practice by focusing on the Self-Managed Concepts, Cost-Benefit analysis or Public Policy analysis for implementing the Buurtzorg approach to other countries such as in Sweden (KPMG 2013).

Descriptive studies can be used as inspiration for others who want to implement features of Buurtzorg into their own organizations. However, it could foster an attitude of imitation and applying the insights as a recipe without respecting the dynamics of the specific context of application or without giving room to a deep understanding of the mechanisms that are really in place for achieving a sustainable outcome. In addition to these studies, this book has provided an explanatory approach for understanding the dynamics behind the client delivery system. Such a scientific approach opens the door for testing the theory in different contexts and provides the possibility for adapting the approach to the contextual constraints as it provides a way of thinking, a way of organizing and a way of integrating these processes at the individual and organizational level. Hopefully such an approach will lead to more sustainable outcomes for others who want to apply the principles either in the community care or outside this industry.

A new way of organizing is an interesting type of innovation (Sundbo 1998). Based on our study, it has become clear that a deeper mechanism of integrating simplification is at the core of its client care focus in which the organizational design is just one part. The mechanism lies at the cognitive context comprising the conversion of our thinking. This refers to the way we perceive, evaluate and construct realities aiming innovative and meaningful solutions for and with the client. Creating knowledge and organizational innovation are important phenomena for the field of entrepreneurship. The Theory of Integrating Simplification contributes to this field of entrepreneurship as well by an elaboration of different deeper levels of knowledge; more holistic ontologies of reality; and pragmatic cognitive approaches for converting the mindset.

Reflections and Conclusion

11

Abstract

In this chapter I will share reflections on the research in regard to the context of management science and a few personal observations and ideas to serve as food for thought to the reader. During a qualitative research approach several additional bits of information pop up that does not directly relate to the main research question. As a scholar one develops his ideas further and several new questions arise as well. The reflections and observations are related to the organizational structure as was found at Buurtzorg, including its possible limitations and spiritual reflections on the sustainability of the approach of organizational innovation, followed by a conclusion.

11.1 Reflections on Management Science

11.1.1 Back to Holistic Human Behavior

In the scholarly field of management several scholars and practitioners address the need for a new management paradigm that is more inclusive and holistic in several ways (e.g. Barrett 2013; Laloux 2014; Fry and Nisiewicz 2013; Nandram and Borden 2010; Bouckaert et al. 2008; Giacalone and Jurkiewicz 2003a, b; Biberman and Tischler 2008; Biberman and Whitty 1997). Some refer to the features of the VUCA world and offer various views as ways to deal with these features, such as conscious capitalism, the triple bottom line, and spiritual-based business. Some think that old solutions have become the new problems (Zuboff 2009) and it is time to build a new paradigm for organizations. Probably not everyone will agree with the statement that we live in a world with unique problems which need to be dealt with and that we are on the edge of huge transformations. We have had such periods in the past as well. When we research management books, we notice that a great part of management is dealing with the same issues it dealt with 50 years ago. Has nothing changed then?

© Springer International Publishing Switzerland 2015   171
S.S. Nandram, *Organizational Innovation by Integrating Simplification*,
Management for Professionals, DOI 10.1007/978-3-319-11725-6_11

We have moved from industrial to knowledge economics, but management is in its original meaning not mainly based on directing, handling, and leading human behavior. Have we ever considered that perhaps we haven't changed that much or even changed at all in the past decades as a human race. And is it the case that at the same time we have ignored the human behavioral factor in our search for excellence and innovative approaches in organizations based on the illusion that we can predict the future and that we can build models that will lead the way to efficiency, effectiveness, productivity, and innovation? Perhaps we have.

If we look back even centuries ago in the works of Kautilya (321–296 BC), in his books on economics 'Arthashastra', he has presented many topics that are still relevant in management today (Nandram 2011c, 2013). In the whole collection of works, the following topics could be found: training and selection, setting up of revenue collection, records, accounts and audit offices, starting of mines and factories, settlement of the countryside, construction of forts, the appointment and the responsibilities of various departmental heads, inspection of officers, agriculture, cattle ranching and trade, main economic resources, legal aspects, issues concerning judges, transactions, filing of law-suits, non—payment of debts, undertaking in partnerships, control, detection and suppression of criminals, punishments and investigation, foreign policy and war.[1] It is said that also in the works of Machiavelli, Plato and Sun Tzu; topics relevant for the management science have been discussed. Taking these works into account we may conclude that we do not need to invent how human beings are and how they perceive and think about the world around them. Rather we acknowledge the way they are and try to move forward to the way we think they should be considering the future of our next generations and the current possibilities we have available due to advanced technologies. Perhaps we can learn from insights from the past on human beings.

What is the role of management science in contributing to empirical insights? Perhaps in ignoring the human behavior we have shifted the question of 'why' (mainly studied for example by psychologist and sociologist) too far to the 'how' (e.g. economics and management). Or those who deal with the 'why' are not concerned enough with the 'how'. But as management is an interdisciplinary field one could expect that both—why and how—are integrated to solve a real life problem that occurs in management.

An interesting article of Colquitt and Zapata-Phelan (2007) revealed that during the past five decades in the issues of the Academy of Management Journal (one of the leading scholarly journal in management) there is an upward trend in theory building and testing over time, however many of the new theories have not been rated as scientifically valid in scholarly articles as they have not been tested or they are being ignored. Scholars seem to prefer testing a theory that has been tested initially after developing it. The motivation to test a new theory is rather low as scholars cannot relate it to an existing theory. Perhaps old theories on organization

---

[1] Possible sources: R.P. Kangle, 'The Kautilya Arthashastra', Motilal Banarasidas (books 1, 2, 3), 1972; Dr Shyama Shastry, Kautilya Arthashastra, Mysore University, 1908.

dynamics do not fit today's reality and we are still stuck in old ways of thinking for ways to organize work and activities.

Suppose we need to adjust our attention in management to bring back the human behavioral aspect: what does it mean for actual management practices? What would the management world look like when managers do the needful for realizing a higher purpose in business instead of what give them power and status? Or when they more often contemplate on what they want to say and to whom before they start speaking as respectful relationships could be an important asset for collaboration? Or if they dare to remove the roles they are 'forced' to play by a competitive mindset and instead start behaving based on their true self? Or what will happen if they show discipline towards their organizational vision and strategic goals but they let go of old habits if things do not work? Perhaps then we would have highly effective, efficient and meaningful organizations.

11.1.2 Management Education Needs New Approaches

What is the consequence of the current developments for management education? Can we continue the way we have taught? With the start of the new millennium, business schools have started to introduce topics such as responsible leaders, stewardship, business ethics, corporate social responsibility, sustainable business management at a much higher pace to address the main problems that are experienced in a VUCA world. As a consequence management education has already faced changes. The question is, whether these changes imply a replacement of old topics by a few of these or whether the education didactics itself has changed. Not much is known about this last topic. Changes in educational didactics usually require a lot of time due the divergent interests of the various stakeholders that are involved. Accreditation agencies have built systems with a high tendency to improve their efficiency in detaching flaws in assessments rather than asking the questions whether human behaviors can be adequately measured with formal objective assessments only. New didactics are explored for virtual learning and the use of social media in class rooms.

What could be the new foundations of management learning? Mueller presents an extensive review of learning theories and positions them in three main paradigms: behavioristic, cognitive and constructivist. She concludes that for management education the context and rapid change are crucial factors (2012). Constructivist learning views seem to fit such modern context. There are several schools within constructivism but in management education social constructivism and adult learning could be important as here the social relationship of individuals who construct the reality and the autonomous learning respecting the particular context, are important features. Mueller concludes that all learning principles in constructivist theories have a common ground in the work of Piaget. The theory of this book, the IST, could be positioned under the label of constructivism. There are several adult learning theories within the constructivism paradigm where the learner is autonomous such as transformational learning. Would management

education gain from a fundamental change for example by introducing transformational learning forms as part of the constructivist paradigm of learning (Nandram
2014a)? Such learning styles activates all our senses, a holistic perception of reality,
intuitive skills, and hence a holistic problem solving. Constructivist learning will
give room for individual mentoring by senior teachers not on a specific management topic but by integrating all aspects of life in their teaching contents and
approaches, tapping from deeper aspects of knowledge such as wisdom. Isn't it
the management science where there could be room for such approaches given the
fact that its nature is interdisciplinary?

11.2   Reflections on the Buurtzorg Practice

11.2.1 Potential Limitations of the Buurtzorg Approach

Buurtzorg is a good practice that inspires many organizations in and outside the
community care industry. The context they face however is not totally similar and
Buurtzorg as well will cope with new contextual dynamics, internally and externally in the years to come. Therefore interesting questions here are: What could be
potential limitations when organizations would like to apply the Buurtzorg
approach? What could be a downside of an organizational structure, such as was
found at Buurtzorg with Self-Managed Teams and no management layers, only
facilitators in the form of coaches and supporting staff and a few directors who
formally have the power to decide for the whole organization? I will mention a few
of these possible limitations.

1. Commander's Intent
In the worst case, the approach could result in a 'commanders intent' if practitioners
blindly follow the Self-Managed Team structure only in their attempts to implement it for gaining the positive results that were realized at Buurtzorg. Such a
commander's intent could as well occur at Buurtzorg in the long-run. Because of
the lack of other managers, except the two directors at Buurtzorg, professionals may
tend to follow and become dependent on their formal decision power. As the
founder is responsible for strategic decision making and he is the one who conducts
all main corporate communication, the tendency to abide to his thinking, may occur
every now and then, as was described in Chap. 8. Such intent could evolve
authoritarian features and finally induce fear amongst employees to follow their
leader. Potentially employees could start only obeying their leader without thinking
about what is effective in given circumstances. They could fall back to rules and
regulations for getting the teams going or by falling back to hierarchic management
and coordination structure at team level to control, with the consequence of an
elimination of autonomy, while this was one of the basic driving forces of the
approach. Therefore the importance here is to stress the integrative nature of the
approach at Buurtzorg. It is not only about the structure, it encompasses much more
as has been shown in the previous chapters. It starts with a universal human

functioning of how we perceive, evaluate and construct reality. The subtle aspects such as trust and freedom are as important as the hard features of decision power, organizing and ICT frameworks.

2. Founder's Dependency

Another impact of the organizational structure is the dependency on the founder. We know in general how important the founder of an organization is, especially in the early stages of the organization's life cycle. Research into life cycles and entrepreneurship however shows that the role could change during the course of the life cycle. Some scholars have suggested that evolving ventures may outgrow the capabilities and qualities of their founders, with founders sometimes being replaced by professional managers (Boeker and Karichalil 2002). But there are also cases where the moment the founder leaves the company, no matter for what reason, the organization experiences a drawback. We know examples of Steve Jobs but also several other examples could be given. There are a few examples of Self-Managed Structures as well and we know how vulnerable the organization could be in such structures. By depending on the founder, who in one hand is the fuel but on the other hand, due to his important role, he becomes the weak wheel in the organization when he is absent. From a rational point of view we may say that such structure is risky, as his strength then becomes his weakness. However, this is not a rule. Organizations can survive and grow with new leaders but perhaps recovery from the departure of the founder, happens faster in a traditional hierarchical organizational structure compared to a Self-Managed flat structure. Considering this, in such cases the leader is the only one with the formal decision authority.

At Buurtzorg, the founder is leading a higher purpose and not an organization, according to the perception of the employees. They do not label him as a manager or a leader. Buurtzorg is also theirs. His priority is serving the community care by initiating the changes he wants to see and he resonates well with this purpose among the professionals. The professionals are not dependent on him for conducting their content-related tasks and they feel attractive to the higher purpose. It seems that, based on their enthusiasm, especially those who are involved already from the start, the majority aims transforming community care. This may make a difference on the long-run in respect to the founder's dependency.

3. Mindlessness

The organization has been awarded several prizes and its organizational outcomes are positive; clients' are extremely positive, employees experience high job satisfaction and pride. If these features become more common and rather a rule than an exception; routine and mindlessness could enter the organization. Also because of its growth, such tendency could occur. It seems like mindfulness is already almost naturally present at Buurtzorg. Due to its growth, here and there in the secondary process of administration, developing and sharing knowledge and a need for standardizing some tasks pop up in discussions. Working along routines is common in almost every organization, although the intensity varies. For example, instead of considering each request of the international audience to visit Buurtzorg teams as unique and aiming to come up with tailor made solutions, from an effectiveness approach it could be wise to search for a balance here. In general if organizations are aiming mindfulness they strive to be alert towards failures and want to create openness to new approaches. Studies find that businesses with a mindful approach have an increased ability to manage the unexpected and avoid catastrophic mistakes (Baker 2007; Coutu 2003). Joyner and Lardner (2008) found that high levels of mindful organizing among front-line employees improves innovation, quality and efficiency. But mindlessness is not per se a bad thing. Levinthal and Rerup (2006) found that conscious or mindful and automatic or less-mindful processes are both needed in organizations. They stated that interruptions trigger a sequential switch from less-mindful to mindful processes and suggest that organizational processes blend the two forms of cognition and behavior on an ongoing basis. However, in practice there may be a conflict between mindlessness and mindfulness. Mindlessness focuses on the role of continuity to preserve accumulated experience whereas mindfulness stresses the importance of novelty to respond to change and unique circumstances. In line with this thinking, Levinthal and Rerup (2006) mention that mindfulness can generate extra costs whereas less mindful, routinized behavior is effective in economizing on scarce attentional resources.

At the moment at Buurtzorg re-constructing reality as has been explained with the Integrating Simplification Theory, is at the heart of its success. If this approach would stop continuing, everyone will operate in their routine modes ending up with no creativity. This in itself, should not be a problem until the needs of clients are met, as that is the core purpose of the organization. But for the long-run the trade-off needs to be made between what could be routinized (mindlessness) and what should have additional degrees of freedom towards tailor made solutions (mindfulness). This requires the attitude to balance between both, which is the twin-principle of Yogic Leadership.

4. "Zeitgeber" Focus

In Chap. 4, I have explained how professionals of Buurtzorg attune to the client's needs and how the client's rhythm works as the dominant pattern in their planning of the tasks, thus as the "zeitgeber". Originally the nursing profession is based on a calling to serve the client in the best possible way. For people in other industries the association with Florence Nightingale resonates with the attunement of a nurse to the client's need as a natural pattern and thus such a focus would not be a big deal. However, for the long run this could lead to burnout among employees. Furthermore, new professionals that are not trained according to the holistic community care view could face this attunement to the client as a big challenge which subsequently could result in disturbances in team dynamics or personal stress and strains. If the challenges develop into serious forms it may turn into an unhealthy situation. Here again a Yogic philosophy could be helpful to cope with such challenges.

5. Closed Ecosystems

In Chap. 6 I have addressed how hiring professionals at Buurtzorg fits in building an eco-system of like-minded people striving for the same value system of serving a higher purpose which is placed above the organizational structure or any specific human resource approach. The eco-system of the Self-Managed Teams is being protected to maintain the cohesion which is one of the strengths for building trust as a core virtue to strive for. The founder protects the internal eco-system by reminding professionals of their autonomy and sharing power. He also strives for protecting them from external overload of information or distraction from the higher purpose. The professionals tap from the community context as well which forms another eco-system mainly maintained by their Craftsmanship and their involvement in the local community. If in the long-run the resources dry up in the local community, teams may need to enter other locations. The question then rises whether others will be open to join with new team members from other locations. Due to the growth at Buurtzorg, in current practice, teams need to split and form additional teams in a location which means that they are usually open to such dynamics. After a while all these systems could develop themselves as closed eco-systems not allowing fresh knowledge. Every possible team problem can occur in Buurtzorg teams as well. They need to deal with human dynamics where consideration of emotions, preferences, likes and dislikes for other members may occur during the work processes. What binds them is the higher purpose to deliver the best possible care but in practice not everyone is involved in the same intensity which may be a cause for issues in a team. Teams are guided in their communication processes to prevent misunderstanding as much as possible, but here again it is not a top down but a bottom up approach which in practice means that teams themselves should take the initiative to receive guidance in problem solving. One may ask whether all these eco-systems need to be refreshed at times to continuously stimulate the process of Integrating Simplification by focusing on the three principles of needing, rethinking and common sensing and actively searching for several types of knowledge to serve the client in the best possible way.

6. Career Block

The research data based on the interviews, the employees' surveys, and the conversation on the Buurtzorgweb shows how positive the majority of employees are. However, in the long-run some professionals could perceive a career block, based on their personal career expectations and drives. While this is not a main issue currently at Buurtzorg, for those who have entered Buurtzorg recently, career development could be an important drive.

It seems that for finding out whether we are well off or not, we often compare ourselves with others. Choosing whom to compare to, then becomes an important factor. Especially in the Western Society, there is a natural tendency to look upward in evaluating oneself. In psychology we call this the upward social comparison. It depends on a person's self-esteem whether he will tend more to upward or downward comparison with others. Those who believe in the Maslow pyramid of needs abide to the notion that people move upward in their needs too and thus do not stay attuned to one specific need. Applied to the Buurtzorg context this may imply that the fit between employee needs and Buurtzorg currently may change in the course of time. In practice this may depend on the life stage of an individual. The more mature a person the less important this upward or downward comparison could be. Then people may even turn to parallel views of comparing with others based on their value and belief systems.

We also know the theory of Deci (1971), Deci and Ryan (2000) which suggests that people can be intrinsically and extrinsically motivated. At Buurtzorg, since there is no upward career development, people are mainly intrinsically motivated in their jobs: they develop perceptions of job pride, gain recognition for their approaches and express commitment to the cause. The majority of the employees is highly educated and professionally mature, which may explain why they tend to be driven by intrinsic motivators. Perhaps, they have different expectations compared to a younger professional for whom the career development means moving upward. While they may eventually discover the intrinsic motivators, it is much harder for them, being in a society where some opinions believe the subjective norm, has a big influence on their own perception and experience of success, happiness and wellbeing. For those who have already walked the 'regular' path, a career at Buurtzorg with mainly intrinsic motivators may not feel as a career block at all.

Another aspect of the career block, next to the required intrinsic orientation, is the specific competences that are developed at Buurtzorg. Human Capital Theory (Becker 1976) states that people develop generic and specific competences for their careers. Organizations tend to develop the specific competences as these are much more required to do the job. We know the tendency of firms to develop on the job training facilities, not only for the current jobs. They often hold the rational perspective that personnel trained in specific competences will not leave the organization easily as their 'economic value' in another context will be low. Companies assure a low employee turnover by offering specific training. As the Buurtzorg way of working is very unique, containing many mature professionals and even change agents, perhaps it can be suggested that these professionals will not easily fit in another existing organization. However, the main reason for a big part of the workforce at Buurtzorg was to make the shift for gaining autonomy and having the feeling that at Buurtzorg they could do the job they were trained for, which is an intrinsic motivator. Hence there is no need to shift jobs for them.

Working in the healthcare has its special feature of experiencing a calling to serve others. Ideas around career development may turn out differently here than in other industries. Next to the distinction between intrinsic and extrinsic motivation, there is a broader view on drives. Barrick et al. (2013) introduce higher order goals or fundamental human strivings that are interesting for this specific context of Buurtzorg. Let us first explain them. *Autonomy striving* motivation is linked to the desire to have control over what to do, when to do it and how to do it. *Status striving* motivation is linked to an individual's motivation to obtain power, influence, and prestige within a status hierarchy. *Communion striving* is a fundamental goal that evolved for survival purposes and represents an individual motivation to obtain acceptance in personal relationships and to get along with others. *Achievement striving* motivation is the desire to complete things in a timely, careful and efficient way. It goes along with a strong focus on getting things done, the desire to increase competency and the desire to enhance oneself (Barrick et al. 2013). These higher order goals partly explain why a person behaves in a certain way. Barrick et al. define them as fundamental, distal and desired motivational objectives that people strive to attain while not always being consciously aware of them (Barrick et al. 2013, p. 135). One could state that if employees feel acknowledged for their communion striving (Barrick et al. 2013) they will tend to seek relational support and enjoy interpersonal activities. If employees feel motivated by status striving motivation they may find the context of Buurtzorg and how things are being organized less attractive for a long period of time as there is no upward mobilization in career. They may survive better in a hierarchic setting. If they tend to achievement striving or autonomy striving motivations they will be encouraged by a Self-Managed Team structure. In general I would state that the career block may be experienced by some but not by all, it depends on the fundamental strivings that one has in life.

11.2.2 Solving Limitations Through a Humane Attitude

These limitations could occur at Buurtzorg on the long-run or as restrictions when applying the Buurtzorg approach in other organizations. Overall, the IST has shown how important simplification both at the individual and organizational levels is by re-constructing reality. Only an integral understanding and implementation by including both levels and the five dimensions enabled by a Yogic Leadership attitude, will give the potential to induce similar results to other organizations as were found at Buurtzorg.

For importing the approach a few basic features are necessary at the humane level.

Leadership Level
Are leaders of other organizations willing to share powers as Jos de Blok does? Are they willing to put humane values, being human and using coming sense above control and bureaucracy? Are others willing to listen to the concerns of their employees and learn from them? Are other leaders willing to listen to and trust their own intuitions, listen to the intuitions of others they work with, and adapt their views and actions to these? Are they ready for converting their mindset? Do they have the skills in doing this? Are they willing to bring others on board for developing new perspectives? Are they willing to learn from others including their clients and improve things for reaching out to realizing the higher purpose of the needs in community care?

Professional Level

Are there professionals available who are aware of their calling and driven to act according to their vocational calling? Are their professionals with mature skills in serving the client in the best possible way? Are there professionals who do not mind to be flexible in their schedules and approaches? Are there professionals who dare to explore towards the unknown? Are there professionals who can contribute to building cohesive teams? Are there professionals who have developed the abilities or who are open to using several types of knowledge, including intuitive knowledge? Are there professionals who can put aside their egos and transcend them towards realizing what is best for their team and clients? Are there professionals who have the courage to express their concerns in open communication for the benefit of the team? Are there professionals who are willing to let go if thing do not work? Are there professionals who are truthful to the organization's mission of serving the client in the best possible way?

These are some initial necessities to create a possibility for Integrating Simplification to take off.

During the study, I have been searching for less favorable factors or flaws as well when I found overwhelming positive results and heard many positive stories from people I interviewed. I must tell how hard it was to find 'negative stories' or people stressing limitations of the approach. If unfavorable factors were shared this had to do with team dynamics and individual preferences or issues that were not solved fast enough due to its Self-Managed Team structure. Team members will hesitate to share negative opinions on others as they are dependent on each other, there is no manager's door to knock on with complaints, and they all benefit if the whole team is in sync. Those things where some hurdles occurred often, were shared stating the following rationale: the time was not right or there was a lack of finding partners, stakeholders in the industry could not be convinced of the approach, there were political constraints in the industry, just because the idea was not favored by the majority in a team or because of its newness it requires more time for others to get used to new approaches of effectiveness, efficiency, growth, all together with humane values. They also stated that the mindset of many seemed to be polluted by mainstream economic driven thinking. Nevertheless, being patient when things did not work, believing in the higher purpose and personal ambitions could be noticed throughout the organization.

I interviewed a few people who were leaving the organization to get their part of the experiences as well. One of the main limitations that was mentioned often was the fear that people are dependent on Jos's decisiveness and the question, how would Buurtzorg look like without Jos in the future. Another limitation was the lack of structure and the high flexibility that was required from the professionals and the incapability of dealing with the provided freedom to teams. Since the organization gets broad international attention a serious concern for some is the visibility of the founder. This was mainly addressed by professionals at the Headquarters of the organization.

Overall we can conclude that there have been some hurdles during the start-up until the point where Buurtzorg is now. One of the main hurdles was how to convince other organizations that it is a new way of working: it is not just a new policy or a new way of doing things or simply a change, but a transformation in thinking, assumptions and humane belief systems, while still applying basic, simple approaches. In early years when Jos shared the experiences he had with the supervisory board he continuously felt not understood when he was trying to tell them what he aimed with Buurtzorg. Discussion took place for hours because the mindset of those in the board was based on the rationalistic profit-oriented economic view of man where there was no place for the client's perspective.

Another reflection is the tendency of people not to be convinced of what is being told about the achievements of Buurtzorg as the approach sounds too simplistic for being real to practitioners. Academics tend to think along complex entrepreneurial and strategic governance models. And since it is a healthcare organization it will catch less of their attention. The mainstream attitude still is the tendency to tell their students the stories of successful entrepreneurs realizing high profits for themselves and their shareholders and fewer stories of successful entrepreneurs who care for a higher purpose. Those who want to adopt the approach tend to import a specific feature and not the whole concept as this requires a new fundamental way of organizing the mindset and the context. While it looks simple in practice it is not that easy to implement, it requires people to go out of their comfort zones and become human, authentic and sincere in communication. These are our gifts by birth and thus could be our natural tendencies but which many of us have lost due to the way we are raised and educated in the society we live in today. Simon's view of the rational man is still dominant in our Western education system. The Yogic Philosophy gives us holistic views that are not opposed to such dominant ideas but which synthesizes the current one-sided views of materialistic drives with spiritual views on man.

11.2.3 Reconciling Spirit and Matter with Yogic Views

Many of the potential limitations that could be thought of are based on a one dimensional rational analysis or on existing theories. These limitations can be moved away from by transforming them with spiritual yogic views. And current good practices can be maintained by these basics of Yogic Philosophy. In practice transformation means going back to our basic human nature where there is both a need for spirit and matter, and the main challenge in life is reconciling both. At Buurtzorg both features are relevant: the materialistic output representing matter and the humane values representing spirit. Here follows a brief explanation of these concepts preceded by positioning Yogic Philosophy.

Yoga is widely practiced worldwide today. It is seen as an effective tool for reducing stress and strain in the business environment, for the prevention of illness, to develop concentration and focus and thus it is used as a tool for a balanced life and good physical health. The roots of yoga go back more than 5,000 years to the Indus Valley civilization. In those times, the techniques were passed on from a teacher or guru to a disciple through direct teaching. This learning system was only accessible to very motivated and able disciples. Yoga is addressed in the ancient Hindu scriptures of the Upanishads. In modern times we owe to Maharisi Patanjali for a systematic presentation of traditional Yoga Philosophy in his well-known Yoga Sutras which went on to inspire many yogic traditions (Karambelkar 2011). The word yoga stems from the Sanskrit word *yuj* which means to join. Yoga has been defined in various ways but in essence it means the path inward toward unity or oneness with the outer world. Various schools of postures and breathing are the main forms of yoga practiced today.

Patanjali's yoga does not solely involve breathing or yoga postures. It is a psycho-spiritual model of development. The philosopher, Sri Aurobindo's (1872–1950) focused on the main principles of the philosophy under the umbrella of Integral Yoga. He gave a holistic explanation of the Yogic Philosophy but did not provide any set of techniques because in his view nature provides the basis for our way of living. He said *"What we propose in our Yoga is nothing less than to break up the whole formation or our past and present which makes up the ordinary material and mental man and to create a new center of vision and a new universe of activities in ourselves which shall constitute a divine humanity or superhuman nature" (Sri Aurobindo, The Synthesis of Yoga, 1993, CWSA, Vol. 23)*. It is a way of relating to the world. Thus Yoga is considered as a way of life in the works of both Patanjali and Sri Aurobindo.

The beauty of the Yoga Philosophy is its wholesome view. This makes it possible for application to physical, social, mental, psychic and spiritual development to be used in professional settings. This way of life can also be applied in understanding why an entrepreneur such as Jos de Blok, focuses on both social and economic entrepreneurial value. And why a professional at Buurtzorg could embrace several values as outcomes rather than solely upward career development, status or other extrinsic rewards. And why for them the care they give should be professional and personal. Sri Aurobindo stressed that we should not deny the material world as it is part of Universal existence (Brahman). He said, that Matter also is Brahman, and from Matter all existences are born, in Matter they increase and enter into Matter when they pass to another stage. The Brahman, resides in all of us, in our material or physical being (Sri Aurobindo 2006). Sri Aurobindo stressed that Matter and Spirit may seem irreconcilable. They may produce the dualistic thinking of Spirit on one end and Matter on the other end but in fact they are part of the same.

Reconciling matter and spirit in a philosophical sense, is not about change but about transformation. Change is mainly a cognitive process. It involves our mind, our beliefs, our attitudes and in turn, our actions. In the business context, change is doing what we do now but in a more efficient way, a more productive way and even a quality enhancing way. In business terms this is often aimed at generating more profit. Change or transition is a fact of life. Maintaining the spirit in the Buurtzorg organization requires maintenance of the Integrating Simplification principles of needing, rethinking and common sensing, which is about transformation. This means transcending our egos and the obstacles they create and reaching out to higher goals, the higher purpose at Buurtzorg. Transcendence is about going beyond dualistic thinking and establishing inclusive thinking and behavior. If we enable ourselves to transcend, we discover and follow our ideal of human life or higher purpose ("*Swadharma*") by identifying and aligning to our authenticity or inner self. This leads to satisfaction and happiness. Our inner side drives the transcendental process; the unfolding to our inner truth and life path. There is a Universal Law to which every human being has the potential to become aligned to. *Dharma* means living in harmony with Universal Law and one's own nature. Rising up or transcending to this Universal Law can occur at all levels: personal, societal, environmental, ecological and universal levels. At Buurtzorg the founders and professionals seem to find it interesting to explore the idea of transcendence at a societal level. Transcendence at a societal level is based on the concept of human welfare ("*Loksangraha*") which assumes that people's actions reflect a desire to be of overall benefit to society. This motivation leads to transcendence of the duality between oneself and others as well.

Such a yogic view provides insights on how to reconcile matter and spirit at a personal level and how to reconcile personal and organizational/societal values to maintain organizational coherence by a continuous focus on the higher purpose. In daily practice it requires the skills of discipline (Abhaysa) and letting go if things do not work (Vajragya). In Chap. 9 I have already explained that such features are already present at Buurtzorg, perhaps not consciously. But a conscious application will open the possibility to prevent the appearance of many of the possible limitations.

Conclusion

Integrating Simplification Theory (IST) is a management theory for organizations aiming a new way of organizing. Its cognitive principles can be applied universally as it is based on human principles of organizing the reality around us. It has foundations of constructing knowledge at the individual level. It follows two assumptions: first, that professionals are able to construct reality and second, they need facilities to discover opportunities for improving their quality of services. The organizing principles are applicable in founding other organizations in several industrial settings as well. Particularly for the community care industry, the organizing principles could be applied as well in transforming existing organizations. The two main assumptions behind the organizing principles are: professionals work effectively if they feel trusted for their knowledge rather than controlled or managed; organizations do not necessarily require many management layers and structures. Ideally speaking the dimensions and expressing the organizing principles are equally relevant. Their properties as discussed throughout the book can be applied in every community care context as well. The outcome of results depends on the public health system in specific countries and the specific cultural beliefs about the quality of life and community care. The leadership approach in the Integrating Simplification framework provides inspiration for other organizations and entrepreneurs. It is based on the assumption that a combination of humane values and entrepreneurial achievement drives, both are necessary for avoiding disintegration in order to realize organizational harmony and sustainable outcomes. The way Integrating Simplification Theory is being applied in the Buurtzorg organization has covered many expressions which could be labeled as the art of management. In management, that manager who manages the least is actually the best manager. But often due to high specialization of tasks and jobs, management itself has become a core concept and thus how to manage complex situation has received a lot of attention in practice and in scholarly works. This has resulted in complex management structures while losing the essence of the art of management. Applied to organizations, the art of management implies that, organizations that manage the least are considered the best organizations. As this is an exception rather than a rule and it introduces a new application of behavioral processes, as well as new organizational and management structures—even if they are very basic—such organizations are considered as organizational innovations.

Appendix A Classic Grounded Methodology

A.1 Classic Grounded Theory

A.1.1 Elements of the Classic Grounded Theory (CGT)

We use the following elements of the Classic Grounded Theory methodology as defined below.

- **Grounded theory**: "the process of data collection for generating theory whereby the analyst jointly collects, codes, and analyzes his data and decides what data to collect next and where to find them, in order to develop his theory as it emerges. The process of data collection is controlled by theoretical sampling according to the emerging theory". (Glaser 1978, Chap. 3).
- **Main Concern**: the research question that you want to address in developing the theory.
- **Core variable** [or category]: "In theoretical sensitivity I said, the goal of grounded theory is to generate a theory that accounts for a pattern of behavior which is relevant and problematic for those involved". The goal is not voluminous description, nor clever verification. The goal is generation of theory around a core category. Without a core category, an effort of grounded theory will drift in relevancy and workability. Since a core category accounts for most of the variation in a pattern of behavior, it has important functions for generating grounded theory: integration, density, saturation, completeness, and delimiting focus" (Glaser 2002, p. 75).
  - The core category in our research is integrating simplification. The theory that we develop is the theory of Integrating Simplification.
  - This theory has been developed with the main concern that we found at Buurtzorg Nederland: The main concern in the study was: 'what does an organization (Buurtzorg) do, to deliver services that are fulfilling the client's or customer's needs and how does it design and organize its activities for realizing a client focused service'.
- **Category**: "A type of concept. Usually used for a higher level of abstraction", (Glaser 2002, p. 39).

© Springer International Publishing Switzerland 2015
S.S. Nandram, *Organizational Innovation by Integrating Simplification*,
Management for Professionals, DOI 10.1007/978-3-319-11725-6

- The Theory of Integrating Simplification consists of three main processes (needing, rethinking and common sensing), and five categories or dimensions:
  Attunement to the client;
  Subtle Craftsmanship;
  Intrapreneurial Team Freedom;
  Pragmatic Will with ICT;
  Leading a Higher Purpose
- **Concept**: "The underlying, meaning, uniformity and/or pattern within a set of descriptive incidents", (Glaser 2002, p. 39).
  - In Integrating Simplification the five categories or dimensions comprise several concepts.
- **Property**: "A type of concept that is a conceptual characteristic of a category, thus at a lesser level of abstraction than a category. A property is a concept of a concept", (Glaser 2002, p. 39).
  - The concepts of the five categories consist of several properties.

A.1.2 Elements Used in the Process of Conducting the CGT

- **Memo**: "The theorizing write-up of ideas as they emerge, while coding for categories, their properties and their theoretical codes". (Glaser 2002, p. 108).
- **Open coding**: "The initial stage of constant comparative analysis, before delimiting the coding to a core category and its properties—or selective coding. The analyst starts with no preconceived codes—he remains entirely open". (Glaser 2002, p. 39)
- **Coding**: "Conceptualizing data by constant comparison of incident with incident, and incident with concept to emerge more categories and their properties". (Glaser 2002, p. 39)
- **Constant Comparative Coding**: "Fundamental operation in the constant comparative method of analysis. The analyst codes incidents for categories and their properties and the theoretical codes that connect them. [...] Two analytic procedures are basic to the constant comparative method of coding. The first pertains to the making of constant comparisons of incident to incident, and then when concepts emerge, incident to concept, which is how properties of categories are generated. The second is asking the neutral, coding question referred to above: what category or property of a category does this incident indicate?" (Glaser 2002, pp. 38–39)
- **Selective coding**: "To selectively code means to cease open coding and to delimit coding to only those variables that relate to the core variable, in sufficiently significant ways to be used in a parsimonious theory. It starts after and only when the analyst is sure that she has found a core variable. The core category simply emerges from the constant comparative coding and analyzing of the data. The core variable then becomes a guide to further data collection and theoretical sampling: the analysis is guided by a core variable. Codes, memo's

and integration start occurring in relationship to the core variable". (Glaser 2002, p. 75)

- **Theoretical coding**: "A property of coding and constant comparative analysis that yields the conceptual relationship between categories and their properties as they emerge. Theoretical codes are conceptual connectors to be used implicitly and explicitly in the way and style in which the analyst writes". (Glaser 2002, p. 39)
- **Theoretical Sampling**: "The process of data collection for generating theory whereby the analyst jointly collects, codes and analyzes his data and then decides what data to collect next and where to find them, in order to develop his theory as it emerges. This process of data collection is *controlled* by the emerging theory". (Glaser and Strauss 1967, p. 45)
- **Theoretical Sorting**: "Begins to put the fracture data and memos back together. It consists of sorting the memos in a theoretical outline in preparation for the writing stage". (Glaser 2002, p. 109)
- **Writing**: "It is a 'write up' of ideas from theoretical sorting". (Glaser 2002, p. 110)

Other terms for clarifications:

- **Induce/induction:** This is a term used in a qualitative research methodology to search for systematic patterns in the data by systematic examination of similarities between various answers of those who were interviewed and within all the data that has been collected to develop concepts or ideas or a theory consisting of concepts and their interrelationships.
- **Respondent:** The persons who were interviewed for the research.
- **Antecedent:** Referring to a variable or factor that explains a phenomenon and that usually precedes the phenomenon of study in time.

A.1.3 Sources of Data for the Classic Grounded Theory

Following Glaser's claim that 'all is data' I have used several sources. For the Classic Grounded Theory the following sources of data were used:

- Interviews: All interviews for the first stage were done face to face; follow up interviews to get more clarification of the primary process, were done by Skype interviews, by phone or face to face. Before additional data was used the concepts had already emerged and the theory was written in draft. From all these interviews field notes were written and immediately after each interview memos were documented and the process of open coding was followed.
- Next to the open coding, handwritten mind maps were prepared to note new ideas and coding was done.
- Notes on observations during the interviews were written immediately after the interview.

- Observations were made and documented during the time spent at the organization in a separate document.
- Additional input was also collected from visits to teams, visits to clients, introductory meeting of employees, meetings with coaches, and a meeting with the supervisory board.
- Three books were used as an additional data source. One of these was written by an external text writer and researcher, it comprises the vision of the founder, weekly diaries of nurses and clients. The other was written by the same researcher and a community nurse. This book gives a detailed description of the processes in community care as it is being practiced at Buurtzorg. Those parts comprise opinions and experiences of clients, nurses and several components of the ICT support. In the stage when the chapters were already written in draft, a third book was included as data to see whether aspects could be clarified or validated. This book was a Ph.D. dissertation based on two cases where Buurtzorg was one of the cases (Van Dalen 2012). As the Ph.D. has followed an ethnographic approach some rich information was found to validate what had already been found in the rest of the data. But as this Ph.D. described patterns and linked them to the literature in the organizational discipline, I wanted to avoid including preconceived thinking in the initial stages of the research.
- Another source for additional input was the blogs of the founder and other news and forms on the website of the organization.
- I also had access to confidential business related information to assess the organizational performance in the past years.
- All written reports and documents on the case were read and relevant input was documented in notes.
- Client and Employee surveys were accessed as well for additional confirmation or adjustments of the draft theory.

Overview of the Data Sources

- In total I have interviewed 40 people, 5 of them more than once to get deeper understanding of some issues or for validation of findings
- I have been present at 3 meetings with teams
- I have been present at 3 meetings with coaches
- I have conducted 2 days client visits
- I have gathered input from 3 teams
- I have been attending two roundtable sessions chaired by the founder with teams, coaches and researchers
- I have spoken with the founder on a regular basis
- I have met and talked to the contact persons in Sweden, USA and Japan who are currently exploring or have set up a Buurtzorg unit in their home countries
- I have been present at 3 informal celebrations (2 birthdays; Christmas)
- I have been present at a meeting with the supervisory board
- I have made use of the results from the Client Surveys

- I have made use of the results from the Employee Surveys
- I have attended one Buurtzorg introduction meeting with the nurses and nurse assistants
- I have attended a Buurtzorg Congress
- For more information on Buurtzorg policy and financial data I have accessed the Business Information (BI) on the web
- For data on communication by the Headquarters and the role of the leader, a summary of the messages was retrieved for me by the ICT expert from the Buurtzorgweb in the period of February 17th, 2008 to March 20th, 2014. When I considered a summary as relevant for getting a deeper understanding or for quotation in a chapter, I retrieved the whole message directly from the blogs on the Buurtzorgweb.
- For validating the results (theoretical sampling) I presented the concepts of the theory and its explanations to the founder, creative thinker, an ICT advisor, a selection of three coaches and two nurses. Due to their role I assumed that not everyone could give additional feedback or confirmations of what I had found on all the five dimensions. The nurses therefore shared mainly their views on Craftsmanship and Attunement to the client.

A.1.4 Guidance When Conducting the Classic Grounded Theory

While doing the study I sought for guidance by Gaetan Mourmant, one of the experts in CGT. We have been working on another study using CGT for the past 2 years. For this current study, because of the geographical distance (Netherlands-Canada) I had several Skype sessions with him in August, September, December 2013, and in January 2014 to get advice especially on the initial steps of the study.

Furthermore I gained insights in the CGT at a workshop with Gaetan Mourmant at Nyenrode Business University, September 19th, 2014.

For more insight and confirmation on how I conducted the current research, the workshop in Paris on April 16th, 2014 at the NEOMA Business School was very helpful to me. This workshop was conducted with experts who discussed several opposed views on CGT and where examples of CGT were presented. The presenting experts were:

- Barney Glaser, the originator of Classic Grounded Theory, *The Grounded Theory Institute*
- Isabelle Walsh, *NEOMA Business School*
- Judith Holton, *Mount Allison University*
- Sébastien Point, *EM Strasbourg Business School*
- Gaetan Mourmant, *IESEG School of Management*
- Valery Michaud, *NEOMA Business School*

I have applied the Classic Grounded Theory for developing a theory on entrepreneurship and decision making when entrepreneurs do not have rational information available or if there is an overload of information. This study has been conducted with 4 co-authors and is being finalized to be submitted to an academic journal. The current study is the second large study with the CGT but the first that I conducted alone.

A.1.5 Methodological Approach for the Research

Please find a synthesis of the classic GTM approach that I have followed in Fig. A.1 and an example of the sorting process.

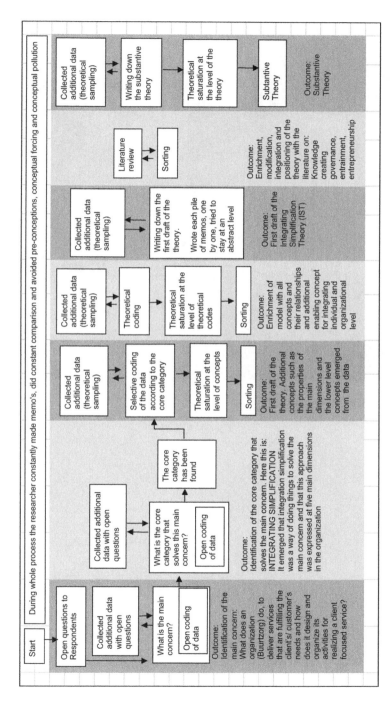

Fig. A.1 Process of CGT of this research

Fig. A.2 Example of sorting

Appendix B Mindful Inquiry for Observations

B.1 Mindful Inquiry

B.1.1 Principles of Mindful Inquiry

Bentz and Shapiro (1998) define Mindful Inquiry, as empowering the researcher both psychologically and philosophically by putting the researcher—rather than the research techniques—at the center of the process. It is about awareness and observation through the inner processes of the researcher and the research subjects, as well as about identifying with these processes. It originates from the Buddhist concept of Mindfulness in combination with phenomenology, critical theory and hermeneutics.

Mindful Inquiry departs from the notion of multi-level ontology (views on reality) and multi-level epistemology (ways of knowing). Referring to the epistemology in Mindful Inquiry next to objective collected knowledge other ways and sources of getting knowledge are also important. Here we talk about the knowledge of our *inner processes* which covers emotions, moods, desires and thoughts. This knowledge is direct but *still separate*. In this mode of knowing we partly identify with the mind and use it to view another part of the mind. The cognitive process separates the knower from the known. This type of knowledge is therefore based on experience. It becomes the person's knowledge; while it is internal and subjective it can be talked about and shared. In research we can ask about these experiences from a third person approach. Mindful Inquiry can be applied to gain this type of knowledge, by self-reports through questionnaires or observations made by the researcher. Another level of knowledge that we include in Mindful Inquiry is the knowledge that we experience our *inner processes and identify* with them. This occurs, for example when we are completely consumed by negative or positive feelings that drive our behaviors. Here the person feels he is directly involved in the experience.

In the context of the current research, I participated in the organization during a fixed period of time to experience a representative number of incidents and to understand the phenomenon of the study. Documentation of the observations I took were helpful for a deeper understanding of the several concepts that had emerged in the research based on the other types of data.

© Springer International Publishing Switzerland 2015
S.S. Nandram, *Organizational Innovation by Integrating Simplification*,
Management for Professionals, DOI 10.1007/978-3-319-11725-6

B.1.2 Mindful Inquiry Attitude

A Mindful Inquiry also required a research attitude based on Integral Yogic Theory (Nandram 2014b) when collecting observations during the study. Below these attitudes are described and an explanation of how they have been applied in the current research is provided:

- **Aspiration**: a deep call to focus on the process rather than on the results. This requires an in-depth analysis and not a superficial observation of what a researcher thinks, feels and experiences when studying communicating processes. I took the following aspects into account during the research: expressions in the culture, expressions during the interviews, the willingness of respondents to contribute easily to the interview, conversations during meetings and at times becoming a part of the Buurtzorg community to experience relevant processes such as birthday celebrations, internal meetings, congress attendance, introductory meeting, meeting with supervisory board, and teams meetings.
- **Rejection**: becoming aware of and withdrawing from all wrong habits and the false identification with the ego when giving meaning to observations, data and feelings. Especially here, while having an extensive research experience and knowledge of the different ways to connect to the literature on organizational theory, I tried to eliminate any pre-conceived theoretical frameworks by deliberately not studying them in the period from the start of designing the research, data collection process and analyzing the data until the core category was found and the underlying concepts, corresponding relationships and lower-level concepts of each property were found and described. Then in the draft chapters, I made notes about linkages that could be made with the literature field and realized that the study could be done using literature from entrepreneurship, intrapreneurship, organizational culture, leadership, innovation, organizational innovation, organizational theory, motivation theory and self-management, as well as philosophical views on human aspiration. The emerged concepts that were obviously linked to existing concepts were added in the draft versions of the chapters and accordingly elaborated and finalized. During the course of the process I realized that such a broad literature study will not result in a comprehensive insight of what is being done at Buurtzorg. Therefore, when rewriting the draft chapters on the concepts and the related data I hardly connected to the literature. In such a way the data got the room to speak for itself. A theoretical reflection based on literature study was done at a later stage and has been separately presented in Chap. 9.

  Another expression of the rejection attitude was the continuous focus on the main concern which I was trying to get an answer for. There is the tendency to get involved in day to day issues while being present at Buurtzorg and therefore the chance of experiencing information overload and confounding data because of that seeing other phenomenon that is not being studied. A mindful attitude requires a focus on the main concern and therefore dealing with the continuous query whether the information being received helps to understand the main concern.

- **Dedication to the phenomena of study:** I was experientially aware of the context of the type of primary process that was present from the perspective of relevant stakeholder, as a family member to such a healthcare organization. In my foreword I have briefly shared my experiences with the Elderly Home Care in the Netherlands before Buurtzorg was founded. Though this experience is based on a single case it covers a period of 10 years with 3 years of extensive experiences with community care in the role of caregiver to a family member (1997–2007).

Overall I can state that while being trained in a positivistic research methodology I have realized that a third person approach with standardized surveys or interviews would not have been sufficient for gaining a deep understanding of the client care focus of Buurtzorg. For follow up studies such an approach can be helpful so that a particular aspect of Integrating Simplification can be studied in more detail.

These Mindful Inquiry attitudes were added to the research design prior to beginning the research and I have communicated about my role with the founder and therefore I was invited to join several internal meetings to get to know Buurtzorg in more depth.

Appendix C Stages in the Study

C.1 Stages in the Research Process

My first interview at Buurtzorg started in November 2011. According to the natural flow between then and setting up the research project of this book several visits, observations, interviews, readings about the case in magazines and media were followed (first stage of the research). I gave two conference presentations based on the findings for international academic audience in India (February 23rd, 2012) and France (May 18th, 2013).

I realized then that the case was very rich and could be studied from several theoretical perspectives. When a research assignment was agreed with the founder, I proposed a Grounded Theory approach because I was convinced that there was much more to learn and even induce to building a new theory. A more intensive process started in Augustus 2013 with a series of interviews and observations (second stage of the research). I dedicated a large amount of time to the whole study. Writing the book and fine tuning the theory until theoretical saturation was experienced also took a large amount of time (third stage of the research).

I have spent about 3 days during office hours (mainly 8:30 am–5:00 pm) in a month during the period of September and December at the Buurtzorg Headquarters. The days and periods were not fixed providing me the opportunity to get a good representative view. I spent this time learning about Buurtzorg, working on the research, participating during a selection of meetings, reporting the interviewed data, and observing the organization dynamics was beneficial to my study. In addition to this, interviews were scheduled either outside the office at convenience places for the interviewees and in a few cases at the Headquarters.

The General Process in the CGT

The general process of CGT as was applied in this study consisted of several iterative steps of coding, sorting, writing and theoretical sampling until theoretical saturation was achieved, concluding with a final substantive theory on Integrating Simplification. The main steps are mentioned in the following paragraphs (See also Fig. A.1):

I started my interviews with open questions to the respondents to formulate the main concern. In the open interviews I wanted to know what they were doing at

© Springer International Publishing Switzerland 2015
S.S. Nandram, *Organizational Innovation by Integrating Simplification*,
Management for Professionals, DOI 10.1007/978-3-319-11725-6

Buurtzorg, about their position and some background about themselves but mainly about their actual activities and their vision on Buurtzorg. I collected additional data with more open questions and used open coding for the data. Once I even entered a few offices at the Headquarters and I ask the employees to fill in a few open questions mainly to express what their activities were for that day and for whom they were doing them.

The open coding with the open questions resulted in the main concern of the study: The main concern in the study was: *'what does an organization do, to deliver services that are fulfilling the client's/customer's needs and how does it design and organize its activities for realizing a client/customer focused service'*.

I collected a new round of additional data through interviews, reading the Buurtzorgweb, attending several visits to clients and meetings with coaches and teams. During the whole process of memoing and conducting several types of coding I worked at my home office after daily meditation and yogic practices to stimulate a relaxed physical state and an open mind. This process was deliberately done outside the Buurtzorg office to avoid getting stimuli or information which could influence the coding process. During the initial stages of the process, memos with reflective ideas were documented also based on observations.

> This resulted in the identification of the core category that solved the main concern on a client care focus. The core category that occurred is Integrating Simplification.

Again additional data was collected (Theoretical Sampling). During this process additional data was gathered mainly in regard to the core category (Selective Coding). They occurred during visits to the Headquarters, when visiting the virtual platform and in meetings with the founder and co-founder or by meeting those who were interviewed for clarifications. Theoretical saturation was reached at the level of the core concepts. Subsequently sorting was done. Several write-ups of the concepts on big sheets of papers were done. It turned out that the core category occurred at several dimensions or levels.

> This resulted in a first draft of the theory and the steps: needing, rethinking, common-sensing. And the several dimensions were included as well in the write-up.

Additional data was collected (theoretical sampling) and theoretical coding was done for each dimension. Theoretical saturation at the level of the theoretical codes occurred. This led to sorting again.

> This resulted in enriching the model with relationships between the concepts. It occurred that there is a process model for integrating simplification with main principles following a simple process. This process seemed to occur at five dimensions: Client Attunement, Subtle Craftsmanship, Intrapreneurial Team Freedom, Pragmatic Will with ICT and Leading Higher Purpose.

Another stage of theoretical sampling was conducted and for each dimension the lower level concepts and their properties were written down in a draft based on the pile of memos, one by one while staying at the abstract level. A validation was built to reflect on the findings with coaches, team members, founder and relevant stakeholders, such as experts from Ecare, the creative thinker and a few nurses.

The result was the first draft of the Theory of Integrating Simplification containing its general principles of the process at the level of each dimension.

Only following this literature studied and sorting was done for each dimension or core concepts of the theory, followed by this same approach for the theory in general including its process.

This resulted in enriching, modifying, integrating, positioning of the theory with the literature in organizational innovation and organizational theory. In the book, the theory has been described without including the literature (in Chap. 3) and again after a reflection on the literature (Chap. 9). This was done to keep enough space for 'non-pollution' by non-preconception of literature input and determining a position within the mainstream literature on organization theory.

Additional data such as: reports on client and employee surveys, web blogs, meetings with two coaches, supervisory board meeting, attendance of the Congress Day at Buurtzorg, interview with the founder's mother and two additional meetings with the founder (theoretical sampling), contributed as a form of validation which resulted in writing the substantive theory. Theoretical saturation at the level of the theory was reached which resulted in *the final substantive theory on Integrating Simplification.*

Appendix D Ancient Views on Subtle Knowledge

Table D.1 Ancient western views on subtle knowledge

Philosophic perspective	Definition of intuition/subtle knowledge
1. Prehistoric and ancient literate societies	Intuitive insights or experiences were regarded as messages from the gods or evidence of the exceptional powers of the seer or oracle (Noddings and Shore 1984, p. 4). The aim was making predictions
2. Chinese Yarrow Stick	Non-rational associations and spontaneous insights gained during performing the ritual of I Ching (Noddings and Shore 1984, p. 4). It was used for understanding the interplay between human insights and physical reality
3. Greeks and Romans	Non-rational sources of knowledge (Noddings and Shore 1984, p. 6)
	It was used for solving real life problems and making connection with the non-material world
4. Pythagoras	A combination of astrology and mathematics leading to the notion that numbers existing in an intuitively apprehended realm, could yield profound knowledge about the universe that was unavailable elsewhere (Noddings and Shore 1984, p. 6)
	It was used for understanding the universe
5. Socrates	Good spirit (Noddings and Shore 1984, p. 6) that guides actions at critical moments
7. Greek philosophy	Knowledge from a vision, an insight or a dream (Noddings and Shore 1984, p. 6)
	It aimed developing views on science, arts, philosophy
8. Plato	Intuition as a reliable source of knowledge (Noddings and Shore 1984, p. 7)
	It was used for developing his ideas on ultimate reality. In his work Republic he used his own intuition about the nature of mankind and society
9. Aristotle	Knowledge that exists without proof which he calls intuitive reason. It is a leap of understanding, a grasping of a larger concept reachable by other intellectual means, yet still fundamentally an intellectual process (Noddings and Shore 1984, p. 7)
	He argued that to begin deductive reasoning, an intuitively

(continued)

© Springer International Publishing Switzerland 2015
S.S. Nandram, *Organizational Innovation by Integrating Simplification*,
Management for Professionals, DOI 10.1007/978-3-319-11725-6

Table D.1 (continued)

Philosophic perspective	Definition of intuition/subtle knowledge
	known truth or an inductive empirical one is needed. He believed that this is ranked above the universals of science and is indispensable for scientific inquiry "No other kind of thought except intuition is more accurate than scientific knowledge" (Noddings, Shore 1984, p. 7)
10. Plotinus	True knowledge is obtained through a special kind of seeing. "To see and to have seen is no longer reason. It is greater than reason, before reason, and above reason, as is also the desire to see... Therefore what is seen is indeed difficult to convey: for how can a man describe as other than himself that which, when he perceived it, seemed not other, but indeed one with himself?" Nodding, Shore 1984, p. 8) The observer has the sensation of union with the object that he or she is contacting
11. Cynics school	Intuitionism: the belief that knowledge of the morally good is directly apprehended by intuition. This is the instinctive sense of what is right and therefore ought not to be confined by laws or conventions of society (Noddings and Shore 1984, p. 9) For this school it was important for creating an ethical system emphasizing virtue
12. Epicurus	Anticipations that give us knowledge with which to evaluate life experiences (Noddings and Shore 1984, p. 9) Intuition served to deal with reactions of the universe
13. Augustine and Aquinas	Spiritual revelation that is non-rational and therefore could be considered an intuitive experience. Intuition is a product of contemplation rather than a distinct way of knowing the real world (Noddings and Shore 1984, p. 11)
14. William of Ockham	Intuitive Cognition: the ability to picture that which is not perceived by the senses (Noddings and Shore 1984, p. 12) He allowed for intuition of non-existing objects (such as ideal objects) through the agency of God
15 Nostradamus	A persistent belief in a seer (Noddings and Shore 1984, p.13) Here again it was used for making predictions
16. Descartes	Rational intuition was the only way to gain certain knowledge. "Intuitive knowledge is an illumination of the soul, whereby it beholds in the light of God those things which it pleases Him to reveal to us by a direct impression of divine clarity in our understanding which in this is not considered as an agent, but only as receiving the rays of divinity" (Noddings and Shore 1984, p. 13) For him it helped to get to better conclusions
17. Spinoza	Intuition is a category in a tripartite division of all knowledge; the others are apprehension and rational thought (Noddings and Shore 1984, p. 13) Intuition was helpful to gain knowledge that is clear and sure and associated with standard knowledge and divorced from mysticism
18. Immanuel Kant	Non-rational recognition and awareness of individual entities. It was linked to sensual perception which is a necessary part of the

(continued)

Table D.1 (continued)

Philosophic perspective	Definition of intuition/subtle knowledge
	whole mental process. He defined two forms of pure sensible intuition: space (Raum) and time (Zeit) (Noddings and Shore 1984, p. 14) Intuition is a source of object knowledge "Without sensibility, no object would be given to us, without understanding no object would be thought, thoughts without content are empty, intuitions without concepts are blind." (Noddings and Shore 1984, p. 15)
19. Jacques Rousseau	Pedagogical intuitionism based on the idea that our true feelings are smothered in us while we are young by the rigorous instruction that children receive (Noddings and Shore 1984, p. 15). It aimed to express our own nature
20. Schleiermacher	"This principle (the intuition of the world) is concerned not only with scientific knowledge, but is the foundation of all intuition and is insofar really the principle of religion, where all knowledge is posited as an intuition of God or in God" (Noddings and Shore 1984, p. 17) He used it as an attempt to link religion and science
21. Vicenzo Gioberti	Knowledge was basically intuitive and in intuition the subject apprehended the object immediately, with no operations performed by subject or object (Noddings and Shore 1984, p. 17) Intuition was learning as a spontaneous event without formalized operations
22. Serafino Sordi	Human ideas are in reality ideas existing only in the divine mind. Intuition is an act, performed by either the subject or the object (Noddings and Shore 1984, p. 17) It is an image in the intuitive person's mind even if the idea has its origin in God
23. Romantics and Pre-Raphaelites	A non-rational way to illumination (Noddings and Shore 1984, p. 19)
24. Schopenhauer	Representations within the human mind (Noddings and Shore 1984, p. 20) It was seen as helping in the quest for meaning in life
25. Heinrich Pestalozzi	The conversion of sense impression into knowledge (Noddings and Shore 1984, p. 20) It was used for stressing the relationships of objects for a clearer understanding
26. Froebel	Intuition will develop by simple concrete objects being presented to the child at the right moment (Noddings and Shore 1984, p. 21) He stressed the psychical context as stimulator of intuitive thinking
27. Henri Bergson	Just as life precedes matter in its reality, intuition precedes intellect (Noddings and Shore 1984, p. 21) Only by entering through feeling into unison with the world of reality one can acquire real truth about it (Noddings and Shore 1984, p. 22)

(continued)

Table D.1 (continued)

Philosophic perspective	Definition of intuition/subtle knowledge
	It was meant for getting a deeper understanding of reality than can be obtained from analyzing data
28. Jung	A function that transmits perceptions meaningfully but unconsciously (Noddings and Shore 1984, p. 25) Jung introduced it for understanding human types
29. Berne	An unconscious source of knowledge, distinguishing it from three other ways of rendering judgments. It is clinical intuition: knowledge based on experience and acquired through the senses (Noddings and Shore 1984, p. 27) He mainly used it in psychiatry
30. Benedetto Croce	Intuition as an artistic faculty
31. Husserl	"A source of authority for knowledge, that whatever presents itself in 'intuition' in primordial form (as it were in its bodily reality), is simply to be accepted as it gives itself out to be, though only within the limits in which it then presents itself" (Noddings and Shore 1984, p. 31)
32. Satre	Non-reflective consciousness (Noddings and Shore 1984, p. 31)
33. Alfred North Whitehead	Intuitive mode: the stage where knowledge is not dominated by systematic procedure (Noddings and Shore 1984, p. 28)
34. Bertrand Lord Russell	Logical intuitions are propositional functions for explaining mathematical entities (Noddings and Shore 1984, p. 28)
35. Butler and James McCosh	Dogmatic intuitionism: it is possible to know intuitively the rightness or wrongness of whole classes of notions or motives (Noddings and Shore 1984, p. 33)
36. Gestalt from Max Wertheimer	Logic itself may not hold the key to the solution of some problems. Instead; association, recollection and an intuitive sense of 'rightness' frequently lead to successful problem solving strategies (Noddings and Shore 1984, p. 35)
37. Bruner	"Intuition implies the act of grasping the meaning, significance or structure of a problem without explicit reliance on the analytic apparatus of one's craft." (Noddings and Shore 1984, p. 37)
38. Fuller	Is the principal tool of humankind in all of its endeavors, it is a positive force that can benefit individuals and society as a whole, and he believes intuition has spiritual content (Noddings and Shore 1984, p. 37)

Epilogue

This book has addressed a qualitative research methodology allowing the Respondents to talk to the reader through me as an author in explaining what they do when putting their clients at the center of their main activities and processes in the organization. I have tried to clarify the theoretical concepts that were drawn from the findings, by using citations from the interviews with the Respondents. Integrating Simplification emerged as the core category of their client care focus. There was a moment while analyzing the findings, when I felt the story needs to be completed by interviewing the mother of the founder of Buurtzorg in addition to the interviews I had with him and the employees of Buurtzorg. The results of this interview are presented in the next section.

I also noticed the broad interest that is being shown by international practitioners and community change agents. Two internationals (Mona and Michele) will briefly explain why they think the Buurtzorg approach could be interesting for implementing in their home countries. Furthermore I have asked the language editor, Shari, who has been helping me with the edits for this book, to give her impressions on the organization. During the editing process at several times, she has mentioned how inspiring the story was. Having dealt with severe injuries and as a consequence receiving treatments both in Canada and the Netherlands she has experienced the Health Care Industry and therefore could place herself in the role of the client. These expressions are presented in the second section of this epilogue.

E.1 About the Founder of Buurtzorg

The author felt that the founder was an important enabler for the pattern that was uncovered in the activities and business processes of Integrating Simplification. In interviews with the founder she could not find a dominant influence for his way of thinking that was hailing from a particular management school of thought, or a philosophical school of thought. It seems as if his tendency towards simplifying, while integrating what is around him, was mainly balancing between activities and aims. It turned out as a natural flow in the way he approaches issues, generates new ideas and starts activities. In that natural flow he entrains or takes along with him many people he works with, who get attuned to his vision and approach on the

© Springer International Publishing Switzerland 2015
S.S. Nandram, *Organizational Innovation by Integrating Simplification*,
Management for Professionals, DOI 10.1007/978-3-319-11725-6

higher goal that the organization has. His own working experiences seemed to have influenced his drive towards reforming community care, a higher goal that works at Buurtzorg.

From the discipline of psychology we know that such high goals do not occur all of a sudden. Even while the workplace influences such a drive, it is assumed that such drives may have been developed during his early years of life. To understand this, I turned to the work of one of the dominant developmental psychological theories, Identity Theory of Erik Erikson. He was the first who developed an eight stage human developmental model which suggests that an individual is facing a certain turning point or crisis that he needs to cope with for moving to a next stage (Erikson 1968, p. 96). In each stage a person develops a dominant basic strength such as hope, will, purpose, competence, fidelity, love, care and wisdom. And in each stage a person has a main existential question. These are in the sequence of the stages: Can I trust the world (0–2 years)? Is it okay to be me (2–4 years)? Is it okay for me to move and act (4–5 years)? Can I make it in this world (5–12 years)? Who am I (13–19 years)? Can I love (20–24 years)? Can I make my life count (25–64 years)? Is it okay to have been me (65 years–death)?

In the instance of the founder of Buurtzorg, the drive of reforming community care could be related to the existential question 'can I make it in this world' which, according to the Identity Theory, was formed at the stage of school between 5 and 12 years where the basic strength of competence is being developed. He recalls the following from his school age which relates to how he started to become aware of his competences and how this influenced his self-confidence. When in primary school he noticed that he was a bright student, he often got bored in the class and could not stay attuned to the teacher's expectations. In his own words:

> It started in the fifth class of the primary school. Two schools in our village merged and became one new school. As of then my tests results were higher than ever before. I started getting usually only A's and I often had the best scores of my class. It was as if I awoke from a sleep. My behavior started to change as well. Due to my results I became self-confident and dared to talk more; could express things more easily if I had an opinion and I experienced some classes as very boring. I easily got distracted and had many associations of more interesting things. As a result I could not stay quiet, as was expected, during classes. Teachers felt that I was disturbing the class, I was chattering too much, and as a result I got punished with detention work. Very often I had to write down the word 'chatter' five hundred times. This happened a few times a week. This attitude continued when I entered high school. And there I was also punished and I recall that I was suspended from school three times. In the last year of my high school I was suspended from various classes. Still if I look back, I believe I was not really tiresome. . . .

The founder showed unique characteristics during his school years. The other important existential question is 'who am I' which according to Erikson's theory was formed at the age of 13 up to 19 years where the basic strength of fidelity is being developed. His ideas about who he is were shaped during the ages of 13–19 when he started to form his own belief system. A main aspect was his concern for humanity and his altruistic attitude (see Chap. 2). The following quote from him expresses this well:

During primary school I was already pondering on 'issues on injustice in the world'. During high school my views on societal issues developed more. I always wanted to discuss and participated in debates about several of these issues but at the same time I wanted to have fun at school. I had a nice time at high school. Actually my ideas about the community issues and the health industry mainly started to develop after high school. I think when I was in my twenties.

Interviewing the founder, only about these stages, may not give a complete picture. Interviewing his mother provided additional insights. These are presented in a summary of quotes in the box. Here follows a few patterns that were found in the interview. The interview revealed that the way he runs Buurtzorg resembles how things were at home. The nature to simplify the world around him already occurred when he was at the age of 8 and decided to do the groceries for his parents in the next village, each Saturday. He was already aware of things other children at that age might not even think of. He noticed that the groceries over there were much cheaper. Being frugal with resources is an important attitude of him. He was the only one in the family who took the responsibility to do the groceries.

Another interesting feature was his position in the family. He is positioned at the center in the family: he has one older sister, one older brother and two younger brothers. Being in the middle gives him a lot of strength. It put him in the position to learn how to balance between several views in the family: when to be strict and when to let go (the Yogic Leadership attitude). When he was still living at home, he had the tendency to mobilize his siblings and felt responsible for being at the center. He also had an altruistic attitude, was a problem solver, was handling things in a pragmatic way and was carrying the feeling of being responsible for others. These characteristics are present still today in his drive to reform community care. In his view both of his parents had an influence on him in shaping his worldview regarding injustice and societal responsibility. Perhaps it was his mother who had influenced him in developing an interest for health care. Perhaps, based on how she handles situations, she has taught him that the world and reality around us can be constructed and should not be treated as a static factor out there. Perhaps this fuelled the idea in him that the world is not *"either-or; yes-but"*. It is rather *"YES-AND; YES-IF"*: the Yogic Leadership attitude.

Box E.1 Excerpt of Interview

Jos is a people person and he is engaged with people's lives. He is interested in how people live and how to improve their lives; he feels sorry for disadvantaged persons. He is not an active devout anymore but I can see how he expresses 'service to others' as a core principle in his work and life.

In the family he is the middle of my five children and it is as if he pulls along everyone with him. He always cared a lot about his siblings and other family members. He feels responsible for others. I think my bit of influence on him is his interest for caring. Everyone in the family except his Dad has work

(continued)

Box E.1 (continued)

that is related to caring for others or service to others. His Dad was a role model for him when it came to his determination, courage and taking responsibility. Actually everyone here has that but somehow Jos has developed that much stronger. Everyone could knock on our door for any kind of help. Both of us were willing to help solving other's problems. I think Jos has seen that from us and experienced how many people felt at ease and at home here.

His Dad was strongly against injustice and Jos has developed this as well. He wants people to be treated well and with justice. He was at an age of 8 or 9 when he started to go for groceries on his small bike at the next village because they were much cheaper. No one else did that but for Jos these things were important. He did this every Saturday. Nowadays as a parent you would not allow your child to travel to another village on his bike at that age. A lot has changed; the world has become very unsafe for children.

Sometimes I think he is too altruistic. He is always willing to help others. All of us at home have that but Jos has a stronger urge to be there for others. When I talk to him on the phone I always want to remind him of not forgetting himself and that he should not overreach himself. If it were up to him he would change the world.

He has a very warm character. For many years he is vegetarian and if he visits us I think carefully what dishes I should prepare. When he was living here, he would easily go and prepare fries for guests. But also when we visited him and he had a young family he was often busy taking care of them, doing the wash or any other activity in the household. He is also very skillful in several other things. Once he restored his house by himself. Nowadays he doesn't have time for such things. When he was a student he was helping people in filling in their tax return forms. He doesn't care about clothes or protocols about how he should dress in the external world. He doesn't like business suits and as far as I can recall he only wore a formal suit during his holy communion. That was a tradition in those days. Then we also called him 'gentleman'. He wants to be true to himself and actually all of us are true to ourselves and I find that an important value.

When there are conflicts he will seek dialogues. Actually he gets along well with everyone but if he doesn't like a person it is mainly because the other is too stubborn or wants to dominate over him or over others and then Jos will either point it out or at times he will avoid contacting such a person.

It is very smart what he has achieved with Buurtzorg. It is very nice to have a Buurtzorg team in our village too and so now and then I hear from others what they think of Buurtzorg. Sometimes Jos sends me newspaper articles or interviews with him about Buurtzorg and its success. I try to keep myself informed about Buurtzorg. It seems like Jos is able to achieve everything he

(continued)

> **Box E.1** (continued)
> *aims with Buurtzorg. With the inauguration of the new office for the Head-quarters I have seen how warmly he socializes with other people. Also in such situations he stays calm while I become nervous. Whatever meeting he enters or whatever achievement he realizes, Jos remains Jos. And that is very good and I know he is able to realize many things but sometimes I wonder whether going abroad with the concept is not too much for him. Without his partner Gonnie he would not have been as successful I think because she contributes a lot to Buurtzorg".*
> (Vogelwaarde, Mother De Blok, 29th May 2014).

E.2 On Buurtzorg by Internationals

E.2.1 Buurtzorg Abroad: Change Agents' Views

It is not so easy to explain everything with a few words.... Why I think the Buurtzorg model is relevant for Sweden is that we have the same fragmentation as you had in Holland before. The elderly have too many different people coming to their homes and they never get to know them well. And the education level is too low and many people who are working in the homecare can't speak Swedish very well and the elderly can't communicate with them. Too many elderly are going to the hospital when it's not needed.

My inspiration to implement Buurtzorg in Sweden was because I worked in a team in Holland before and I knew how good the Buurtzorg concept worked. I knew there was a big difference between the Buurtzorg concept and other big organizations. We have now two teams in two different municipalities here in Sweden and it's working very well. Only the financial part is difficult because of the Swedish system. The payment from the municipalities is too low to have only highly educated nurses. I have had many discussions with politicians and they know the problem, so I hope they are going to do something about it. I think it will take some time for them to understand that in the end it will be cheaper for the whole country to have better home care with well-educated nurses who can prevent all the unnecessary visits by the house doctors and the hospital.

Mona Lindström Leg.sjuksköterska/Verksamhetschef
Grannvård Sverige AB

In 2017, more than 50 % of the population of the United States will be over the age of 50, and yet the U.S. is inadequately prepared to address what is expected to be an enormous demand for long-term care services. A fragmented system delivers uneven quality across a wide variety of services—from nursing homes to assisted living facilities to home care and more—that are often extremely expensive, inadequately staffed and not easily accessible.

Studies have shown that home care is the most preferred option by all ages in need of non-acute or post-acute health care services, whether it is recovering from a hospital stay, managing a chronic condition, or simply dealing with the affects of aging. It is also the least expensive, and yet both private and public insurers continue to focus higher reimbursement levels as a percentage of funding on institutional care.

In recent years, key U.S. policymakers and long-term care advocates at both the federal and state levels have been looking for solutions. First introduced to the Buurtzorg model as I worked to improve long-term care services for older Americans in Minnesota, I found it immediately intriguing. Could the promise of higher quality home care at a lower cost already realized by this nurse-led innovation in the Netherlands be achieved here in the United States?

We are about to find out. Together with Buurtzorg's first team of nurses in Stillwater, Minnesota, I am excited to be working to implement Buurtzorg's model of community nursing here in the United States. A simple proven concept that works beautifully can be the answer to the problems created by a complex fragmented system. I believe this—and many colleagues at both the state and national level representing important patient and health care organizations believe this, too. The Buurtzorg model of neighborhood nursing can potentially change health care delivery for millions of Americans and provide what is truly needed—higher quality at lower costs from a dedicated, professional workforce. Home care the way it was meant to be.

Michele H. Kimball is the Co-Founder and CEO of Buurtzorg USA.

E.2.2 Language Editor's Impressions

While reading this book I have been taken on a journey of education, inspiration, insight and hope. The book introduces many technical management terms, theories and ideologies meanwhile humanizing the concepts and the values they represent, in perspective of a successful business model, Buurtzorg Nederland. There were times in this book, when I felt overwhelming emotion by the input from founders, clients, employees and the author, Sharda Nandram's observations and other times when my mind just absorbed the principles, philosophies and lessons. We all face challenges in life and health over the years, as we get older I am sure there will be more to encounter, but learning about Buurtzorg gives me a little peace of mind and hope about the future I age into. The ambition to not only inspire and change the community healthcare industry but actually create a working model, with client focus and professional care and take that into a 'caring community of care' is remarkable. The pride and determination Mr. de Blok and team invest with true passion and belief in humanity is powerful and proving successful. Many people have power, many have beliefs; few have the power to believe they can make a difference and are willing to share their will and help others, help them to make it happen. I would say that Buurtzorg's aim to create a 'healthcare community that cares and provides the best possible care' is a higher purpose that must succeed.

Shari Leibbrandt-Demmon

About the Author

Dr. Sharda S. Nandram, born in Suriname, Person of Indian Origin from Jodhpur, Rajasthan, India and resident of the Netherlands as of 1985. Sharda is Associate Professor at Nyenrode Business University and founder of Praan Solutions. She has earned two bachelors and two masters (one in Psychology and the other in Economics (both at the University of Amsterdam). She has also earned her PhD in Social Sciences at the Vrije University at Amsterdam. Her topics of interests are: entrepreneurship, organizational innovation, spirituality in management and Indian leadership. In her former positions she was professor of Entrepreneurship at the HAN University of Applied Sciences and Senior Researcher at the Nyenrode Forum for Economic Research. She is member of the steering committee of the European SPES Institute; supervisor of SJOAL (new perspectives on entrepreneurial education) and advisor to Skerpe Jeugd (mental development of young athletes). Her two other books at Springer are: The Spirit of Entrepreneurship (Nandram and Samsom 2006); Spirituality and Business (Nandram and Borden 2010).

© Springer International Publishing Switzerland 2015
S.S. Nandram, *Organizational Innovation by Integrating Simplification*,
Management for Professionals, DOI 10.1007/978-3-319-11725-6

Review of the Book by Scholars

Enjoy this book on one of the most talked about and innovative cases in community care: the successful and award winning practice of Buurtzorg.

Insights are shared in the development of entrepreneurial professionals and in the functioning of self-managing teams at Buurtzorg. Some 8000 professionals working in about 700 teams are driven by their values, guided by no more than 2 managers. Operational co-ordination is done with the help of sophisticated I-Pad based software and internal governance is extremely simplified by building on trust and a collective ambition. There is only one simple focus: the wellbeing of the client.

Prof. Dr. Mathieu Weggeman, professor of Organization Science and Organizational Innovation at Eindhoven University of Technology, the Netherlands.

All grounded theories are asymptotic, that is as close to perfection as possible. Sharda has come very close to achieving a perfect Grounded Theory, especially for her first effort at Grounded Theory research. Read well and enjoy the conceptual level and integration of concepts!

Barney G, Glaser, PhD, Hon. PhD
Founder of the Classical Grounded Theory Methodology, USA.

There is a tendency to conclude that if a theory isn't working there must be something wrong with reality. Not reality is wrong but theoretical foundations on the model of man needs reconsideration as they do not fit today's reality. This book plays an important role through developing the Integrating Simplification Theory and in a lucid and convincing way, it shows how constructing reality based on different sources and processes of knowledge results in new organization creation.

Prof. Ikujiro Nonaka, Leading scholar in the field of knowledge management, Japan.

This book written by Sharda Nandram offers a distinctive concept of management that can be universally used in founding or transforming organizations, initiating social change or encouraging innovation.

Integrating Simplification framework is interesting as it has seamlessly combined the Eastern and Western philosophies to explain human principles of organizing the reality around us. The book has truly brought out the "art of management" by clearly laying out a framework revolving around the holistic

© Springer International Publishing Switzerland 2015   213
S.S. Nandram, *Organizational Innovation by Integrating Simplification,*
Management for Professionals, DOI 10.1007/978-3-319-11725-6

aspect of problem solving by deftly delving into social relationship of individuals while maintaining the autonomy of the individual.

Dr. Madhumita Chatterji, Director

Chairperson- Centre for Social Entrepreneurship and Management, IFIM Business School, India

Sharda Nandram's book on Buurtzorg, an exemplary health care organization in The Netherlands, clearly shows that true client-centeredness and genuine care in a service organization require adopting a holistic perspective and employing intrinsic motivation. The humanistic leadership of Buurtzorg has been influenced by the Yoga Philosophy which transcends the duality of matter and spirit as well as the duality of self and others. The result is the emergence of radical simplicity in organizational structure and functioning. The book is a fascinating analysis of a fascinating case.

Laszlo Zsolnai, Professor and Director, Business Ethics Center, Corvinus University of Budapest, Hungary and President European SPES Institute, Leuven, Belgium.

References

Adams, J. S. (1965). Inequity in social exchange. In L. Berkowitz (Ed.), *Advances in experimental social psychology*. New York, NY: Academic.

Adams, R., & Thompson, M. J. (2013). *Suited monk leadership: Leading with wisdom and purpose in a complex and uncertain world*. London: WOW Books.

Adizes, I. (1979). Organizational passages—diagnosing and treating lifecycle problems of organizations. *Organizational Dynamics, 8*(1), 3–25.

Altinay, L. (2005). The intrapreneur role of the development directors in an international hotel group. *The Service Industries Journal, 25*(3), 403–419.

Ancona, D., & Chong, C. L. (1996). Entrainment: Pace, cycle and rhythm in organizational behavior. In B. M. Staw & L. L. Cummings (Eds.), *Research in organizational behavior* (Vol. 18, pp. 251–284). Greenwich, CT: Jai Press.

Antoncic, B., & Hisrich, R. D. (2001). Intrapreneurship: Construct refinement and cross-cultural validation. *Journal of Business Venturing, 16*(5), 495–527.

Archer, D. (1985). Social deviancy. In G. Lindzey & E. Aronson (Eds.), *The handbook of social psychology* (Vol. 2, pp. 413–483). New York, NY: Random House.

Argyris, C. (1973). Organization man: Rational and self-actualizing. *Public Administration Review, 33*(4), 354–357.

Aschoff, J. (1979). Circadian rhythms: General features and endocrinological aspects. In D. Krieger (Ed.), *Endocrine rhythms* (pp. 1–61). New York, NY: Raven Press.

Ashmos, D. P., & Duchon, D. (2000). Spirituality at work: A conceptualization and measure. *Journal of Management Inquiry, 9*(2), 134–145.

Aurobindo, S. (2007). *The synthesis of yoga* (Fifth impressionth ed.). Pondicherry: Sri Aurobindo Ashram Trust.

Baker, L. T. (2007). *The relationship between mindfulness, strategic decision process and small business performance*. Dissertation Abstracts International.

Bandsuch, M. R., & Cavanagh, G. F. (2002). Virtue as a benchmark for spirituality in business. *Journal of Business Ethics, 38*, 109–117.

Bandura, A. (1977). *Social learning theory*. Englewood Cliffs, NJ: Prentice-Hall.

Barrett, R. (2013). *Liberating the corporate soul*. London: Routledge.

Barrick, M. R., Mount, M. K., & Li, N. (2013). The theory of purposeful work behavior: The role of personality, higher-order goals, and job characteristics. *Academy of Management Review, 38* (1), 132–153.

Bass, B. (1985). *Leadership and performance beyond expectations*. New York, NY: Free Press.

Bass, B. M. (1990). From transactional to transformational leadership: Learning to share the vision. *Organizational Dynamics, winter*, 19–31.

Bass, B., & Avolio, B. (1994). Transformational leadership and organizational culture. *International Journal of Public Administration, 17*, 112–121.

Becker, G. S. (1976). *The economic approach to human behavior*. Chicago, IL: University of Chicago Press.

© Springer International Publishing Switzerland 2015   215
S.S. Nandram, *Organizational Innovation by Integrating Simplification*,
Management for Professionals, DOI 10.1007/978-3-319-11725-6

Benefiel, M. (2005). The second half of the journey: Spiritual leadership for organizational transformation. *The Leadership Quarterly, 16*, 723–741.

Bentz, V. M., & Shapiro, J. J. (1998). *Mindful inquiry in social research.* Thousand Oaks, CA: Sage.

Bhal, K. T., & Debnath, N. (2006). Conceptualizing and measuring gunas. Predictors of workplace ethics of Indian professionals. *International Journal of Cross Cultural Management, 6*(2), 169–188.

Biberman, J., & Tischler, L. (Eds.). (2008). *Spirituality in business: Theory, practice, and future directions.* New York, NY: Macmillan.

Biberman, J., & Whitty, M. (1997). A postmodern spiritual future of wok. *Journal of Organizational Change Management, 10*(2), 130–138.

Birkinshaw, J., Hamel, G., & Mol, M. J. (2008). Management innovation. *Academy of Management Review, 33*(4), 825–845.

Block, J. (1982). Assimilation, accommodation, and the dynamics of personality development. *Child Development, 53*, 281–295.

Block, P. (1996). *Stewardship: Choosing service over self-interest.* San Francisco, CA: Berrett-Koehler.

Bluedorn, A. C. (2002). *The human organization of time. Temporal realities and experience.* Stanford, CA: Stanford University Press.

Boeker, W., & Karichalil, R. (2002). Entrepreneurial transitions: Factors influencing founder departure. *Academy of Management Journal, 45*, 818–826.

Borch, O. J., Huse, M., & Senneseth, K. (1999). Resource configuration, competitive strategies, and corporate entrepreneurship: An empirical examination of small firms. *Entrepreneurship: Theory and Practice, 24*(1), 49–70.

Bouckaert, L., Opdebeeck, H., & Zsolnai, L. (Eds.). (2008). *Frugality: Rebalancing material and spiritual values in economic life* (Vol. 4). Bren: Peter Lang.

Burgelman, R. A. (1983). Corporate entrepreneurship and strategic management: Insights from a process study. *Management Science, 29*(12), 1349–1364.

Burns, J. M. (1978). *Leadership.* New York, NY: Harper and Row.

Caldwell, C., Hayes, L. A., Bernal, P., & Karri, R. (2008). Ethical stewardship–implications for leadership and trust. *Journal of Business Ethics, 78*(1–2), 153–164.

Chakraborty, S. K., & Chakraborty, D. (2008). *Spirituality in management: Means or end?* New York, NY: Oxford University Press.

Chesbrough, H. W. (2003). *Open innovation: The new imperative for creating and profiting from technology.* Boston, MA: Harvard Business Press.

Chesbrough, H. W. (2006). The era of open innovation. *Managing Innovation and Change, 127*(3), 34–41.

Chesbrough, H. (2012). Why companies should have open business models. *MIT Sloan Management Review, 48*(2).

Colquitt, J. A., & Zapata-Phelan, C. P. (2007). Trends in theory building and theory testing: A five-decade study of the Academy of Management Journal. *Academy of Management Journal, 50*(6), 1281–1303.

Cooper, A. (1981). Strategic management: New ventures and small business. *Long Range Planning, 14*(5), 39–45.

Coutu, D. L. (2003). Sense and reliability: A conversation with celebrated psychologist Karl E. Weick. *Harvard Business Review, 18*, 84–90.

Covin, J. G., & Slevin, D. P. (1986). The development and testing of an organizational-level entrepreneurship scale. *Frontiers of Entrepreneurship Research, 1*(1986), 626–639.

Covin, J. G., & Slevin, D. P. (1989). Strategic management of small firms in hostile and benign environments. *Strategic Management Journal, 10*(1), 75–87.

Covin, J. G., & Slevin, D. P. (1991). A conceptual model of entrepreneurship as firm behavior. *Entrepreneurship Theory and Practice, 16*(1), 7–25.

Currie, G., Humphreys, M., Ucbasaran, D., & McManus, S. (2008). Entrepreneurial leadership in the English public sector: Paradox or possibility? *Public Administration, 86*(4), 987–1008.

Dane, E., & Pratt, M. G. (2007). Exploring intuition and its role in managerial decision making. *Academy of Management Review, 32*(1), 33–54.

Davis, J. H., Schoorman, F. D., & Donaldson, L. (1997). Toward a stewardship theory of management. *Academy of Management Review, 22*(1), 20–47.

De Blok, J. (2011). Buurtzorg nederland: A new perspective on elder care in the Netherlands. *AARP international the Journal* (Summer).

De Blok, J., & Pool, A. (2010). *Buurtzorg: Menselijkheid boven bureaucratie.* Den Haag: Boom Lemma uitgevers.

Deci, E. L. (1971). Effects of externally mediated rewards on intrinsic motivation. *Journal of Personality and Social Psychology, 1971*(18), 105–115.

Deci, E. L., & Ryan, R. M. (2000). The 'what' and 'why' of goal pursuits: Human needs and the self-determination of behavior. *Psychological Inquiry, 11*, 227–268.

Dent, E. B., Higgins, M. E., & Wharff, D. M. (2005). Spirituality and leadership: An empirical review of definitions, distinctions, and embedded assumptions. *The Leadership Quarterly, 16* (5), 619–622.

Eisenhardt, K. M. (1985). Control: Organizational and economic approaches. *Management Science, 31*(2), 134–149.

Erikson, E. (1968). *Youth: Identity and crisis.* New York, NY: W. W. Norton.

Ertel, C., & Solomon, L. K. (2014). *Moments of impact: How to design strategic conversations that accelerate change.* New York, NY: Simon and Schuster.

European Commission. (2006). *Key competences for lifelong learning. European reference framework* (p. 12). Luxembourg: Office for Official Publications of the European Communities.

Festinger, L. A. (1957). *Theory of cognitive dissonance.* Stanford, CA: Stanford University Press.

Fry, L. W. (2003). Toward a theory of spiritual leadership. *The Leadership Quarterly, 14*, 693–727.

Fry, L. W. (2005). Introduction to the leadership quarterly special issue: Toward a paradigm of spiritual leadership. *The Leadership Quarterly, 16*, 619–622.

Fry, L., & Kriger, M. (2009). Towards a theory of being-centered leadership: Multiple levels of being as context for effective leadership. *Human Relations, 62*(11), 1667–1696.

Fry, L., & Nisiewicz, M. (2013). *Maximizing the triple bottom line through spiritual leadership.* Stanford, CA: Stanford University Press.

Fry, L. W., & Slocum, J. W., Jr. (2008). Maximizing the triple bottom line through spiritual leadership. *Organizational Dynamics, 37*(1), 86–96.

Gergen, K. (1999). *An invitation to social construction.* Newbury Park, CA: Sage.

Giacalone, R. A., & Jurkiewicz, C. L. (2003a). Toward a science of workplace spirituality. In R. A. Giacalone & C. L. Jurkiewicz (Eds.), *Handbook of workplace spirituality and organizational performance (pp. 3–28) Armonk: M.E* (pp. 3–28). Armonk: M.E. Sharpe.

Giacalone, R. A., & Jurkiewicz, C. L. (2003b). Right from wrong: The influence of spirituality on perceptions of unethical business activities. *Journal of Business Ethics, 46*, 85–97.

Giacalone, R. A., & Promislo, M. D. (2013). Broken when entering: The stigmatization of goodness and business ethics education. *Academy of Management Learning and Education, 12*(1), 86–101.

Glaser, B. G. (1978). *Theoretical sensitivity: Advances in the methodology of grounded theory.* Mill Valley, CA: Sociology Press.

Glaser, B. (2002). Constructivist grounded theory? [47 paragraphs]. Forum qualitative sozialforschung. *Forum: Qualitative Social Research [On-line Journal], 3*(3).

Glaser, B., & Strauss, A. (1967). *The discovery of grounded theory 1967.* London: Weidenfield & Nicolson.

Gourlay, S. (2006). Conceptualizing knowledge creation: A critique of nonaka's theory. *Journal of Management Studies, 43*(7), 1415–1436.

Greenleaf, R. (1977). *Servant leadership.* New York, NY: Paulist Press.

Gueldenberg, S., & Helting, H. (2007). Bridging 'the great divide': Nonaka's synthesis of 'western' and 'eastern' knowledge concepts reassessed. *Organization, 14*(1), 101–122.

Hackman, J. R., & Oldham, G. (1975). Development of the job diagnostic survey. *Journal of Applied Psychology, 60*, 159–170.

Hart, S. L. (1997). Beyond greening: Strategies for a sustainable world. *Harvard Business Review, 67–76*.

Hernandez, M. (2008). Promoting stewardship behavior in organizations: A leadership model. *Journal of Business Ethics, 80*(1), 121–128.

Hernandez, M. (2012). Toward and understanding of the psychology of stewardship. *Academy of Management Review, 37*(2), 172–193.

Hisrich, R. D., & Peters, M. P. (1998). *Entrepreneurship: Starting, developing, and managing a new enterprise* (4th ed.). Chicago, IL: Irwin.

Hong, J. F. (2012). Glocalizing Nonaka's knowledge creation model: Issues and challenges. *Management Learning, 43*(2), 199–215.

Horney, N., Pasmore, B., & O'Shea, T. (2010). Leadership agility: A business imperative for a VUCA world. *Human Resource Planning, 33*(4), 34.

Hornsby, J. S., Kuratko, D. F., & Zahra, S. A. (2002). Middle managers' perception of the internal environment for corporate entrepreneurship: Assessing a measurement scale. *Journal of Business Venturing, 17*(3), 253–273.

House, R. J., & Mitchell, T. R. (1974). Path goal theory of leadership. *Journal of Contemporary Business, 3*, 81–97.

Jain, N., & Mukherji, S. (2009). Communicating a holistic perspective to the world: Kautilya on leadership. *Leadership and Organization Development Journal, 30*(5), 435–454.

Johansen, B., & Euchner, J. (2013). Conversations: Navigating the VUCA world: An interview with Bob Johansen. *Research Technology Management, 56*(1), 10–15.

Jones, M. R., & Boltz, M. (1989). Dynamic attending and responses to time. *Psychological Review, 96*(3), 459–491.

Jones, G. R., & Butler, J. E. (1992). Managing internal corporate entrepreneurship: An agency theory perspective. *Journal of Management, 18*(4), 733–749.

Joyner, P., & Lardner, R. (2008). Mindfulness: Realising the benefits. *Loss Prevention Bulletin, 201*, 22–27.

Karakas, F. (2009). Spirituality and performance in organizations: A literature review. *Journal of Business Ethics, 94*, 89–106.

Karambelkar, P. V. (2011). *Patanjala yoga sutra*. Lonavla: Kaivalyadhama.

Kathuria, R., & Joshi, M. P. (2007). Environmental influences on corporate entrepreneurship: Executive perspectives on the internet. *International Entrepreneurship and Management Journal, 3*(2), 127–144.

Katzenbach, J. R., & Smith, D. K. (1993). *The wisdom of teams*. Boston, MA: Harvard Business School Press.

Kearney, P. (1999). Enterprising ways to teach and learn. A series of books: Book 1:"Enterprise Principles". *Enterprise Design Associates, North Hobart Tasmania Australia, Pty Ltd ISBN 0, 958*(5663), 0.

Kearney, C., Hisrich, R., & Roche, F. (2008). A conceptual model of public sector corporate entrepreneurship. *International Entrepreneurship and Management Journal, 4*(3), 295–313.

Kelemen, M., & Peltonen, T. (2005). Spirituality: A way to an alternative subjectivity. *Organization Management Journal, 2*(1), 52–63.

Kernis, M. H., & Goldman, B. M. (2006). A multi-component conceptualization of authenticity: Theory and research. In M. P. Zanna (Ed.), *Advances in experimental social psychology* (pp. 284–357). San Diego, CA: Elsevier.

Knight, G. A. (1997). Cross-cultural reliability and validity of a scale to measure firm entrepreneurial orientation. *Journal of Business Venturing, 12*(3), 213–225.

KPMG. (2013). *The Swedish market for Home-based care: Desktop analysis of the case for expanding Buurtzorg's operations in Sweden*. White paper study.

Kreitzer, M. J., Monsen, K. A., Nandram, S. S., & De Blok, J. (2014). Buurtzorg Nederland: A global model of social innovation, change and whole systems healing. To be published in *Global Advances*.

Krishnakumar, S., & Neck, C. P. (2002). The 'what', 'why' and 'how' of spirituality in the workplace. *Journal of Managerial Psychology, 17*(3), 153–164.

Kulkarni, S., & Ramamoorthy, N. (2011). Leader–member exchange, subordinate stewardship, and hierarchical governance. *The International Journal of Human Resource Management, 22* (13), 2770–2793.

Kuratko, D. F., Montagno, R. V., & Hornsby, J. S. (1990). Developing an intrapreneurial assessment instrument for an effective corporate entrepreneurial environment. *Strategic Management Journal, 11*, 49–58.

Laloux, F. (2014). *Reinventing organizations*. Brussels: Nelson Parker.

Lawrence, A. T., & Weber, J. (2008). *Business and society: Stakeholders, ethics, public policy.* Boston, MA: Tata McGraw-Hill Education.

Leferink, A., De Blok, J., Nandram, S., & Hotta, S. (2014). Buurtzorg Nederland and ICT innovation: The shift from bureaucracy to accountability. *Hospitals, 73*(6).

Letiche, H., & Hagemeijer, R. E. (2004). Linkages and entrainment. *Journal of Organizational Change Management, 17*(4), 365–382.

Levinthal, D., & Rerup, C. (2006). Crossing an apparent chasm: Bridging mindful and less mindful perspectives on organizational learning. *Organization Science, 17*(4), 502–513.

Lim, S., Ribeiro, D., & Lee, S. M. (2008). Factors affecting the performance of entrepreneurial service firms. *The Service Industries Journal, 28*(7), 1003–1013.

Lovrich, N. P. (1989). The Simon/Argyris debate: Bounded rationality versus self-actualization conceptions of human nature. *Public Administration Quarterly, 12*, 452–483.

Lumpkin, G. T., & Dess, G. G. (1996). Clarifying the entrepreneurial orientation construct and linking it to performance. *Academy of Management Review, 21*(1), 135–172.

MacMillan, I. C. (1986). *To really learn about entrepreneurship, let's study habitual entrepreneurs*. Wharton School of the University of Pennsylvania, Snider Entrepreneurial Center.

Mair, J. (2002). *Value creation through entrepreneurial activity: A multiple constituency approach (No. D/468)*. IESE Business School.

Marques, J. F. (2006). The spiritual worker. An examination of the ripple effect that enhances quality of life in- and outside the work environment. *Journal of Management Development, 25* (9), 884–895.

Maslow, A. H. (1943). A theory of human motivation. *Psychological Review, 50*(4), 370.

Maslow, A. H. (1954). *Motivation and personality*. New York, NY: Harper and Row.

McClelland, D. (1953). *Human motivation*. Cambridge, MA: Cambridge University Press.

McCraty, R., Atkinson, M., Tomasino, D., & Bradley, R. T. (2009). The coherent heart: Heart-brain interactions, psychophysiological coherence, and the emergence of system-wide order. *Integral Review, 5*(2), 10–115.

McGrath, J. E., & Rotchford, N. L. (1983). Time and behavior in organizations. *Research in Organizational Behavior*.

McGrath, J. E., Kelly, J. R., & Machatka, D. E. (1984). The social psychology of time: Entrainment of behavior in social and organizational settings. *Applied Social Psychology Annual, 5*, 21–44.

McGregor, D. (1960). *The human side of enterprise*. New York, NY: McGraw-Hill.

Menzel, H. C., Aaltio, I., & Ulijn, J. M. (2007). On the way to creativity: Engineers as intrapreneurs in organizations. *Technovation, 27*(12), 732–743.

Miller, D. (1983). The correlates of entrepreneurship in three types of firms. *Management Science, 29*, 770–791.

Miller, E. D. (2004). The development and validation of a new measure of spirituality. *North American Journal of Psychology, 6*(3), 423–430.

Miller, D. W., & Ewest, T. (2011). *Present state of workplace spirituality: Literature review of context, theory and scales and measurements*. Submission 15995 for Academy of Management Annual Meeting, Texas.

Monsen, K. A., & De Blok, J. (2013a). Buurtzorg: Nurse-led community care. *Creative Nursing,* *19*(3), 122–127.

Monsen, K. A., & De Blok, J. (2013b). Buurtzorg Nederland: A nurse-led model of care has revolutionized home care in the Netherlands. *The American Journal of Nursing, 113*(8), 55–59.

Mourmant, G. Niederman, F., & Kalika, M. (2013, May). Spaces of IT intrapreneurial freedom: A classic grounded theory. In *Proceedings of the 2013 annual conference on computers and people research* (pp. 33–44). ACM.

Mueller, S. (2012). *The mature learner: Understanding entrepreneurial learning processes of university students from a social constructivist perspective.* Ph.D. thesis at Robert Gordon University.

Nandram, S. S. (2010a). Spirituality and business. In S. S. Nandram & M. E. Borden (Eds.), *Spirituality and business: Exploring possibilities for a new management paradigm* (pp. 17–32). Heidelberg: Springer. doi:10.1007/978-3-642-02661-4_2. ISBN 978364202667.

Nandram, S. S. (2010b). Synchronizing leadership style with integral transformational yoga principles. In S. S. Nandram & M. E. Borden (Eds.), *Spirituality and business.* Heidelberg: Springer.

Nandram, S. S. (2011a). Spirituality, economics and leadership: Integral yoga model. *The International Journal's Research Journal of Social Science and Management, 1*(7). www.theinternationaljournal.org

Nandram, S. S. (2011b, August–September). Spirituality and business: From a profit maximizing model to a social economic DNA. *The European Financial Review.* August-September issue. pp. 30–33.

Nandram, S. S. (2011c). Kautilya the first management Guru rediscovered. *NHRD Journal*

Nandram, S. S. (2012). In search for the spiritual innovation at the Dutch elderly home care organization Buurtzorg Nederland. *Amity Case Research Journal,* 1–6.

Nandram, S. (2013). Schumacher and kautilyan economics from an integral view: A sustainable approach. *Advances in Management, 6*(5), 29.

Nandram, S. S. (2014a). Vedic learning and management education. *Journal of Management Development* (scheduled Fall, in press).

Nandram, S. S. (2014b). Mindful inquiry. In D. Coghian & M. Brydon-Miller (Eds.), *Encyclopedia for action research.* London: Sage.

Nandram, S. S., & Borden, M. E. (2010). Introduction: Exploring possibilities for a new paradigm. In S. S. Nandram & M. E. Borden (Eds.), *Spirituality and business: Exploring possibilities for a new management paradigm.* Heidelberg: Springer.

Nandram, S. S., & Koster, N. (2014). Organizational innovation and integrated care: Lessons from Buurtzorg. *Journal of Integrated Care, 22,* 174–184.

Nandram, S. S., & Samsom, K. J. (2006). *The spirit of entrepreneurship: Exploring the essence of entrepreneurship through personal stories.* New York, NY: Springer.

Noddings, N., & Shore, P. J. (1984). *Awakening the inner eye. Intuition in education.* New York, NY: Teachers College Press, Columbia University. 10027.

Nonaka, I. (1991). The knowledge-creating company. *Harvard Business Review, 69*(6), 96–104.

Nonaka, I. (1994). A dynamic theory of organizational knowledge creation. *Organization Science, 5*(1), 14–37.

Nonaka, I., & Takeuchi, H. (1995). *The knowledge-creating company: How Japanese companies create the dynamics of innovation.* New York, NY: Oxford University Press.

Nonaka, I., Toyama, R., & Konno, N. (2000). SECI, Ba and leadership: A unified model of dynamic knowledge creation. *Long Range Planning, 33*(1), 5–34.

Nonaka, I., & Toyama, R. (2002). A firm as a dialectical being: Towards a dynamic theory of a firm. *Industrial and Corporate Change, 11*(5), 995–1009.

Nonaka, I., & Toyama, R. (2003). The knowledge-creating theory revisited: Knowledge creation as a synthesizing process. *Knowledge Management Research and Practice, 1*(1), 2–10.

Nonaka, I., & von Krogh, G. (2009). Perspective—Tacit knowledge and knowledge conversion: Controversy and advancement in organizational knowledge creation theory. *Organization Science, 20*(3), 635–652.

Ouchi, W. G. (1981). *Theory Z: How American business can meet the Japanese challenge.* Reading, MA: Addison-Wesley.

Pandey, A., & Gupta, R. K. (2008). A perspective of collective consciousness of business organizations. *Journal of Business Ethics, 80,* 889–898.

Pandey, A., Gupta, R. K., & Arora, A. P. (2009). Spiritual climate of business organizations and its impact on customers' experience. *Journal of Business Ethics, 88*(2), 313–332.

Pérez-Nordtvedt, L., Payne, G. T., Short, J. C., & Kedia, B. L. (2008). An entrainment-based model of temporal organizational fit, misfit, and performance. *Organization Science, 19*(5), 785–801.

Piaget, J. (1950). *The psychology of intelligence.* London: Routledge and Kegan.

Piedmont, R. L., & Leach, M. M. (2002). Cross cultural generalizability of the spiritual transcendence scale in India: Spirituality as a universal aspect of human experience. *American Behavioral Scientist, 45*(12), 1888–2002.

Pinchot, G. (1985). *Intrapreneuring: Why you don't have to leave the corporation to become an entrepreneur.* New York, NY: Harper & Row.

Pool, A., Mast, J., & Keesom, J. (2011). *Eerst buurten, dan zorgen: Professioneel verplegen en verzorgen bij Buurtzorg.* Den Haag: Boom Lemma Uitgevers.

Radjou, N., Prabhu, J., & Ahuja, S. (2012). *Jugaad innovation: Think frugal, be flexible, generate breakthrough growth.* San Francisco, CA: Jossey-Bass, Wiley.

Read, S., & Sarasvathy, S. D. (2005). Knowing what to do and doing what you know: Effectuation as a form of entrepreneurial expertise. *The Journal of Private Equity, 9*(1), 45–62.

Renking, D., Labbo, L. D., & McKenna, M. C. (2000). From assimilation to accommodation: A developmental framework for integrating digital technologies into literacy research and instruction. *Journal of Research in Reading, 23*(2), 110–122.

Sánchez, J. C., & Loredo, J. C. (2009). Constructivism from a genetic point of view: A critical classification of current tendencies. *Integral Psychological Behavior, 43,* 332–349.

Sandra, D., & Nandram, S. S. (2013). The role of entrainment in the context of integral leadership: Synchronizing consciousness. *Advances in Management, 6*(12), 17–24.

Sarasvathy, S. D. (2000). Seminar on research perspectives in entrepreneurship (1997). *Journal of Business Venturing, 15*(1), 1–57.

Sarasvathy, S. D. (2001a, August). Effectual reasoning in entrepreneurial decision making: Existence and bounds. In *Academy of management proceedings* (Vol. 2001, No. 1, pp. D1–D6). Washington, DC: Academy of Management

Sarasvathy, S. D. (2001b). Causation and effectuation: Toward a theoretical shift from economic inevitability to entrepreneurial contingency. *Academy of Management Review, 26*(2), 243–263.

Sarasvathy, S. D. (2004). Making it happen: Beyond theories of the firm to theories of firm design. *Entrepreneurship: Theory and Practice, 28,* 519–531.

Scharmer, C. O. (2000). Conversation with Ikujiro Nonaka. *Reflections, 2*(2), 24–31.

Schein, E. H. (2004). *Organizational culture and leadership.* San Francisco, CA: Jossey-Bass.

Schneider, B., Ehrhart, M. G., & Macey, W. H. (2013). Organizational climate and culture. *Annual Review of Psychology, 64,* 361–388.

Schollhammer, H. (1981). The efficacy of internal corporate entrepreneurship strategies. *Frontiers of Entrepreneurship Research, 451–456.*

Schollhammer, H. (1982). Internal corporate entrepreneurship. In C. A. Kent, D. L. Sexton, & K. H. Vesper (Eds.), *Encyclopedia of entrepreneurship* (pp. 209–223). Englewood Cliffs, NJ: Prentice Hall.

Schwartz, M. S. (2006). God as a managerial stakeholder. *Journal of Business Ethics, 66,* 291–306.

Shi, W. S., & Prescott, J. E. (2012). Rhythm and entrainment of acquisition and alliance initiatives and firm performance: A temporal perspective. *Organization Studies, 33*(10), 1281–1310.

Simon, H. A. (1967). *Models of man social and rational: Mathematical essays on rational human behavior in a social setting.* New York, NY: Wiley.

Simon, H. A. (1973). Organization man: Rational or self-actualizing? *Public Administration Review, 33,* 346–353.

Skinner, B. (1950). Are theories of learning necessary? *Psychological Review, 57,* 193–216.

Soriano, D. R. (2005). The new role of the corporate and functional strategies in the tourism sector: Spanish small and medium-sized hotels. *The Service Industries Journal, 25*(4), 601–613.

Spears, C., & Lawrence, M. (2002). *Focus on leadership.* New York, NY: Wiley.

Sri Aurobindo, G. (1993). *The integral yoga: Sri Aurobindo's teaching and method of practice* (pp. 396–397). Pondicherry: Sri Aurobindo Ashram.

Sri Aurobindo, G. (2006). *Life divine* (7th ed.). Pondicherry: Sri Aurobindo Ashram.

Standifer, R., & Bluedorn, A. (2006). Alliance management teams and entrainment: Sharing temporal mental models. *Human Relations, 59*(7), 903–927.

Steers, R. M., & Porter, L. W. (1987). *Motivation and work behavior.* New York, NY: McGraw-Hill.

Stevenson, H. (2000). The six dimensions of entrepreneurship. In S. Birley & D. Muzyka (Eds.), *Mastering entrepreneurship.* London: Pearson.

Stewart, G. L., Manz, C., & Sims, H. (1999). *Team work and group dynamics.* New York, NY: Wiley.

Strogatz, S. H., & Stewart, I. (1993). Coupled oscillators and biological synchronization. *Scientific American, 269*(6), 102–109.

Sundbo, J. (1998). *The theory of innovation: Entrepreneurs, technology and strategy.* Cheltenham: Edward Elgar.

Timmons, J., & Spinelli, S. (2004). *New venture strategies: Entrepreneurship for the 21st century.* Burr Ridge, IL: Irwin-McGraw-Hill.

Van Dalen, A. (2012). *Zorgvernieuwing: Over anders besturen en organiseren.* Den Haag: Boom Lemma Uitgevers.

Van Dam, K., Schipper, M., & Runhaar, P. (2010). Developing a competency-based framework for teachers' entrepreneurial behaviour. *Teaching and Teacher Education, 26*(4), 965–971.

Vaughan, F. E. (1997). *Awakening intuition.* New York, NY: Doubleday.

Venkataraman, S., Sarasvathy, S. D., Dew, N., & Forster, W. R. (2013). Of narratives and artifacts. *Academy of Management Review, 38*(1), 163–166.

Vermeer, A., & Wenting, B. (2012). *Zelfsturende teams in de praktijk.* Amsterdam: Reed Business.

Vesper, K. H. (1990). *New venture strategies.* University of Illinois at Urbana-Champaign's academy for entrepreneurial leadership, historical research reference in entrepreneurship.

Von Glasersfeld, E. (1996). *Radical constructivism: A way of knowing and learning.* Falmer: Routledge.

Von Glasersfeld, E. (1982). An interpretation of Piaget's constructivism. *Revue Internationale de Philosophie, 36*(4), 612–635.

Von Krogh, G., Nonaka, I., & Rechsteiner, L. (2012). Leadership in organizational knowledge creation: A review and framework. *Journal of Management Studies, 49*(1), 240–277.

Vroom, V. H. (1964). *Work and motivation.* New York, NY: Wiley.

Wegner, D. M., & Vallacher, R. R. (1977). *Implicit psychology: An introduction to social cognition.* New York, NY: Oxford University Press.

Werner, A., & Pool, A. (2013). *Diversiteit in de verpleegkundige zorg: Handreiking voor wijkverpleegkundigen bij de zorg voor migranten.* Den Haag: Boom Lemma uitgevers.

Zahra, S. A. (1991). Predictors and financial outcomes of corporate entrepreneurship: An exploratory study. *Journal of Business Venturing, 6*(4), 259–285.

Zahra, S. A. (1993). Environment, corporate entrepreneurship, and financial performance: A taxonomic approach. *Journal of Business Venturing, 8*(4), 319–340.

Zahra, S. A. (1999). The changing rules of global competitiveness in the 21st century. *The Academy of Management Executive, 13*(1), 36–42.

Zahra, S. A., Neilsen, A. P., & Bogner, W. C. (1999). Corporate entrepreneurship, knowledge and competence development. *Entrepreneurship: Theory and Practice, 23*(3), 169–189.

Zellmer-Bruhn, M., Waller, M. J., & Ancona, D. (2004). The effect of temporal entrainment on the ability of teams to change their routines. *Research on Managing Groups and Teams, 6*, 135–158.

Zuboff, S. (2009). The old solutions have become the new problems. *Business Week, 2*, 1.

Index

A

Abhyasa, 155
Accommodation, 141, 152–154
Acknowledging humane values, 53–54
Activist's attitude, 86, 88–89
Adjustment, 20, 33, 34, 42, 48, 49, 53, 55, 61,
    66, 71, 74, 76, 79, 89, 90, 99, 100,
    169, 184
Affordable loss principle, 86, 88, 150
Ancient views, 146–147, 154, 197–200
Antecedent, 7, 65, 83, 86, 89, 91, 153, 164, 183
Argyris, C., 23–25
Assimilation, 141, 152–154
Attunement, 2, 6, 32–35, 37, 39, 42, 43, 45–63,
    76, 80, 93, 98–99, 102, 126, 129, 140,
    157, 158, 162, 172–174, 182, 185, 194,
    201, 202
Awareness conflict interests, 47, 58–59

B

Balanced team composition, 71–74
Belief system, 6, 7, 29, 33, 35, 36, 84, 111–117,
    127–129, 136–137, 143, 163, 174,
    176–177, 202

C

Category, 2, 4, 26, 27, 37, 88, 98, 157, 158,
    161, 162, 181–183, 190, 194, 201
Causal reasoning, 148, 149
Change agent, 13, 42, 117, 174, 201, 205–206
Christiaan Huygens, 47
Classical grounded theory (CGT), 2, 4, 25–27,
    47, 133, 181–188, 193, 209
Coding, 2, 26, 181–183, 193, 194
Coherence, 57, 79, 88, 93, 179
Community care, 3, 8, 12–13, 16, 17, 20, 21,
    25, 41, 65, 66, 71, 76–80, 87, 102,
109–111, 114, 116–117, 125, 126, 129,
    132–134, 138–139, 163, 165, 166,
    170–172, 175, 179, 184, 191, 202, 203,
    206, 209, 210
Community coherence, 47, 57–58
Company life-cycle, 85–86
Complexity, 2, 5–7, 16, 19, 26, 29, 31, 37, 40,
    41, 51, 60, 61, 95, 98, 103, 121, 129,
    132, 159–163, 177, 180, 206
Concept, 2–8, 13, 14, 20, 24–27, 34–43, 45–49,
    61, 62, 65–66, 74, 76, 77, 79, 80, 82–89,
    95–97, 99, 107, 111, 121–126, 128, 129,
    133–135, 137, 139–142, 146–148,
    153–155, 157, 158, 161–163, 166, 177,
    179–183, 185, 189, 190, 194, 195, 201,
    205, 206, 209, 210
Constant comparative coding, 182
Constructivist approach, 102
Context attunement, 47, 50, 56–59, 163
Conversing thinking, 166
Conversion, 5, 27, 48, 61, 101, 112, 119, 153,
    160–161, 166, 190
Core category, 2, 4, 26, 27, 157, 158, 181, 182,
    190, 194, 201
Core concepts, 2, 5, 26, 40, 45, 95, 157, 158,
    163, 180, 194, 195
Core variable, 181–183
Corporate entrepreneurship, 82–85
Craftsmanship, 2, 3, 5–7, 33–35, 37–43, 65–80,
    95, 135, 147, 148, 156–158, 162, 165,
    173, 182, 185, 194
Creative causal reasoning, 148
Cues, 5, 6, 29, 35, 50, 51, 58, 65, 76, 79–80,
    138, 142, 144, 145, 147, 152, 153, 162

D

Dharma, 179
Differentiation, 53, 86, 88, 134, 152–154, 174

S.S. Nandram, *Organizational Innovation by Integrating Simplification*,
Management for Professionals, DOI 10.1007/978-3-319-11725-6

CPSIA information can be obtained at www.ICGtesting.com
Printed in the USA
LVOW05*1451041214

417192LV00011B/186/P

9 783319 117249